ACCLAIM FOR
JUST TELL ME I CAN'T

"JUST TELL ME I CAN'T has it all. It is loaded with grit and heart and soul. It is written with sweet smoothness and insight. It is also the best book I have ever read on the psychology of that complex and marvelous creature called the pro athlete."
—Buzz Bissinger, author of *Father's Day*, *Three Nights in August*, and *Friday Night Lights*

"Fascinating. Once the mind breaks out of its prison, anything, anything is possible: even a 49-year-old, throwing no harder than the kid who lives down your block, pitching in the bigs! Ahhh, but how the mind makes that escape and how it yearns to pass that secret on, that's a book in itself . . . the book laying in your lucky hands." —Gary Smith, *Sports Illustrated*

"Jamie was a great competitor and a guy who persevered despite being told 'you can't' time and again. That competitive spirit and belief in himself coupled with a tough stubbornness resulted in a remarkable career that we can all learn from."
—Cal Ripken Jr.

"Captivating . . . a fascinating view inside America's game and inside the head of a pitcher who understood it as well as anyone." —*Philadelphia Inquirer*

"With his nearly singular combination of competitive will and pitching guile, it seemed as if Jamie Moyer's big league career would never end. Now that it finally has, I have only one regret: There goes the last active player whose iPod playlist might be similar to my own." —Bob Costas

JUST TELL ME I CAN'T

How Jamie Moyer Defied the Radar Gun and Defeated Time

JAMIE MOYER AND LARRY PLATT

GRAND CENTRAL
PUBLISHING

NEW YORK   BOSTON

Grand Central Publishing
Hachette Book Group
237 Park Avenue
New York, NY 10017
www.HachetteBookGroup.com

Printed in the United States of America

RRD-C

Originally published in hardcover by Hachette Book Group.

First trade edition: September 2014

10 9 8 7 6 5 4 3 2 1

Grand Central Publishing is a division of Hachette Book Group, Inc.
The Grand Central Publishing name and logo are trademarks of Hachette Book Group, Inc.

The Hachette Speakers Bureau provides a wide range of authors for speaking events. To find out more, go to www.hachettespeakersbureau.com or call (866) 376-6591.

The publisher is not responsible for websites (or their content) that are not owned by the publisher.

The Library of Congress has catalogued the hardcover edition as follows:

Moyer, Jamie.
 Just tell me i can't : how Jamie Moyer defied the radar gun and defeated time / Jamie Moyer and Larry Platt.
    pages cm
 Includes bibliographical references and index.
 ISBN 978-1-4555-2158-6 (hardcover)—ISBN 978-1-4555-2159-3 (ebook) 1.
Moyer, Jamie. 2. Baseball players—United States—Biography. 3. Pitchers (Baseball)—United States—Biography. I. Platt, Larry. II. Title.
 GV865.M69 2013
 796.357092—dc23
 [B]

                                    2013004654

ISBN 978-1-4555-2157-9 (pbk.)

For Harvey Dorfman

CONTENTS

How old would you be if you didn't know how old you are?

—Satchel Paige

JUST TELL ME
I CAN'T

JULY 2010

INTRODUCTION

It had been many years since Jamie Moyer was unable to quiet the chattering distractions of his own mind. But now, on a sweltering St. Louis night, the oldest athlete in all pro sports was in trouble on the mound. No matter how often he pleaded with himself to just *focus*, the doubts, laced with fear, kept coming.

His first pitch in the first inning had been a down-and-away two-seam fastball to Cardinals leadoff hitter Felipe Lopez; the two-seamer, gripped along (as opposed to across) the ball's stitches or seams, looks like a straight fastball—before its angled spin causes it to suddenly sink. Moyer, who has kept notes on every batter he's ever faced, knew that Lopez was often tempted to chase sinkers that sizzled and dipped toward his ankles. Upon releasing the pitch, however, with his trusted left arm raised to its three-quarters release point above his shoulder, Moyer felt something. It wasn't a searing pain; it was more as though there were a rubber band inside his elbow, and it was stretching and expanding and elongating…and then, as if on cue after the release, the pain came. And so did the ball. Lopez flailed at the pitch and weakly tapped it back to the pitcher. Moyer grabbed it while instinctively trying to hide that his arm felt like it had exploded.

The ball in his glove presented a problem. *How do I get*

this to first base? Moyer wondered. In a fraction of a second, his mind raced. He thought about sprinting the ball over to first baseman Ryan Howard, but Lopez was already halfway down the line. Should he underhand it? That was too far. Now Lopez was two-thirds of the way there. Moyer raised his throbbing left arm and lobbed the ball, a soft toss that Howard caught for out number one.

As Moyer went for a slow walk around the mound, the thoughts kept coming. *Will I be able to pitch batting practice to my boys? Is this the last time I'll be on a mound? Will I go on the DL?*

Moyer knew these thoughts for what they were: negative self-talk. Two decades earlier, he was a losing pitcher in his early thirties with a career 34–54 record who had been cut by three teams. The mound was a scary, powerless place; is there a more solitary spot in sports? The pitcher stands elevated, exposed, part of a team while simultaneously apart from it. He's alone with his thoughts, emotions, and countless other voices; on the mound, the withering doubts of others—fans, media, managers—can often drown out the game's actual sound. Those voices have crippled more pitchers than any actual succession of line drives.

But then he made a pilgrimage to the man a whole generation of ballplayers had come to refer to as "baseball's best-kept secret." Harvey Dorfman was the raspy-voiced guru who had practically invented the field of sports psychology. Dorfman, who passed away at seventy-five early in 2011, had helped some of baseball's biggest names shed their self-consciousness. Among the disciples of the Cult of Harvey: slugger Alex Rodriguez, pitchers Roy Halladay, Greg Maddux, and Jim Abbott, and many more. None, however, were greater devotees than Moyer. Ever since that first meeting in 1991, Dorfman's acerbic aphorisms were with Moyer on every mound, in every jam, preceding every pitch.

And so on that St. Louis night, when the end of his career seemed imminent and the fearful thoughts came in waves, Moyer did as Harvey would have him do. He drew a deep breath, slowly exhaling. And he listened for that gravelly voice that for nearly twenty years had comforted him on the mound.

Focus on the task at hand.

Establish a short-term goal.

One. Pitch. At. A. Time.

Digging into the batter's box was centerfielder Randy Winn, Moyer's onetime teammate in Seattle, who had hit Moyer hard the last few years. With each pitch, the rubber band inside his elbow was pulling even more now. Moyer's changeup was in the dirt; the curveball didn't have its finish, that outward, looping wrist snap that causes the ball to arc away from lefthanded batters. In the middle of the count, Winn hit a cutter to third base for out number two.

Another out, another walk around the mound. How had he gotten here? Moyer, the thirty-sixth winningest pitcher of all time, was currently in search of his tenth win of the still-young season; he was on pace to record more wins than he had since his 16–7 record led his team, the Philadelphia Phillies, to the World Series championship two years prior, and possibly as many as he'd had seven years earlier, when his 21–7 record for Seattle made him an All-Star. He'd become something of a folk hero in Philadelphia, where middle-aged men with paunches would stop him in restaurants or on the street to share how his inspirational example had gotten them back into the gym.

Having won far more games in his forties than in his twenties, and doing so with an 81-mile-per-hour fastball and a changeup that lived on the black corners of home plate, Moyer had come

to enjoy testing himself against testosterone-fueled twentysome-
things; he'd gotten expert at using young hitters' machismo
against them. After each called third strike or weak grounder
to short, they'd take the walk of shame back to their dugout,
befuddled and embarrassed that this seeming thrower of junk
had once again bested them. "Jamie carved us tonight," Atlanta
Brave Chipper Jones said after Moyer threw a two-hit shutout
against his team in May 2010. "The guy is eighty-seven years
old and still pitching for a reason. He stays off the barrel of
the bat. He changes speeds, changes the game plan, keeps you
guessing."

Oh, sure, his teammates would razz him; shortstop Jimmy
Rollins would call him "Grandpa," and on "Turn Back the
Clock" uniform nights, someone would invariably joke that this
wouldn't be the *first* time Moyer wore a 1929 uniform. But that
was all in good fun. He'd come to embrace his role, as he put it,
"representing the fortysomethings."

But now it was all suddenly in jeopardy—the pursuit of 300
wins (he was 33 shy of the magic number that assures a spot in
Cooperstown), the folk hero status, the very way he'd defined
himself his whole life. He knew what Harvey would say: *Shut
up and breathe.*

Moyer inhaled deeply and reminded himself: *Every pitch
with purpose.*

Next up was only the best hitter in the National League, Al-
bert Pujols. He took ball one, down and away. After a fastball
at the knees, Moyer came inside with a cutter. This version of
the cutter was Moyer's newest pitch, and it was largely why his
2010 season had thus far defied expectations. During the 2009
World Series his boyhood idol, Phillie great Steve Carlton, was
to throw out the first pitch of game four, with Moyer catching
him. As they warmed up before the game, Carlton started toss-

ing his legendary slider. "Can you show me that?" Moyer asked. For the next half hour, he received a tutorial on the slider, which differs from a cutter only in degree; the slider's spin is tighter. Moyer had thrown a cutter since the early '90s, but this one was vastly dissimilar, with a different grip and more bite. Moyer worked on the pitch all off-season—without telling anyone on the Phils' coaching staff. When he got to spring training, it took a while before pitching coach Rich Dubee asked, just what was that pitch that seemed to be fooling so many hitters?

Moyer tried to jam Pujols with the cutter, a difficult enough proposition when the hitter *isn't* the best in baseball. The plate, after all, is a mere seventeen inches wide, framed along the outside by a thin black strip. The goal for a non–power pitcher like Moyer in what he calls the "ultimate game of truth or dare" is to keep hitters off balance by consistently hitting the plate's black corners. When a pitcher says he made a "mistake," it's often because he has thrown "white on white": the white ball over the white part of the plate. Moyer's pitch to Pujols was barely off, catching perhaps a half inch of the white, enough for the slugger to swing and muscle a bloop base hit over the infield.

The next hitter, leftfielder Matt Holliday, mimicked Pujols, fighting off an inside cutter for a soft single. Moyer took another walk, letting his arm pain subside. Rightfielder Allen Craig was a rookie who had never seen Moyer before. Early in the count, the runners stole second and third.

Moyer went for another walk, looked around the stadium. *God, I love it here*, he thought to himself, looking up at the stands, taking in the scene—in case this was his last time on a big league mound. Harvey's voice in his head caught it:

You think you're focusing, but are you? Are you really?
Return to your breath. Slow it down.

Dorfman used to say that the adrenaline rush when in a

jam on the mound was not unlike scurrying around doing last-minute chores while getting ready to go somewhere. You get nervous and tense; a modicum of doubt can result in a *deficit*— a Harvey word—of conviction behind the pitch. And a pitch that lacks conviction is a pitch asking to be punished. In Baltimore in 1993, while lessons from Harvey were still sinking in, Moyer heard his teammate Doug Jones say that when things got loud, he'd get softer. When the fans are screaming and your thoughts are racing, the tendency is to grip the ball harder, rear back, and throw with all your might. Instead, Moyer learned, throwing it softer is the more aggressive act.

His arm throbbing, Moyer started Craig with soft stuff, away. Then he decided to throw a four-seam fastball—his only straight pitch, gripped across the ball's horseshoe-shaped stitches—right down the middle, white on white. *Here it is, let's see you hit it.* Allen hit a tame fly ball to Shane Victorino in centerfield to end the inning.

Walking into the dugout, Moyer called over pitching coach Dubee and manager Charlie Manuel. And then he said the three hardest words he'd ever had to say, words that, when he'd recall them months later, would still bring a quiver to his voice: "I can't throw."

So began the most improbable of comebacks, in a life filled with them. Most mere mortals would have quit when cut by the Texas Rangers in 1991 with a career 34–49 record. Or a year later, after an 0–5 season. Or the season after that, when the Chicago Cubs offered him a job as a pitching coach. Instead, he took a flyer on handling mop-up duty for the Toledo Mud Hens for all of $12,000.

Moyer persevered after all those setbacks, but now—with a

serious arm injury that would require Tommy John surgery in 2010—was this the end? Not hardly.

I first met Moyer and his wife, Karen, just weeks after the injury in St. Louis. It was Phillies Alumni Weekend, and we met in a hotel bar to talk about collaborating on a book. Moyer was lukewarm; he'd read athlete autobiographies, and he'd never liked them. "I'm not a me, me, me kind of guy," he said apologetically.

Besides, he may not have been done on the mound. Phillies general manager Ruben Amaro and virtually every sports yakker on the airwaves had loudly proclaimed his career to be over. But I got the sense that Moyer was still penning his own type of cliffhanger. "He's already plotting his comeback," Karen said, only half joking. As we chatted, none other than Steve Carlton stopped by. For hours, the two legends talked pitching. They talked about Cole Hamels's arm slot: "He's really seeing those lanes," Lefty said.

"He's dialed in," Moyer agreed.

Members of an elite, exclusive club, they spoke in a cryptic, knowing shorthand. Each one seemed to know precisely what it was like for the other; *What it's like*. That's the book, I thought; not Jamie Moyer's life story so much as a biography of a master craftsman. Not some linear career blow by blow, but a travelogue of critical points of challenge, small moments examined closely.

I had just finished reading Christopher McDougall's compelling *Born to Run*, which in its profile of the record-breaking distance running of the Tarahumara Indians of Mexico's Copper Canyon, illustrated the power of mind over matter. Now, as Moyer and Carlton compared notes—596 major league wins between them!—it struck me that they spoke far more about the mental side of the game than the purely physical. As the beer flowed into the night, modern-day pitchers were dissected as much for their perseverance and focus as for their movement and velocity. Moyer and Carlton were indeed talking craft, but they spoke in clipped sentences about the *psychology* behind the act.

Later, approaching last call, I made this observation to Moyer, and it struck a nerve. He'd learned firsthand the wisdom in the legendary Yogi Berra Zen koan: "Ninety percent of this game is mental, and the other half is physical." Moyer had learned, he said, that "pitching takes place from the neck up." He excitedly started walking me through all he had learned at Dorfman's knee. How important having a persona is, for example. There had long been two Jamie Moyers. One, the Clubhouse Gentleman, was the thoughtful, accessible favorite of the media pack due to his willingness to hold forth like an academic on pitching. The Clubhouse Gentleman, who never refused an autograph and who, with his wife, heads a charity foundation that is the model for how pro athletes can make a difference, had long been regarded throughout the game as a loyal teammate and a class act.

And then there's the Inner Warrior. It's the Inner Warrior who comes to the fore when Moyer, his eyes narrowed to intense slits, refers to the pitching mound as "*my* f'ing circle."

Moyer learned, as Carlton had before him, that a pitcher's body language was inextricably linked to his success. He'd watched an early mentor, Nolan Ryan, walk off the mound during an away game only to have a rabid heckler drench the flamethrower in beer. But the indomitable Ryan never even broke stride, his hard-edged sneer firmly in place, while the opposing dugout looked on. The game, at that point, was over. For Moyer, it was an object lesson: if you let opposing batters see you sweat, they'll race each other to the on-deck circle. And if they think you have an otherworldly composure and nerves of granite, they'll begin to doubt themselves, if even slightly.

Jamie was now coming around to the thought of a different kind of sports book. One that told the story of his forthcoming comeback attempt, but that also, in alternating chapters, flashed back to moments of critical challenge throughout his long career: in short, a chronicle of his continuing education. Turns out, he wasn't done learning. A few months after our first meeting came arm surgery, followed by exhaustive rehab. That was followed by one of the most audacious comebacks in sports history—a forty-nine-year-old pitcher with a rebuilt arm making one last stand on the mound. This is the story of that comeback, but of many others as well.

It's the story of what it takes to come back, time and again, in the pressure cooker of professional sports, when you find yourself a punch line on *SportsCenter* or dismissed time and again by the purveyors of conventional wisdom. Is there more of an Everyman on the sporting scene than Moyer? When he's on the mound, he looks like us; all sweat and struggle, graying hair at the temples, lines creasing his face; in the last couple of years, he has found himself middle-aged, with his two eldest children off to college, while he defiantly stares down a potential forced retirement. That temerity has long characterized Moyer. If he had listened to others—high school coaches, pro scouts, major league managers, his own relatives, sabermetrician devotees—he would have been out of baseball years ago.

It's also the story of the ultimate battle that all athletes wage—the one against the calendar. In recent years, we've seen Michael Jordan, Brett Favre, and Roger Clemens all fight the clock; all were, if not tarnished in the attempt, certainly diminished. We may have admired their effort to reclaim past glory, but when Jordan missed that dunk in the 2003 NBA All-Star

Game or when Favre limped off the field after that last flurry of interceptions, we were saddened by the spectacle. Moyer, on the other hand, is arguably the first star athlete who actually kept getting *better* deep into his forties. Hall of Fame pitcher and three-time Cy Young winner Tom Seaver, for example, posted a 66–64 record between the ages of thirty-seven and forty-one. At the same ages, Moyer was 74–44, including two 20-win seasons, at thirty-eight and forty. Between the ages of forty-four and forty-seven, Moyer's record was 51–38.

Of course, the Seaver trajectory is the norm. The careers of great athletes tend to be contracted versions of the typical life span. Major league pitchers peak at twenty-seven; most are out of baseball by their midthirties. Moyer's Seattle teammate Ken Griffey Jr. played until he was forty, but his peak power years were from ages twenty-six to twenty-nine. Even a legend like Joe DiMaggio, who retired at thirty-six, had his best year at twenty-two. Dwight Gooden pitched until he was thirty-five, but never came close to the season he had at twenty. Moyer, though, has defied the script. His Inner Warrior has spent the last decade giving the middle finger to mortality.

But this is also the story of what pitching *is*—the mystery and mastery of it, as seen through the eyes of its most cerebral, seeking student. It's a story deep inside the ever-elusive mental side of sports, in today's Moneyball-dominated culture of spreadsheets and analytics. And most of all, it's the story of two men, professional sports' ultimate odd couple, the unlikely All-Star pitcher with his 80-mile-per-hour fastball, and the unlikely psychologist with his in-your-face observations (*"I know your act, kid!"*) and absence of sentiment.

NOVEMBER 1991

CHAPTER ONE

A great deal of talent is lost in this world for
want of a little courage.

—Harvey Dorfman

As it was for many ballplayers, the idea of seeing a psychologist—a shrink!—was total anathema to Jamie Moyer. But there
he was, on a crisp, sunny day, wandering the baggage claim
area of Phoenix's Sky Harbor International Airport, looking for
his last and best hope at salvaging the only career he'd ever
wanted. He was twenty-nine years old, with a wife and infant son
at home, and he was without a baseball team for the first time
since he was eight years old.

Back then, Moyer would tell whoever would barely listen that
he was going to be a major league pitcher. There were plenty
of doubters, even as he dominated in high school and college.
But he'd made it to the Show, using the naysaying as psychic
fuel along the way. But when the call came from Tom Grieve,
general manager of the Texas Rangers, on November 12, 1990,
how Moyer had always defined himself was suddenly no longer
applicable. With six terse words—"We don't see you helping

us"—Jamie Moyer became a former big leaguer. And one with a desultory 34–49 career record.

Rock, meet bottom.

So Moyer thought, *What do I have to lose?* before flying to Arizona to meet someone his agent, Jim Bronner, thought could be of help. As Karen said before sending Jamie on his way, "Treat this as a learning experience."

He was here to meet Harvey Dorfman, who was arriving on another flight. Together they would drive to Dorfman's home in Prescott, Arizona, about ninety miles away, for a weekend of sessions that...what? Would have him unearth long-dormant resentments about his mother while he was lying on a couch?

In truth, Moyer had read and been intrigued by Dorfman's classic book *The Mental Game of Baseball: A Guide to Peak Performance*, and he'd heard good things about Dorfman from players in the Oakland organization, where Dorfman was on staff and in the process of revolutionizing the subterranean world of sports psychology. But Moyer had grown up in the tiny blue-collar hamlet of Souderton, Pennsylvania, not exactly a New Age zip code.

Plus they weren't a particularly emotive bunch, the Moyers. They expressed themselves through a shared love of baseball. Neighbors would pass the nearby ball field and see those baseball-crazy Moyers—mom Joan, sis Jill, and Jamie all in the outfield, shagging dad Jim's fly balls. Jim, a former minor league shortstop, served as Jamie's coach throughout American Legion ball. Souderton, a working-class suburban town of some 6,000 residents an hour outside Philadelphia, was where Moyer's baseball education took hold—as well as his values. His early baseball journey was nurtured by an entire town that seemed to jump right out of some idealized version of America's past; the same folks who cheered on his three no-hitters his junior year of high school populated Friday night's football games *and* prayed together at church on Sunday. He'd gone from that atavistic world into the macho realm of the professional baseball clubhouse, where introspection is traditionally looked upon with suspicion.

"Hi, I'm Harvey Dorfman," a waddling, croaky-voiced fifty-something said, approaching with outstretched hand. Dorfman didn't look like an athlete, with his hunched shoulders, gimpy gait, and baggy sweatshirt, but Moyer knew that during the season he was in the dugout in an Oakland A's uniform. And anyone—even a shrink—who wore the uniform deserved the benefit of the doubt.

On the awkward ride to Dorfman's house, the two men made small talk. Dorfman asked open-ended questions about Moyer's upbringing and his history in the game, and soon Moyer was unburdening himself:

"I can't throw my curveball for strikes."

Dorfman said nothing.

"I got to the major leagues because of my changeup, but I just show it now. I don't throw it for strikes."

Dorfman said nothing.

"When I'm on the mound, I can't stop thinking about being pulled. Or released."

Dorfman said nothing. He simply smiled.

Isn't this guy going to tell me what to do? Moyer wondered.

A few months before Moyer's pilgrimage to Prescott, *Saturday Night Live* broadcast an uproarious skit featuring guest host Michael Jordan. Called "Daily Affirmations with Stuart Smalley," it was a classic send-up of what happens at the intersection of self-help culture and jockdom. Al Franken played

Smalley, a cable TV host described as a "caring nurturer" and "member of several twelve-step programs," who was looking to provide gentle encouragement to "Michael J.," an anonymous basketball player.

Jordan is coaxed into admitting that sometimes before big games he gets nervous. Smalley tells Jordan to look in the mirror and quell those "critical inner thoughts" by reciting his daily affirmation: "I don't have to dribble the ball fast, or throw the ball into the basket. All I have to do is be the best Michael I can be. Because I'm good enough, I'm smart enough, and doggone it, people like me!" The skit ends with a hug between the best athlete in the world and this comical, cliché-ridden would-be therapist.

Harvey Dorfman was the real-world anti–Stuart Smalley. He knew that the calm, nurturing counselor, with that soothing NPR voice, was a total nonstarter in sports. Unlike other sports psychologists, he knew he had to have a macho persona in order to break through to the modern-day athlete. Even though Dorfman was a bibliophile who could deconstruct the novels of Somerset Maugham in great detail, ballplayers just knew him as a foulmouthed taskmaster. "I don't care about your *feelings*," Dorfman would tell them. "I care about what you *do*."

The character of SNL's Stuart Smalley was everything Dorfman disdained about those in his own profession: too precious, too solicitous. But the skit did nail the crisis in confidence world-class athletes inevitably face. Dorfman had had a procession of major league ballplayers walk through the door to his study over the years, all doing battle with their internal demons, all—no matter the runs batted in or hitters fanned—feeling like, as Smalley would say, imposters. Dorfman knew, of course, that they weren't imposters—just works in progress. But try telling that to an athletic prodigy who, through achingly dull repetition, is raised to train his muscle memory so that the physical act becomes something done by rote. Without fail, ballplayers—and for that matter the wider, retro world of baseball—had never contemplated the possibility that the same type of discipline might be needed to train the mind, so its overactive chatter could get the hell out of the muscles' way. Dorfman adopted an in-your-face persona, more tough-love coach than shrink, designed to jump-start his clients into awareness and action. As he'd tell them, "Muscles are morons. Self-consciousness will screw you up."

Not exactly Freudian wisdom. But then Dorfman wasn't even a shrink. No, he'd been a high school English teacher and basketball coach at Burr and Burton Academy in Manchester, Vermont, where he coached the girls' team to a state title. He was equal parts jock and man of letters, as likely to quote Shakespeare as to dissect the virtues of the two-hand chest pass. He contributed columns to the local paper, slice-of-life profiles of local characters. A baseball column he penned for the *Berkshire Sampler* led him to profile minor leaguers on the Pittsfield Rangers, a Double A farm team of the Texas Rangers. He and top draft pick Roy Smalley sat for hours, sharing psychological insights. Smalley, who had attended the University of Southern California, recommended the book *Psycho-Cybernetics*, by Maxwell Maltz. When Dorfman indicated he'd already read and liked the book, Smalley knew he'd found a kindred spirit.

Once he made the Show, Smalley introduced Dorfman to Karl Kuehl, a coach with the Minnesota Twins. Kuehl, who passed away in 2008, had noticed that players excelled when they were able to simply stay in the moment and set aside their doubts and fears. Dorfman partnered with Kuehl in researching the mental side of the game, and the two began working on a book that would become the bible of sports psychology. *The*

Mental Game of Baseball was published in 1989, and dog-eared copies fast became a staple in baseball clubhouses throughout the major and minor leagues.

When Kuehl became the Oakland A's farm director in 1983, he persuaded general manager Sandy Alderson to hire Dorfman. Alderson, as documented by Michael Lewis in *Moneyball*, would later take on the baseball establishment by playing a critical role in the embryonic stages of the sabermetric revolution. A former Marine and Harvard Law grad, Alderson didn't come up through the baseball ranks and was wired to challenge the game's conventional wisdom. Putting Dorfman in uniform, placing him in the dugout, and making him responsible for, as Harvey put it, everything above the shoulders on every player was a move ahead of its time.

The same could be said of Dorfman's theories. In the last decade, the science of the mental side of sports has become a popular topic among the intelligentsia. In 2000, the *New Yorker's* Malcolm Gladwell wrote an article entitled "The Art of Failure." In it, he defines "choking"—the worst kind of athletic failure—as the opposite of panic. He might as well have been quoting Dorfman from the 1980s. "Choking is about thinking too much," Gladwell writes. "Panic is about thinking too little." In 2012, writer Jonah Lehrer cited in *Neuron* a study by a team of researchers at Caltech and University College London, in which escalating monetary rewards were offered to players of a simple arcade game. As the stakes got higher, player performance significantly worsened.

Intellectuals like Gladwell and Lehrer buttressed their writings with reports from the front lines of neuroscience research, which had become all the rage, but their findings echoed Dorfman from the '80s. Only Dorfman didn't need to don a white coat in order to discover the degree to which self-consciousness altered athletic outcome. His laboratory was Major League Baseball itself, and after Alderson gave him the opportunity, the ensuing years found him developing his unique approach and putting his theories into practice.

There was, for example, the mano a mano with Jose Canseco in the minors, after the phenom failed to run out a grounder. There Dorfman was, right in the slugger's face after Canseco nonchalantly shrugged off his lack of hustle by chalking it up to "normal" frustration.

"*Normal?*" Dorfman shrieked. "You want to be *normal?* You're an elite athlete. You're already exceptional—and that's what you should want for yourself. To be extraordinary, not ordinary."

Canseco, backing down, asked how he should have handled his emotions. "Just train yourself by saying, 'Hit the ball, run. Hit the ball, run. Hit the ball, run,'" Dorfman explained. "It'll become an acquired instinct. It doesn't matter how you *feel* during combat; you fight."

Just a year and a half prior to Moyer's visit, Dorfman had been instrumental in settling down A's pitcher Bob Welch. Welch, a recovering alcoholic, had always been a jumble of nerves, fidgeting on the mound to the point of distraction, especially when the pressure mounted. "You can make coffee nervous," Dorfman told him. Welch would become frenetic on the mound, in a rush to get the ball back from his catcher. Dorfman and catcher Terry Steinbach conspired together. When Welch would walk to the front of the mound, waving his glove in order to get the ball returned—*now!*—Steinbach wouldn't throw it. That, Dorfman told his pupil pitcher, would trigger the signal in Welch's mind to take a deep breath, exhaling slowly, bringing himself down.

To the ballplayers, Dorfman was as in-your-face as the other coaches, it's just that he provided practical *mental* tips. Welch joked, "If you told Harvey you just killed somebody, he'd say, 'What are you going to do about that?'"

Dorfman's emphasis on practical tactics was an actual psychological school of thought he was the first to apply to baseball: semantitherapy. Freudians, Dorfman believed, in their search for the long-dormant cause of a patient's fear or neurosis, forgot to treat the manifestation of those fears. Perhaps the root of a fear of flying *is* in a patient's childhood in the form of a long-ago traumatic experience. But just as real are the current-day sweaty palms and heart palpitations as the plane readies for takeoff. In baseball, Dorfman realized, if you conquer the symptoms, you kill the disease.

Now this kid Moyer presented with some familiar indications. Fear, doubt, lack of confidence, distracting thoughts. For the better part of three days, Dorfman would give the kid the full treatment. He and Anita, Dorfman's wife of thirty-one years, a schoolteacher who'd grown used to and welcomed these visits from shy, awkward athletes, lived in a house at the top of a hill on a secluded cul-de-sac. He and Moyer would do multiple two-hour sessions in Dorfman's study each day, go for long walks in the Arizona hills, and have breakfasts of oatmeal and bagels with Anita. Dorfman didn't usually work with players who weren't in the A's system, but this was a favor to Moyer's agent, Jim Bronner. The kid was nearly thirty and had a losing record. There was a lot of work to be done.

At least there's no couch, Moyer thought, entering Dorfman's study. Dorfman settled in behind a big oak desk, in front of a bookcase that housed many of the inspirational quotes and anecdotes that Dorfman would pepper his life lessons with.

Moyer would hear those gems over the next twenty-odd years; they'd seep into his consciousness much like Harvey himself, everything from Cromwell's "The man who doesn't know where he's going goes the fastest" to Marcus Aurelius's "If you are distressed by anything external, the pain is not due to the thing itself but to your own estimate of it; and this you have the power to revoke at any moment."

Moyer didn't know what was in those books, and he didn't know what to think. He was about to pick up the conversation where he'd broken it off in the car—with a recitation of all that he was doing wrong—when Dorfman lurched forward.

"There are a couple of things you need to know, kid," Dorfman said. "First, this doesn't work if you're not honest with me. I don't have time for you if you're not going to level with me. And second, none of this goes back to your agent or your club or the media. This is just you and me."

Just you and me. The words washed over Moyer. The mound, once a calm escape, had become frightening in its solitariness. On it, he was keenly aware of *them*: the fans, the manager, the teammates. He'd hear them, or he'd imagine what they were thinking about him. When a fan heckled him for his lack of speed, he'd carry on an angry pretend dialogue in his head: *You think this is easy?* When runners got on, he'd wonder what his teammates were thinking, he'd decipher the body language of his catcher—was he against me now too? He sensed—or invented—collective doubt all around him, and it led him to wonder, *Do I belong?* But now here was someone who actually wore a major league uniform saying he was there *with* him.

Moyer returned to his narrative, cataloging all that he can't do on the mound. Can't get ahead of hitters. Can't throw the changeup, once his money pitch. Can't stop furtively glancing into the dugout to see if the skipper is on the phone to the pen.

He talked about how the middle twelve inches of the seventeen-inch plate belong to the hitter, but how the umps rarely consistently gave him what he believed to be rightfully his: the outer inches on either side. Finally, Dorfman, who'd been listening with his eyes locked on Moyer's, had heard enough.

"Bullshit."

Pause. "Excuse me?"

"Bullshit. You have control over that. Over all of it."

"I do? How?"

"By changing your thought process. You gain control over all of it by acknowledging that you have no control over any of it, the umpire, or the manager, or what other people think, and by taking responsibility for what you can control."

Moyer wasn't getting it. "Are you aware of how you talk about yourself?" Dorfman asked. "It's all negative. 'I can't, I can't, I can't.' I've seen your act, kid, and you need to get better. You need to change your thinking. Your process needs to be *positive*. You have to train yourself to hear a negative thought, stop, let it run its course, and then let it go. 'Cause it doesn't mean crap. The only thing that matters is focusing on the task at hand, which is making that pitch. The task at hand."

It's a page right out of classic Zen meditation—stop, label the distracting thoughts, and return to your breath. Dorfman reminded Moyer of one of baseball's most infamous cases of the yips, when Dodgers second basemen Steve Sax suddenly, inexplicably could no longer make the rudimentary throw from second to first. If, when Sax fielded the ball, he thought to himself, *I'm not going to throw this ball away*, he might have *thought* he was thinking positively. But he was actually focusing his mind on committing an error—in effect, directing his body to do just that. A better thought, Dorfman explained, would be, *I'm going to hit the first baseman with a throw that's chest high.*

To get there, though, the player has to learn to think about what he's thinking. To reformulate his thoughts. Dorfman suggested an exercise. "I want you to rephrase everything you've already told me, taking out all the 'can't' stuff, all the negativity. Restate it. Go ahead. I challenge you."

This is going to be hard, Moyer thought. How do you positively observe that you can't throw your curveball for strikes? He stammered and stuttered, started and stopped. Finally, he came to this: "I'm going to throw a sweeping curveball that catches the inside corner to a righthanded hitter."

Dorfman seemed pleased. But, he said, just stating that isn't enough. "You need to *see* it," he said. "You need to visualize the flight of that curveball before you throw it. So you say it, you see it, and then you throw it."

In this way, Dorfman explained, the mind was as much a muscle as any other on the pitcher's body: "We're training it."

Moyer's own idol, Steve Carlton, was the master of such training. Carlton considered pitching nothing more than a heightened game of catch between him and his catcher; the batter was merely incidental. On days that he'd pitch, Carlton would lie down on the training table after batting practice and close his eyes. Teammates would laugh, thinking he was napping. In reality, he was imagining his "lanes" in the strike zone—an outer lane and an inner lane. He'd imagine the flight of his ball within those lanes, over and over. The middle of the plate didn't exist in his mind's eye, and nor did any menacing hitters or rabid fans. He was fixated on those lanes. He was focused, as Dorfman would say, on "the task at hand."

The moral of the Carlton example? "It's not about anyone else," Dorfman said. "It's all about *you*. You're the one with the ball in your hand. You're the one everyone else reacts to. You're in charge."

It had been so long since Moyer felt in charge on the mound. He had always wanted to be Steve Carlton, who, miraculously, he'd beaten in his major league debut for the Cubs five years earlier. Growing up in Souderton, Jamie would be in front of the big color TV every fifth day in the living room of that modest house on North Fourth Street, watching Lefty, who always seemed so in control of his emotions and surroundings. He might not have Carlton's heat or his world-class slider, but he could certainly emulate his mastery of the mental game.

It had been two hours. "Go relax in your room, watch TV," Dorfman told him. Instead, Moyer flopped on the twin bed in the Dorfmans' guest room and flipped open a notebook. He hurriedly scribbled notes, fearing he'd forget what he just learned, even as he was excitedly unsure about precisely *what* he was learning.

Jamie Moyer had never before been fearful on the mound. Even as he dominated in high school and at St. Joseph's University in Philadelphia, there were doubters, but he'd never let them get to him. In fact, early on, like so many successful athletes, he'd not only hear but catalog the criticisms, compiling a type of internal roster of slights in order to drive his own narrative of retribution. "All I heard growing up was 'You can't, you can't, you can't,'" he says. "Every time I heard someone doubt me, I'd just use it to push me more."

Ironic, isn't it, how the doubts caught up to him after five years of failure in the big leagues? He'd had setbacks, of course, but no real crisis of confidence—until now. It was as if the thought of failure hadn't occurred to him in his youth, so he was immune to the fear of it. Dorfman knew that Moyer wasn't alone. Scores of ballplayers confront their first crisis of confidence after they've already made it to the big leagues. He'd seen players who are so crippled by anxiety that they can't perform, or who protect what modicum of self-esteem they have left by not trying hard. Not putting anything on the line is actually the safer course. You wouldn't know it to look at these strapping young ballplayers, but their psyches were often in torment. In the same way that many of us, in our Little League days, would silently hope that the ball wouldn't come our way, Dorfman had found that the best baseball players in the world were similarly paralyzed by such self-fulfilling fear. He'd quote former outfielder Enos Cabell, whose best years were with the Houston Astros in the '70s and '80s: "I don't want to be a star, they get blamed too much." That's a scared player, Dorfman knew.

Dorfman, on the other hand, was schooled early in fear. Moyer's youth was spent outdoors, playing sports and competing. Dorfman's formative years were spent in bed in a Bronx apartment, a sickly asthmatic whose overprotective mother would fuss over him all day, gripping his clenched fists as young Harvey would sit upright, struggling for one more breath. Dorfman rebelled; he raged against his sickness as well as the comfort and security of his loving home. Growing up surrounded by fear—it was in the air, with the cataloging, each morning, of whether little Harvey had had a good or bad night—he learned how to tell it to get lost. Like any schoolyard bully, fear backed down when you stood up to it.

So it was that the baseball prodigy encountered debilitating fear as he approached thirty, and sought solace and counsel from the aging psychologist who had stared fear down as a sick child. Now Dorfman gave Moyer the three-point plan that he'd spent a lifetime developing. He had Moyer write this down: "1). Awareness (Define the Problem). 2). Forming a Strategy (What Has to Be Done?) 3). Act It Out. (Do It)." And he told him,

"To aspire to great achievement is to risk failure. It's a package deal."

Again and again, Dorfman emphasized to Moyer that, as the pitcher, *he* was in charge—*he* set the tempo. "That mound is your f'ing circle, and you need to have that attitude about it," Dorfman said. Moyer's eyes widened. Later, in his room, he scribbled down the phrases "My f'ing circle" and "Knock somebody down."

They talked about the difference between anger and aggression on the mound, about how to identify distractions, take a deep breath, and just let them go. "Timing is important," Dorfman said. "Our minds are at peak efficiency for about six seconds, and then we have to refocus our attention. If you rush your thinking, you'll have a rushed delivery." Dorfman schooled Moyer in what he called the "mental windup." Let distracting, negative thoughts run their course by giving them time to leave your mind, he said. Then come back to your breath and a visual image of the outcome you desire.

They talked about Moyer developing a set routine on days that he pitches—so that his focus narrows to laserlike precision by the time he takes the mound. Until now, Moyer's game-day routine had been angst-ridden. He'd sit in front of his locker, his stomach roiling, obsessing. He was focused on outcome, not process. "You lose control when your feelings and thoughts center on consequence," Dorfman said. Instead, they mapped out a routine centered on Moyer controlling what he could control, one that built his level of concentration to its peak by game time. It was methodical—from the time that he lifted three-pound weights to when he put on his mesh shirt and stretch undershorts—all designed to mentally lead him to a familiar state of confidence and preparedness.

They talked about "strong eyes" versus "weak eyes"—the difference between a passive persona on the mound and one who is intently locked in on his catcher, lost in (here's that phrase again) the task at hand. They talked about Moyer's changeup—the pitch he learned at St. Joe's, the pitch that got him to the major leagues, the pitch he now didn't have enough confidence in to throw over the plate.

"Your lack of speed is your weapon," Dorfman proclaimed. "Be aggressive with it!" A changeup from Jamie Moyer was, in other words, akin to a fastball from Nolan Ryan. Instead of just showcasing it to keep hitters honest, go after them with it— *throw it with conviction!*

And then Dorfman said the thing Moyer would say for years, whenever he was asked to define his pitching style: "You're not going to blow guys away," he said. "You are who you are. Accept who you are. You have to outthink batters. You have to use their egos against them. They come up there thinking they can crush your pitch. *Use that.*"

More breathless notes.

After three days, Dorfman took Moyer to the airport. The pitcher felt exhilarated, but also a bit confused, like he'd gotten a glimpse, but only a glimpse, into a whole new way of thinking. How would he ever figure this thing out by himself? Dorfman sensed his inner tumult. Dropping Moyer off at the terminal, he extended his hand. "I'm only a phone call away, Jamie," he said.

SEPTEMBER 2011

CHAPTER TWO

> To aspire to great achievement is to risk failure.
>
> —Harvey Dorfman

Feeling like more of a suspect than a prospect, Jamie Moyer eyes the specimen of athletic prowess before him. Perci Garner is a 6´3˝, 225-pound literal definition of prospect. He's twenty-two years old, broad-shouldered and thick-legged, with a quick, wide smile. His fastball has been clocked at 93 and 94 miles per hour, and has reached 97.

Moyer looks Garner up and down. "I don't know if you're ready for it yet," he says with mock solemnity. "But are you a reader?"

Garner says he is, so Moyer starts evangelizing. "There's a book called *The Mental ABC's of Pitching*, by a fellow named Harvey Dorfman. He also wrote a book called *The Mental Game of Baseball*. These are the best books about the game of baseball because they deal with this"—Moyer points to his head—"and teach you how to use it. They'll teach Perci how to get out of Perci's way."

It's the fall of 2011 and they are here, the veteran and the phenom, in the Clearwater, Florida, clubhouse of Bright House Field, the Philadelphia Phillies' spring training complex, for reasons both alike—to work on their respective games—and vastly dissimilar. Garner, drafted in 2010 by the Phillies in the second round out of Ball State University, is here trying to make the transition from thrower to pitcher. Moyer is here, nine months after Tommy John surgery, to find out if he'll ever be a major league pitcher again.

The Phillies, his former team, have offered the use of their facility and trainers for this quixotic exercise. Moyer can't bring himself to call it a comeback, not yet, though those around him know that's exactly what it is. He's taking things one step at a time, as he does on the mound. Like pitching, his rehab is a process. He has thrown long toss without pain, but hasn't tried to really pitch, save one disastrous batting practice session from forty feet on flat ground to a group of fourteen- and fifteen-year-olds, including his son Hutton, who were trying out for summer league back in Seattle last spring. There, the ball seemed in open rebellion upon each release; it was merely forty feet, and yet a man who had been able to deliver a baseball within centimeters of a target for decades now had no idea where it was going. One pitch bounced to the plate. Another sailed over the catcher's head. He struck one fifteen-year-old batter in the torso, the kid's eyes morphing in one panic-stricken instant from excitement to terror. Then he did it again. (What a story *that* kid would have to tell!)

Of fifty pitches, six were hittable. Two hit the kid. And forty-three were nowhere near the hitting zone. After five minutes, embarrassed and flustered, Moyer slinked away and went home to crack open a beer and wonder if that was that—if, despite the surgery, he was done. Though his arm had been remade, maybe his *ability* had somehow gotten lost?

He'd heard the stories. How in some 15 percent of Tommy John cases, the thing that is gone, the thing that never comes back, is control. That said, Moyer told himself not to read too much into this debacle. After all, he had never been very good at throwing batting practice, where the goal is to give the hitter something he can hit square on the barrel of the bat, an exercise wholly at odds with Moyer's desire to keep the hitter off balance by preventing him from getting good wood on the ball. Besides, for the last quarter century he'd had a similar feeling every time he first took the mound each spring to face a live batter—that the ball in his hand, far from being an extension of his arm and mind, mocked him in its refusal to go where he was used to putting it. He'd always been able to work through it; he'd always been able to rouse his muscle memory. Eventually, he always became Jamie Moyer again. Could he be that person again at forty-eight, with a surgically repaired arm and, for the first time in memory, a bit of a middle-age paunch?

Tomorrow, he'll pitch off a mound for the first time in ten months, since the night in the Dominican Republic in the fall of 2010 when, trying to come back from the injury initially sustained on that steaming St. Louis night in July 2010, he blew out his arm. He'd been befuddling the Dominican hitters when he threw a cutter down and in to a righthanded batter. It snapped his ulnar collateral ligament *and* his flexor pronator clean off his elbow, the black-and-purple bruise developing quickly, like the exposure of a Polaroid photograph.

He mentions Dorfman's book to Garner because yesterday the two men played catch. To Moyer, a game of catch is never just a game of catch. He learned at an early age that catch *is* work—not some idle act between batting practice at-bats. Long toss, in particular, is a rite of spring. Typically, a pitcher and his throwing partner will begin at twenty feet apart, softly throwing to one another. As the players limber up, they move back in roughly ten-foot increments, topping out at somewhere around a hundred feet. As Moyer and Garner warmed up, Garner's ball sizzling through the air and thudding into Moyer's glove, Moyer noticed that *both* of Garner's feet faced him. "Do you always play catch like that?" he asked, approaching the pupil. "You don't pitch like that, so why would you play catch like that?"

Moyer moved Garner so his back foot was perpendicular to the target, just like it is on the pitching rubber. Garner's ball rocketed through the air, but seldom did two consecutive throws arrive at precisely the same spot. Some throws sailed overhead, some hit the ground short of Moyer. After a particularly wild and high bullet, Garner chastised himself under his breath: "C'mon, you're playing with a big leaguer!"

Finally, Moyer stopped. "The big question for you is, 'How am I gonna teach myself good muscle memory?'" he said. "You play golf?"

"Trying to," Garner said, smiling broadly again.

"Well, you can figure it out, then," Moyer said. "Golf is all about tempo. If my body is ahead of my hands, I'm not going to hit the ball right. If my body is behind my hands, I'm not going to hit the ball right. But if my body and my hands are working together, I'm going to hit the ball right. When you're playing long toss, you've gotta *feel* when you make a good throw, visualize where your arm slot is, and recall that feeling time after time. Because I guarantee you there are times during a season where you're gonna lose your arm slot. So the repetition now helps you find it then. Think about throwing the ball *through* me. Take your fingers and reach into my belly button. You want to get extension. It doesn't have to be hard, just create carry to the ball, and backspin."

The two went back to throwing, quietly basking in the sounds of catch, with Moyer occasionally breaking the silence with "Better!" or "Arm slot!" or "Through me!"

Today, Moyer introduces his accidental pupil to a game, one he grew up playing. The two stand some sixty feet from one another, roughly the distance between pitcher and catcher; one positions his glove as a target for the other. If the receiver has to move his glove to catch the other's throw, it's a point against the thrower. First one to 21 loses. Game after game, Garner's glove doesn't move. When he offers a low target, Moyer whistles. "You don't want to go there," he says. "That's where I live."

Here now, with each throw, it's becoming clear to Moyer that—the summer tryout disaster notwithstanding—he can still make accurate throws. And with each admonition from Moyer to "have an awareness of your body" and to "reach through me," Garner's throws get more accurate.

Still, the kid loses 21–8 and 21–6, and is frustrated. Moyer can see it. "Listen, if you learn one thing about the game every time you come to work, you'd be a pretty good player, right?" he says. "One thing—about the game, or about pitching, or about hitters, or about base runners. To me, that's our goal. Even at my age, that's the goal. Learn one thing a day, and learn it well. That gives you a chance to get better, because any problem can be solved. Any setback is temporary, and you can learn from it, if you do the work."

If you spend any amount of time with Moyer when he is in baseball mode, you start to hear his Inner Harvey come out. He has spent so long inculcating Dorfman's lessons that he doesn't even hear them as Harvey's when they leave his mouth. So it is now: thumbing through my copy of Dorfman's book, I find it. "Any problem is solvable. Any setback is temporary and instructive." In Moyer's own copy of the book, it's one of the underlined phrases.

Afterwards, back in the empty clubhouse, Garner admits to Moyer that he's nervous playing catch with him. Moyer tells the wide-eyed hurler, "You're creating that. All physical acts start with a thought." He tells his newfound protégé that it's okay to be nervous or afraid—so long as you attack that fear and make it work for you. And you do that, as Harvey used to say, by changing your thinking, by acknowledging that the pressure you feel is self-made. And if you've created the pressure, you can discard it. Again, it's Harvey speaking: "A physical performance is the outcome of a thought," or "It's hard to see the picture when you're inside the frame."

Later, over beers at Clearwater's Tilted Kilt sports bar, I ask Moyer if he was aware that he'd been quoting Harvey to the kid. Though Moyer is a hard-bitten old-school baseball man who guards his emotions on the mound, he is quick to sentiment off it. Now he takes a pull on his beer and his eyes mist over at the mention of his friend, who passed away earlier in the year. In keeping with who Harvey was, there was no public funeral or memorial service. Moyer was at home, recovering from Tommy John surgery, when Roy Halladay called, having just heard the news.

"Was he even in the hospital?" Moyer asked.

"I don't know. No one knows," Halladay replied.

Shortly thereafter, Brad Lidge was on the line: was there any information? There wasn't. But there was, for days, a series of commiserating phone calls among big league players, all in search of information, all trying to figure out how to say goodbye to their mentor. He never wanted it to be about him.

Moyer moped around the house, angry that he hadn't had a chance to bid a proper farewell and tell Harvey what he'd meant to him. At the same time, he knew Harvey wouldn't have been one for grandiose exit scenes. Harvey's players had long known he was sick, but that's about all they knew. In the late '90s, after having worked for the A's, the Florida Marlins, and the Tampa Bay Devil Rays, Dorfman went to work counseling the clients of agent Scott Boras. Boras would send ballplayers to see Dorfman because Harvey could no longer travel.

For years after their initial weekend meeting in Prescott (Harvey and Anita had since moved to Brevard, North Carolina), Moyer would call Dorfman at least every month and unburden himself. Dorfman would dissect his language—"Whaddya mean, you *can't?*"—and not let Moyer lapse into scapegoating. In the latter stages of his career, Moyer had internalized so much of Dorfman's wisdom that he no longer *needed* to call, which Dorfman had long predicted. "You already know the answers," he'd say. "It's just a question of changing your thinking." Still, Moyer would call just to check on Harvey's health and ask after Anita. Even in his late forties, a funny thing would happen to Moyer when Dorfman would answer the phone: upon hearing that scratchy and cough-laden voice, a warm wave of comfort would wash over him. More than once, Moyer jokingly wondered to Karen whether Harvey had hypnotized him years ago.

Moyer didn't know that Dorfman had had a serious congenital respiratory issue, having battled severe asthma his whole life. He just knew to call his friend in the mornings because by afternoon Harvey could barely speak through his coughing fits. Still, when asked about his health, Dorfman would deadpan, "My streak goes on."

"What streak is that, Harv?"

"Consecutive days alive."

Now, back in the bar, Moyer takes his eyes from the Marlins game on the big screen before us. "I'm enjoying talking to Perci about this stuff," he says. "But it's also a way for Harvey to be talking to me. I may be coaching Perci, but Harvey's coaching me, too."

It is a strange dynamic, a situation faced by every elite athlete at some point or another. You have millions of people watching you succeed or fail at the most tender of ages, and then, when others your age are still looking forward professionally, you're faced with the end of a career.

What's next? What *could* be next? What could rival the excitement, the challenge, the competition? After being the best athlete in the world, Michael Jordan searched compulsively for something to replace the thrill of playing basketball professionally. He even got into motorcycle thrill racing on the deserted streets of Chicago at 3 a.m., so addicted was he to recapturing the adrenaline rush of his youth. His friend Charles Barkley, who retired from the NBA at thirty-seven ("Now I'm just what America needs—another unemployed black man"), says he initially looked forward to playing golf every day. "At some point, I said to my wife, 'Hey, how long have I been retired?'" he says. "She said, 'About six weeks.' I said, 'Uh-oh.'"

After the cheering stops, most athletes stare into an existential abyss. *What now?* Moyer knows ballplayers who have hung up their cleats and turned to alcohol or substance abuse, spurred by a sudden, pounding sense of loss. The very way they've always defined themselves, after all, was no more.

But Moyer, in his year and a half away from the game, wasn't in mourning. Back home in Rancho Santa Fe, just outside San Diego, he fell into a comfortable, stable routine. The Moyers—Jamie, wife Karen, and their eight kids, including two Guatemalan adoptees, who range in age from twenty to five—live amid a sort of baseball diaspora. Retired players Vince

Coleman, Trevor Hoffman, and Mike Sweeney all live nearby. In fact, Sweeney coached eight-year-old Mac Moyer—who brought gas against eleven- and twelve-year-olds. (Phils manager Charlie Manuel likes to joke that Mac *already* throws harder than his old man.) Moyer found himself enjoying playing Mr. Mom and being a talking head analyst on ESPN, appearances that met with good reviews.

Still, Karen sensed that something was missing. Every day, when the dishwasher would complete its cycle, her husband would bound off the sofa as if the bullpen phone had just rung with orders to start throwing. It was a comical Sportsworld version of the final scene of *The Hurt Locker*, in which Sergeant First Class William James, played by Jeremy Renner, is back from war and shown going through the motions of domestic life—grocery shopping, tucking in the kids—only to realize he can't live without the action promised by another tour of duty. The film begins with the quote, "The rush of battle is a potent and often lethal addiction, for war is a drug"; the same could be said of sports, especially at the highest levels of American pop culture. Like Renner's character, world-class athletes like Moyer are addicted to team camaraderie, and to the adrenaline rush of competition. Is that what's driving Moyer to be here, in Florida, at nearly forty-nine, following a year off, following reconstructive arm surgery, contemplating a comeback that none of the game's punditocracy can fathom?

Given Moyer's present-tense mind-set—courtesy of Dorfman—it's not always clear what is driving him. Though the charity work he and Karen do, helping kids in distress, never fails to move him to tears, he has long been stoic when it comes to the game. During a streak when he threw three consecutive no-hitters his junior year of high school, he'd come home and his mother, Joan, would ask, "Did you win?" To which, he'd simply reply, "Yeah." She had to hear the minor detail that he'd thrown a no-hitter from neighbors.

So it is today. When asked why someone who has achieved so much and earned $83 million over his career would attempt a comeback at such an advanced age, Moyer thinks for a moment and then simply states, "Because I can." He doesn't spend a lot of time inspecting his own motivations—that's for the know-it-alls in the media to do. Over the next year, as he makes his way back, there will be further insights as to why he refuses to go gently; for now, it's enough to reference another Harvey-ism: "Believe it and you will become it." Moyer suspects he can still get batters out. Far from refusing to let go, he's still looking forward.

What is clearer is what's *not* driving him. Moyer doesn't seem interested in posterity; he doesn't even know how many career wins he has (267, thirty-sixth all-time), or how that compares to others who are in the Hall of Fame. (Jim Kaat is not in with 283 wins; Bert Blyleven is, with 287.) Nor does his other career options—like broadcasting—seem to excite him. When he was at ESPN's Bristol, Connecticut, campus last season, he'd think of something Tommy Lasorda used to tell his players, that there are three types of people: those who make things happen, those who watch what happens, and those who wonder what the hell just happened. He was not yet ready to be merely commenting on the action; he still felt the yearning to be in it.

So here he is, away from his close-knit family, holed up in a Clearwater Holiday Inn Express, rousing himself out of bed every day at 6 a.m. to put in three hours of rehab work—arm strengthening with light weights, running in four feet of water on a hydraulic-powered treadmill, countless "Jobe" exercises, named after Dr. Frank Jobe, the legendary sports orthopedic surgeon. One of the keys to Moyer's longevity has been the premium he's placed on working his serratus anterior muscle. That's the ridgelike muscle that runs from the upper eight or nine ribs at the front of the rib cage and attaches to the winglike bone at the back of the shoulder blades. The serratus generally gets ignored in the typical weight room routine, but it's critical to the upward shoulder rotation that is part of the pitching process.

Moyer calls this going to work every day. Its reward is to play long toss or throw a bullpen; if you want Jamie Moyer to come alive, ask what he's working on in his bullpen session. Like the neighboring men back home in Souderton who spent their Saturdays in their muscle Ts with their garage doors up and their bodies hunched over their car's precious engine, Moyer's bullpen sessions are when he tinkers and experiments, playing with new grips or infinitesimally nuanced tweaks to his windup. As much as he loves the competition of pitching against the best hitters in the world—and he's faced an astonishing 8.9 percent of all major league hitters in the entire history of the game—he may love those solitary bullpen sessions more, with their sense of trial and error and discovery.

Moyer is nothing if not a zealot about the notion of pitching as process. Baseball, as he's seen it and as he's lived it, is a game that rewards the steady application of principle; if you do the right, unselfish things—move runners along, pitch to contact, make adjustments based on the evidence before you—the results will come during the course of a long season. Paradoxically, if you're *only* focused on those results, they'll be heartbreakingly elusive.

Another partial—but only partial—explanation of why he's here is his lifelong passion for proving his doubters wrong, an utterly common motivation among elite athletes. There was, for instance, the high school basketball coach who told him he'd talked to Bill White, the former broadcaster and president of the National League, whose son played for a rival Pennsylvania school. The word came back: despite his three no-hitters his junior year, Moyer was a good high school pitcher who didn't throw hard enough to have a future in the game. There were the back-to-back releases from the Rangers and Cardinals organizations, respectively, in the early '90s. "We don't win when you pitch," Joe Torre, St. Louis's manager at the time, explained to the 0–5 Moyer, whose initial thought was, *That's quite obvious*.

And there was, shortly thereafter, his own father-in-law, legendary college basketball coach Digger Phelps, suggesting he could call a good friend who sold RVs—maybe there was a sales position available. Moyer had immense respect for Phelps; at the same time, he told himself that his father-in-law knew basketball, not baseball. He reminded himself that in *his* sport, lefties mature late. When Digger made the RV offer, rather than feeling discouraged, Moyer was energized. *Okay, you're another one of those people who doesn't believe*, he said to himself.

It's a sports story as old as our sports, really: the athlete who turns the doubts of others into an internal I'll-show-you narrative. It's Michael Jordan, years later, summoning the pain of being cut from his high school team to fuel an otherworldly drive. It's Mike Schmidt, jump-starting a Hall of Fame career by replaying in his head the boos of his hometown fans, in order to prove them wrong. And it's Moyer, a losing pitcher cut multiple times, resolving in his early thirties that if his career were to flame out, he wouldn't go down without a fight. "This isn't how it's going to end for me," he told Digger.

But coming back now, at nearly forty-nine, requires something deeper than responding to critics. It demands a reservoir of energy—much of it mental—that is all too uncommon among athletes in their twilight years. Steve Mix, who played thirteen seasons in the NBA and retired at age thirty-five, says he knew when it was time to go. "I was playing for Los Angeles and I saw a rebound come off the rim and I thought to myself, 'I can get that,'" he recalls. "And then I thought, 'Aw, screw it. I'll get the next one.'"

Mix is more the norm. Oftentimes the aging athlete still has the physical skills to succeed, but, having nothing left to prove, he lacks the intensity of his youth. "A lot of times, the competitive fire in guys goes out," says former manager Tony La Russa. "Jamie's fitness level is amazing, but more impressive than that is his mental commitment. His fire is still burning bright. That's what I shake my head at."

Moyer feels he owes it to himself to explore whether he can still get guys half his age out. He still tears up when he thinks about those words he uttered to Charlie Manuel on that 2010 night in St. Louis: "I can't throw." It's the difference between giving something up voluntarily—and having it ripped from your grip. If he's going to go out, Moyer wants it to be on *his* terms.

Before leaving for Florida, Moyer spoke to Pat Gillick, his general manager during the peak years in Seattle and in Philly. Gillick stressed something that Moyer's career had always shown, that there's a difference between command and control on the mound. Having control means throwing strikes and not walking guys. Having command means "living on the black": working the count by consistently attacking the black corners of the plate, which are not only tough pitches to hit, but also tough pitches for umpires to call balls. Pitchers call it "hitting your spots," and it's often the difference between hitter's counts (2–0, 2–1, 3–0, 3–1) and pitcher's counts (0–1, 0–2, 1–2, 2–2). That difference can make all the difference: in 2009, major league hitters hit .391 when ahead 2–1 in the count and just .171 when behind 1–2. That's the difference of one pitch; baseball truly is a game of quarter-inches.

Moyer has always had good control, but it has long been his command that has set him apart. Gillick reassured Moyer that he could pitch *well* into his fifties—provided he still had it. "If you can still hit your spots, you'll be fine for years to come," Gillick said.

Tomorrow, Moyer will face his first major step in this very deliberate process. There will be no fanfare, and hardly any witnesses, yet thirty pitches—mostly four-seam fastballs with a handful of two-seamers thrown in—might be all that's keeping Jamie Moyer from being a former big league pitcher.

Rollie DeArmas has the look of a lifer, one of those career baseball men who, though their names aren't widely known, are the keepers of the game. DeArmas is sixty years old and has spent much of his playing career in the minors. Since the late '70s, he's primarily been a minor league manager and coach, including a stint with the Phillies as their minor league catching instructor in 2005–6, when a Spanish-speaking converted second baseman named Carlos Ruiz was still learning the position.

When DeArmas got a call from one of the Phillies trainers to come by today and catch Jamie Moyer, he didn't know what to expect. Wasn't this guy retired? Now, crouching behind home plate, his eyebrows rise in surprise when the first fastball hisses in. For all the jokes about Moyer's lack of velocity, up close, a baseball traveling at roughly 80 miles per hour still seems fast. But it's not the speed that surprises DeArmas—it's the location. Right over the black part of the plate, down and in to a righthanded batter.

On the mound, Moyer is wearing a red Phillies cap and work-out shirt. He is pitching out of the stretch, with a free and easy delivery that's notable for its lack of grunts or violent, Lincecum-like gyrations. His mechanics seem effortless. To the untrained eye, it would seem that he might be barely trying.

Pitch number two hits the same spot. He's in a rhythm now. Pitches three through six all catch the same corner.

"How am I doing, Rollie?" Moyer asks.

"Outstanding!" DeArmas yells back. "Just like 2008!" Moyer led the world champion Phillies with 16 wins that year, to go with a 3.71 ERA.

Around pitch twelve, a fastball is up and over the plate. "Damn!" Moyer calls out upon its release, before it's even smacked DeArmas's glove. But then he's back on the edge, or just barely off it until pitch fifteen, when he signals DeArmas to the other corner. He's just as accurate on that side, the ball hit-ting DeArmas's glove either over the black or an inch inside to a lefty batter. Before quitting, he throws some two-seamers; they look like a straight fastball, only to drop at the last possible in-stant before reaching DeArmas. All in all, he's thrown thirty-five pitches, and for at least thirty of them, DeArmas didn't have to move the target.

Baseball lifers are not prone to bluster. They've been on too many all-night bus rides, in so many rinky-dink parks, seen so many phenoms that never pan out, to get too excited about a single throwing session, no matter how promising. Yet as they prepare to leave the field, DeArmas's face is frozen in a wide smile as he shakes Moyer's hand. "Outstanding!" he exclaims.

Moyer walks the empty hallway leading to the trainer's room, where he'll have his shoulder and arm loosened and worked on before doing another half hour on an elliptical machine. He whistles as he walks, tossing the ball to himself, kidlike, as he goes. As he's on the trainer's table, his shoulder being stretched, DeArmas comes bounding in, still buzzing.

"I am in total shock!" the coach says. "I didn't expect you to throw *that* good."

"How was the sink, Rollie?" Moyer asks.

"The sink was outstanding, unbelievable. And the velocity— it was *better* than in '08."

"Yeah, well, I'm brand-new now," Moyer says, laughing at DeArmas's excitement. As a lifer himself, Moyer will play it closer to type. He's encouraged by his command today, but he knows there is a long way to go. He had his fastballs today. Now on to the next challenge: over the next three weeks he'll reintroduce each one of his pitches, until he has command of his full repertoire.

Moyer essentially throws four pitches. He thought he'd have no problem rediscovering the four-seamer, but he's extra pleased that the sink of his two-seamer impressed Rollie. It's the grip that causes that action on the ball. The seams are on a baseball for a reason; when you hold a ball along them, with your fingers actually resting on them, you create backspin, which makes the ball suddenly drop.

Next will come the changeup, which Moyer first learned from a teammate in college. The first time he tried throwing it, a series of pitches went sailing over the backstop. The challenge is to maintain the same arm speed as the fastball, otherwise the hitter will pick up on the decreased speed before the pitcher even releases the ball. So how is it that Moyer's changeup is typically ten miles per hour slower than his fastball? Grip, again: he holds the ball with the three nondominant fingers of his left hand. But his index finger and thumb aren't pushing behind the pitch, thereby reducing its force and increasing its deception.

Once the change is complementing the fastball, Moyer will seek to find his looping curveball, which he's had since high school. He's one of the last to throw a spiked curve, with the fingernail of his index finger wedged into the seam of the ball.

The wild card, and final pitch to rediscover, will be the cutter—a version of Moyer's idol Steve Carlton's legendary slider. Because of its sharper snap than the curve and a barely noticeable lower release point than his other pitches, the cutter is tougher on the arm than Moyer's other pitches. A part of him wonders if it's more than coincidence that the very year he started throwing the cutter as a de facto out pitch—in his 2010 five-hit win over the Yankees at Yankee Stadium, he befuddled Derek Jeter and his teammates by throwing over sixty cutters— is the year he blew out his arm.

Moyer will test his command by, as he puts it, "pitching to the Xs." Four-time Cy Young winner Greg Maddux, who, like Moyer, was drafted by the Cubs in 1984, was the first pitcher Moyer had heard talk about "the Xs," and it's how he's thought of pitching ever since.

He imagines two large Xs on the low part of the strike zone and on either outer side, or lane, of the plate. When he has his command, the respective flights of his cutter and two-seam fastball should form an X to a righthanded hitter. The cutter breaks in to the righty, and the two-seam fastball appears to be coming straight at the righty but breaks down and away from (or "backdoors") the batter at the last instant. When those two pitches are combining to make that X on the corner, he can add another look with his straight four-seam fastball. That's three different looks for the batter to worry about on effectively two pitches— the fastball (both four- and two-seam) and cutter.

"Now go to the opposite side, the lefthanded side of the plate," Moyer explains. "I can sink the ball in on the lefty, or throw a two-seamer below the hitting zone, or back-door the hitter with a cutter so the ball is breaking from off the plate onto the plate. So now he's either going to give up on it or he's going to be messed up by the movement of it."

And that doesn't even get to his curveball, which Moyer calls a "depth pitch." It ought to not quite reach his imaginary Xs. "You don't want the curve breaking over the middle of the plate, you want it breaking short of the plate. Some guys who have good control with a firmer breaking ball throw it to the hitter's back foot, if it's a lefty versus a righty. But I throw it as a depth pitch, meaning I want guys swinging over the top of it."

Of the seventeen-inch plate, Moyer considers the middle twelve inches the hitter's property. Mistakes are made when you encroach on their turf. The remaining part of the plate—where the Xs are—are Moyer's, as he sees it, which makes the umpire arguably more important for Moyer's success or failure than when the pitcher is someone with a blazing fastball who can get away with more mistakes. The cat-and-mouse game between pitcher and hitter is all about establishing these lines of demarcation.

It's commonly agreed that the hardest act in sports is hitting a baseball. That's because the hitter has roughly 0.4 seconds to hit a round ball with a cylindrical piece of wood that has a mere three-inch sweet spot. As a result, even the best hitters have to guess where the ball is going and at what speed. This is known as "cutting off half the plate"; they look for a pitch either inside or outside. On top of that, they have to anticipate either a fast pitch or an off-speed one. It's virtually impossible to be looking for something slow and outside and react quickly enough to squarely hit something fast and inside.

Moyer excels at messing with hitters guessing pitching pat-
terns, both in terms of location and speed. When asked what advice he'd give to someone trying to hit off Moyer, Lou Piniella,
his manager in Seattle, once said, "Think backwards." He
means that on the counts that are typically considered hitter's
counts, Moyer won't give in and throw fastballs over the hitter's
part of the plate, even though, according to *Baseball Prospectus*,
93.8 percent of pitchers throw either a two-seam or four-seam
fastball when behind in the count 3–0. Precisely *because* the
hitter is looking for a fastball closer to his zone, Moyer won't
oblige. Ever since he and Dorfman first started talking in the
early '90s about using hitters' egos against them, Moyer has actually gotten *more* aggressive—throwing softer and with more
precision toward the corners, especially inside, when the conventional wisdom is to the contrary. The result has been that he
keeps hitters off balance, or, as hitters like to say, "off the barrel
of the bat." It's also why Moyer induces a particularly high number of infield pop-outs.

Moyer hasn't thrived for twenty-five years in the big leagues
because he's like other pitchers, in other words. He's thrived because he's so different. Much is made of his velocity, or lack
thereof, but it's quite intentional: he flusters batters by going
from slow to slower to slowest. (In 2010, Moyer's fastball averaged 81 miles per hour. Early in his career he was clocked in
the mid-80s, as reported in the scouting report that Chicago
Cubs scout Billy Blitzer prepared prior to the Cubs' selection of
Moyer in the sixth round of the 1984 draft. Moyer still carries
the report with him, in his shaving kit. Blitzer praised Moyer's
poise and baseball smarts, while noting that he topped out at 84
miles per hour.)

As he struggled in the majors, Moyer would try to throw
harder, pushing off his back leg with more and more force. Oc-

casionally, he'd add a mile or two or three, but the results never improved. "Me throwing at 86 or 87 miles per hour was still below average compared to the league, but to reach that velocity, my ball would be higher in the strike zone," he realizes now. It wasn't until Dorfman finally gave him permission to accept who he is—a smart, soft-tossing lefty who could still be aggressive without being fast—that the results started to come.

He learned, in other words, that on the mound, speed often kills. To one degree or another, depending on the quality of their stuff and their mind-set, this "pitch to contact" lesson is something all successful pitchers go through—even the hardest throwers. "I became a good pitcher when I stopped trying to make them miss the ball and started trying to make them hit it," none other than Sandy Koufax (another late-blooming lefty) once observed.

Because of his lack of speed and his cerebral nature, Moyer is commonly, and erroneously, thought of as a "nibbler," a pitcher who fears the hitter, and as a result "nibbles cautiously" around the strike zone. Early in his career, Moyer nibbled; he'd rarely throw his changeup for strikes, even though it had been his best pitch in college and the minors, and he'd rarely come inside. When Dorfman started pointing out that the pitcher is the only player on the defensive field who is actually an *offensive* player—"You act," his guru would say. "The batter *reacts*. You're in control"—it liberated Moyer to assert his will, to make the batter hit *his* pitch. It meant taking control of the pitcher/hitter relationship, which begins to happen before even taking the mound.

Inspired by Dorfman's aphorism, "Failure is wanting without work," Moyer began keeping copious notes on every batter he'd face, so he'd always have at the ready his own scouting report to review prior to every game. He first got the idea after seeing his Cubs teammate Vance Law, an infielder, scribbling in a notebook in the dugout during games. Law was logging the pitchers and pitches he faced, what fooled him, what he had solidly struck. Eventually, Moyer started doing the same as a pitcher, first in a series of notebooks and then on the clubhouse lineup card itself. Before every game, he goes over the notes with his catcher and pitching coach. So if they're facing the Yankees, there is his scribbled strategy scrawled next to Derek Jeter's name: "First ball fastball swinger. Climb the ladder. Start low." Translation: Moyer would start him with a fastball below the strike zone, hoping he chases. Then, because Jeter doesn't adjust well to having to change his eye level, he'd "climb the ladder," throwing something at mid-thigh, though not over the white. He'd follow that with something above the letters.

On another page, there are notes for facing pinch hitter extraordinaire Matt Stairs, a lefty. If an opposing team has sent a lefty to pinch-hit against him, Moyer knows it's because they think he can hit his breaking ball. Stairs will be looking for something soft, away. So he's written, "Pound in, pound in, cutter away, backdoor change."

A couple of pages later, there's the secret to success against White Sox leadoff hitter Ray Durham: "Pitch backwards, start him with soft, wants ball up and out over plate. After establishing away, will chase breaking balls down with two strikes."

Then there's slugger David Justice: "If you go in, he will look away next pitch. May take a lot of first pitches. Cutters away, breaking balls down and away. Hard on hands. Likes ball down and in. Change away, sinker away. Occasional front door cutter, off his body. Throw it to his hip."

On the mound, Moyer juggles the information from his own notes with, as he puts it, what the batter is (unwittingly) telling him. If, for example, Moyer knows that the batter likes to slap first-pitch fastballs on the outer part of the plate to the opposite field for base hits, that doesn't necessarily mean he'll shy away from a first-pitch fastball away—as a true nibbler, guided by fear and caution, might. Instead, Moyer will throw a fastball outside—but rather than being on the outside third of the plate, maybe it will be an inch or two off the plate, or an inch below the hitter's preferred zone. This is why Moyer says pitching takes place from the neck up: "You're trying to keep him from getting what he wants, at the same time that you're trying to lull him into thinking that he *is* getting what he wants," he says.

Moyer's aggression, then, lies in his ability—in a Zen-like fashion—to turn hitters' aggression against them. It's not *just* about hitting his spots; it's about hitting his spots *and* thereby seizing on hitters' frustration. "If a guy takes a swing at an outside fastball and hits off his front foot and fouls it off, I know I have the advantage," Moyer says. "If he couldn't get around on that, it means he was looking for the change. If he couldn't get around on something away, he won't get around on something in, so I'll jam him with a cutter, get him to hit the ball above the label, foul it off. Now he's pissed off, thinking, 'I should've hit that ball.' Now, in hitting my spots, the game within the game has begun. I can bust him inside again or get him to swing over something soft or come back and back-door him on the outside corner. Now I've got him second-guessing himself. I've gotten inside his head."

He and Garner are continuing to play catch and talk pitching every day. Moyer has always felt that this is what a pitching coach should do; start out each spring with a couple weeks of playing catch and holding classroom-like staff tutorials. Instead, the pitching coach position at the major league level has often become an administrative, as opposed to a teaching, post. Spring training is when an organization's veterans mingle with its minor leaguers; why not make it a learning experience for both groups? In his last year with the Phillies, he addressed the pitchers in this very clubhouse and urged the young ones to take advantage of the moment. "Ask me questions," he implored them. "Pick the brain of Roy Halladay. Or Brad Lidge."

Only one young pitcher—Mike Zagurski—felt comfortable enough to take the advice, asking Moyer to show him the grip on his cutter. If Moyer had his way, teams would create an atmosphere for staff growth. "You get the pitchers to come down ten days early and you condition the heck out of them, you play catch and long toss, and then you bring them into a classroom environment and you talk about pitching," he says. "Kind of like what Perci and I are doing here every day."

Now, as a result of their daily sessions, it's starting to dawn on Garner just how much work he has in front of him. One day in the clubhouse he asks Moyer how many pitches he throws.

"Eight," Moyer responds, barely withholding a smile. He knows what's coming next. Garner's whole body seems to freeze, his mouth opens but no words come out. He's just gotten a lesson in the difference between Class A ball and the Bigs: Garner effectively throws only two pitches.

"Four pitches on either side of the plate," Moyer explains. "That's eight."

Garner thinks for a minute. "I never thought of it that way," he says, finally.

Again and again, because he needs to hear himself say it, Moyer tells the young pitcher that you can only control what you can control. It's another Harveyism, of course: "You can control your approach, and you can control your response, but you can't control the result." Long ago, Moyer took that to heart, and ever since, he's done all he can to ensure that he'll never regret not going all-out after what he wants. Maybe that's why he's here, coming back—and now that the pitches have been rediscovered, it *is* a comeback. "If I didn't try, I'd always wonder if I could have done it," he says.

Moyer's getting in shape, losing the extra few pounds put on during his months of recovery. With each passing day, the thought that he's not yet a former pitcher becomes more real; the exhortations he offers to Garner on the field and in the clubhouse—"How many coats of paint are you ready to apply today, Perci?"—double as positive self-talk too.

One day the two men are throwing, hitting each other's gloves with ease. Garner has improved and is seeming more confident.

Moyer is quick to smile this morning, and why not? It's a beautiful Florida day and the only sound to be heard is the soundtrack of his youth, the hum of a ball and its crack into their leather gloves. Moyer breaks the silence. "How old are you?"

"Twenty-three."

"I wish I had your body at twenty-three," Moyer says.

Garner, hearing this from someone who has won 267 big league games, breaks into that smile. "Really?"

There's a pause. "Yeah," Moyer says. "But I'll stick with my mind at forty-eight."

SOUDERTON, PENNSYLVANIA, 1972

CHAPTER THREE

> No one can make you feel like a failure with-
> out your consent.
> —Harvey Dorfman

At 6 p.m., the Moyer Dry Cleaning van would turn onto North Fourth Street from Reliance Road, and there he'd be. Little Jamie, ball and glove in hand, parked on the front step of the modest two-story house the Moyers had built in the late '60s. He'd already have played a couple of hours of wiffle ball after school with Scooter Myers, from a block away, on Summit Street. Scooter was four years younger than Jamie, but the two were like brothers: Moyer and Myers.

Sometimes Scooter would stay for dinner, but most times he'd go home when that van would make that turn. Because that's when Jim Moyer, after a day of picking up and delivering dry cleaning, would go inside and fetch his beat-up old catcher's mitt and crouch down against his garage door, while Jamie took to his pretend mound at the driveway's end, some forty feet away. And son would commence to throw to father. Jim's glove was small, with no webbing and no thumb. But it had a loud sweet spot, and Jim knew how to catch his son's ball right on it, so that a loud *thwack* would ring out.

Eventually, as he got bigger, Jamie would be throwing from the middle of the street and the nonplussed drivers of passing cars would make sure to swerve in order to avoid the pitching prodigy; they knew it was just the Moyer kid, throwing again. Such was life in Souderton, the small, working-class town just an hour outside of Philadelphia.

Jamie was always throwing. And when he wasn't throwing, he always seemed to be *about* to throw. He'd carry a ball with him wherever he went, tossing it to himself, or just holding it, getting a feel for it in his left hand. A baseball, after all, is an amalgam of cowhide, rubber, and hand-stitching; even today, Moyer likes to spend hours holding baseballs, because each one has a distinct feel. One may feel bigger in his hand, the next smaller. Another might seem to have bulging seams, the next hardly any at all.

Jim Moyer coached Jamie in Little League through American Legion ball, and he would catch his son in that driveway every night, calling out balls and strikes. He knew that—especially at the Little League level—the game was about getting the ball over the plate. So he'd call every pitch as if there were live hitters at bat; after twenty-seven punch-outs, the two would go around back to play the fielding drill pepper, with the elder Moyer hitting brisk grounders for his son to scoop up until inevitably one would crash off Jamie's shin and he'd run crying into the house, where Joan would be preparing supper. After dinner, especially on nights that Jamie's idol, Steve Carlton, pitched, the Moyer family—including older sister Jill, who was a musical prodigy—would sit before the big color TV in the living room and Jamie would be transfixed by the lefty on the screen.

In 1972, Steve Carlton was having arguably the most dominant pitching season of the modern era. He'd win a miraculous 46 percent of his team's games that year, going 27–10 for a horrible team that would win only 59 times. Carlton's ERA was 1.97; in games he didn't pitch, the team gave up nearly twice as many earned runs.

But it was less about the results than the aura of Carlton that captivated Moyer so deeply. To the nine-year-old Moyer, the big number 32 on his TV screen represented everything that intrigued him about throwing a baseball; here was a larger-than-life mystery, an enigma who didn't speak to the press and had a mercenary sense of purpose on the mound. And just like Jamie, Carlton was a lefty.

Dissecting his hero every fifth night, Moyer started to get a sense of just how complicated pitching was. He'd watch and try and solve the puzzle: What made a pitch move like that? Why throw a slider there, on that count? His apprenticeship had begun. Studying Carlton, Moyer saw a fierce competitor who was always looking for an edge. Carlton, in fact, was well ahead of the times in his mental approach to the game. His guru—his Harvey, if you will—was Gus Hoefling, the Phillies' strength and flexibility coach, who was a lifelong student of the martial arts. Hoefling introduced Carlton to kung fu—and to meditation. In the dank basement of Veterans Stadium, where the Phillies played, Hoefling set up a soundproofed, softly lit "mood room," where Carlton would recline, rest, and listen to relaxation tapes prior to his starts.

Moyer would pore over the articles in the Philadelphia newspapers that touched on Carlton's unique preparations. He'd go to bed filled with baseball dreams and wake up to the giant Carlton poster on the back of his bedroom door. One time, a teacher told the Moyers that their son had refused to do a homework assignment. Jamie had decided he'd never need to know

the material. "I'm going to play professional baseball," he declared.

Baseball is the sport that fathers hand down to their sons, to be
handed down to theirs. And in Jim Moyer, Jamie had the ultimate mentor. The elder Moyer was a fast-pitch softball pitcher
until he turned fifty, and then spent weekends umpiring
semipro games. He also coached his son and the neighborhood
kids up through American Legion ball. The dry cleaning business may have been Jim's job, but baseball was his passion. And
always by his side was little Jamie. After a game, there he'd be,
begging his dad to let him bang the mud off his cleats. When
the elder Moyer didn't have a game, he'd take the whole family down to the field off Reliance Road, back behind Moyer Oil
and Storage—no relation—and neighbors would laugh as Joan,
Jill, and Jamie shagged fly balls. *Those Moyers.*

Jim, born and raised in Souderton, had been a pro player
himself whose dreams of diamond glory just barely came up
short. In 1950, the legendary NBA ref and baseball scout Jocko
Collins saw Moyer play. Though he was barely 5′7″ and 145
pounds, the shortstop seemed to be all over the field, playing
with an awareness of the game far beyond his years.

"You wanna play ball, don't ya?" Collins asked Moyer.

"Yessir, I sure do," Jim said.

Collins, at the time a Phillies scout, signed Moyer for $150
per month. He played for the Phillies affiliate in Carbondale,
Pennsylvania, and earned an invite to spring training in Fort
Lauderdale. The last week of camp, one of the coaches took
him aside. "I like the way you play, but the team has $5,000 on
that kid over there," the coach said. "You're out of here."

Two years later, the St. Louis Cardinals gave Jim a chance

and signed him. Once again, he survived the first couple rounds of cuts at the Cards' Albany, Georgia, camp, before he again became a casualty of baseball's unforgiving system. And that was it. Back home, Jim bought the dry cleaning business from his dad and set about raising a family—while figuring out a way to remain connected to the game for the rest of his life.

Jamie was part of that plan, though Jim never pushed Jamie toward the game. He didn't have to. The Moyers have a photo of Jamie at sixteen months, hitting a wiffle ball with a plastic bat in the backyard, making solid contact. It helped that Jamie was a natural athlete, able to pick up and master any sport. As he got older, a legend surrounding Jamie Moyer started to take hold in Souderton. As a fourteen-year-old, he was a star quarterback, before giving up the game upon entering high school so as not to risk injury that would sideline him from baseball. On the basketball court, he was the quickest player, the most adept dribbler. His golf swing was pristine.

But everyone knew baseball always came first. One day in the junior high gymnasium, Moyer was throwing and a crowd gathered. "One of the teachers was there and I remember him calling other teachers over and telling them, 'Look at this, look at how this ball moves,'" recalls Tim Bishop, who starred with Moyer on the Souderton Area High and American Legion baseball teams, and went on to play pro ball before becoming the Baltimore Orioles' strength and conditioning coach, where he was reunited with Moyer in the 1990s. Back in that junior high gym, Bishop and the others saw a ball that moved almost cartoonishly: breaking wildly, fluttering in midair. "We were from a small town. No one had seen anything like that before."

Nor had Souderton seen Moyer's type of dominance before. By the time he got to high school, he was a wiry six-footer with—ironically—a speedier fastball than anybody in the Bux-

Mont League was used to and a big, sweeping curve that, thanks to all those driveway sessions with Jim, he could throw for strikes. In fact, in a bit of hyperbole that would later come to seem even more ironic, local writers often referred to Moyer's fastball as "blazing"; Bishop and others suggest that it may have been 84 miles per hour, a good ten miles per hour faster than the high school norm. He won 22 of 25 games in his high school career and averaged nearly two strikeouts an inning. His ERA was 0.59.

In his junior year, en route to a 10–0 record, Moyer threw three consecutive no-hitters. The stands were packed not to see the games, but to see whether the opposing team could even make contact against the phenom. In his senior year, Moyer not only hit .375, but also went 8–1 with a 0.54 ERA. Major league scouts sent letters, including one from Martinez Jackson, Reggie's father, who was a tailor in Philadelphia and a scout for the California Angels. Jackson would visit Souderton often. "My boss has heard about you, Jay," Jackson wrote to Jamie. "He's anxious to see you in action."

By then, baseball wasn't just Moyer's passion; it was his obsession. Never a good student, he did just enough to get by in school. And he wasn't much into girls, either. When she learned her son had a date for the prom, Joan Moyer was shocked. Scooter Myers remembers Moyer having a beer now and then, but mostly he was fixated on baseball like it already *was* his profession. When it had rained all night before a big game, the local paper reported that Moyer was on the field at 7:30 a.m., trying to dry it off himself. That kind of commitment has never really left him, even as a pro. Moyer is always the first out of the dugout, sprinting to the mound each inning. Bishop and other Souderton teammates have seen that throughout the years, and they smile, recognizing a Jim Moyer dictum in action.

"Jamie tried everything to get better," remembers Bishop. "He knew about cuff and scapula stabilization exercises, doing these crazy arm motions, before any of us. I remember going to some massage guy on his recommendation. In Souderton in 1980, guys didn't get massages, but Jamie was always learning, always looking for the next thing."

In 1980, Moyer's senior year, the Souderton Area High School team posted a 15–6 record. Yet that summer, virtually the same group of players went undefeated—18–0, with Jamie going 11–0—in American Legion ball. The difference? Jim Moyer.

On game days, the kids would show up at the Moyer house on North Fourth Street, hours before they were to leave, and sit in the Moyer front yard under the big tree. Jim wouldn't even be home yet. As she saw the boys gathering outside, Joan would bring them lemonade and have Jim's uniform ready for him to slip into when he pulled up. The kids couldn't wait for the games, because Coach Moyer made playing the game fun, while still stressing fundamentals. Though soft-spoken, the elder Moyer was no pushover. If you missed a game because you went to a dance or were in a play, it would probably take you a while to crack the lineup again. At the start of each season, he'd lead his players around the bases, peppering his never-ending commentary with the details that could make the difference between winning and losing.

"Look," he'd say, taking a lead off first base, before quickly hopping a foot or two back toward the outfield. "If you're not stealing, you can take a step back once the pitcher is in his motion toward home plate and give yourself a better angle to round second and get to third on a base hit."

Instead of the drudgery of mandatory wind sprints, Coach Moyer would line the boys up at second and hit fly balls for them to chase and catch. "That was our running," Jamie re-members. "Only we didn't know it then."

The town was wildly supportive of Jamie, but there were plenty of question marks. He heard the doubters—and never failed to take note of the doubts. Early in his senior year, during basketball season, he and teammates Tom Shutt and Scott Bishop were invited to the Bucky Dent baseball camp in Boca Raton, Florida. It would have meant missing some basketball games, which hoops coach Jarinko was none too happy about. That's when, no doubt trying to discourage his point guard from taking the time off, the basketball coach told Moyer of the conversation he'd had with former big leaguer Bill White. "He says you're good, but you don't throw hard enough to be in the majors," the coach said. That sealed it: he'd go to the camp. And he'd add his coach and White to the list of the nonbelievers. He'd show them.

Yet despite his dominant numbers, Moyer's name didn't get called in that summer's Major League Baseball draft. The town expected him to be drafted. "Jamie has done nothing but get people out all his life," Jim Moyer said in the local paper. "He's shown that he's never had trouble doing that at any level."

The baseball scout, though, doesn't look at results so much as potential. And Jamie Moyer, at seventeen, was rail thin and threw comparatively slow. "The two things that go against him are size and speed," one scout was quoted at the time. "He could be a prospect when he's 21, 22 years old. But he's got to get a little faster. That comes from development, physical growth, maybe squeezing a rubber ball to build up strength."

Setbacks were becoming nothing new for Moyer. That summer, shortly after the draft, major league scouts held a tryout in nearby Pottstown to determine who, among all American Legion players, had pro potential. Moyer faced three batters and set them down on nine pitches. When the names of those who would move on to the tryout's next phase were posted, there it was: Jamie Moyer, Pennridge. Wait: Pennridge? That was another high school, in another league. And that team, it turned out, *also* had a kid named Jamie Moyer, who was mistakenly chosen in a bad mix-up. Jamie Moyer—the one from Souderton, who was as can't-miss a prospect as the region had recently produced—didn't make the cut owing to a mistake by the tryout organizers.

It was perplexing that by midsummer after his senior year of high school, Moyer's once-promising future was still unknown. It looked like he'd be enrolling at Montgomery County Community College and playing next spring for the Mustangs—not exactly the dream Moyer or his hometown had long harbored. But neither Moyer nor his boosters knew then that this would ultimately be the story of Moyer's career—that nothing would come easily. Skip Wilson, the legendary coach for Temple University in Philadelphia, took a ride that summer to Souderton. Under Wilson, Temple had played in the College World Series in 1972 and 1977 and had received four other NCAA bids in the '70s. Now here he was, in the Moyer living room, making his pitch for Jamie to come and play for the Owls. Joan, however, wasn't impressed, not with the College World Series appearances or the NCAA bids. Wilson, you see, had worn shorts and sneakers with no socks—*no socks!*—to her home.

When St. Joseph's head coach, George Bennett, came to visit, he wore socks; Joan liked him right away. And Jamie liked that Bennett was offering the chance to start as freshman, something the more competitive Temple program couldn't guarantee. But there was a catch: "We'll give you a scholarship, but you've got to work as hard for me in the classroom as you do on the baseball field," Bennett said. Moyer would be a night student his first semester and then upgraded to full-time status if he could carry a 2.5 grade point average. Moyer saw it as a challenge.

When the academic year rolled around, Moyer realized how quickly fortunes can change. Just a couple of months prior, he'd been dreaming of being drafted and of playing minor league baseball by now. Instead, he got a day job working for the Town of Souderton. He'd spend his days mowing ball fields, collecting leaves, and tarring roadways. At quitting time, he'd drive his parents' blue Pinto up the turnpike to Philly for night classes at St. Joe's.

But at least he had a team, a baseball home, and a scholarship. After hearing all the doubts about his game and after not getting drafted, he got his first lesson in the sheer power of perseverance. Years later, after he had become a star for the Seattle Mariners, an attendant named Tom stationed outside the clubhouse door would slip him a piece of paper that read:

PRESS ON

NOTHING IN THE WORLD CAN TAKE THE PLACE OF
PERSISTENCE

TALENT WILL NOT; NOTHING IS MORE COMMON THAN
UNSUCCESSFUL MEN WITH TALENT

GENIUS WILL NOT; UNREWARDED GENIUS IS ALMOST A
PROVERB

EDUCATION WILL NOT; THE WORLD IS FULL OF EDUCATED
DERELICTS

PERSISTENCE AND DETERMINATION ALONE ARE
OMNIPOTENT.

The scrap of paper immediately found a place in Jamie's vaunted shaving kit, where he keeps his motivational reminders, for Moyer knew not only how true it was, but how it could just as easily have been penned by the seventeen-year-old Jamie Moyer who, at the eleventh hour, got a baseball scholarship, *and* by the forty-eight-year-old Jamie Moyer who would try and defy the game yet again by coming back from Tommy John surgery.

Like Jamie Moyer, Harvey Dorfman fell in love with baseball at the youngest of ages. Unlike Moyer, though, Dorfman didn't dream so much of playing the sport as of escaping into it. Little Harvey, six years old in 1941, was bedridden in his family's Bronx, New York, apartment with extreme asthma, surrounded by an overprotective mother and two doting older sisters. He took solace in the re-created teletype games that played on his bedside Emerson radio.

As it would be in the Moyer household, the father gave his son the game. Mac and Harvey Dorfman would listen to games on AM radio, Harvey keeping score in a school notebook. When he wasn't gasping for breath, it was as though he was in suspended animation, waiting for his life to start. "There I was, a child—having comfort without ever having had challenge; having order without discipline; ritual without responsibility; entertainment without effort," he'd recall much later, in *Persuasion of My Days*, one of the three memoirs he would write. "Indulged, protected, feared for and cared for by loving adults."

Harvey went to his first game at the Polo Grounds, the Cubs versus the Giants. The eight-year-old was transfixed by the experience, but not like other kids. Moyer, for example, caught the bug early and knew he wanted to *do* this thing. Not Dorfman. He wasn't addicted to the game so much as his own curiosity about its players. This child—sequestered, surrounded by fear—found himself touched by, as he put it, the "physical freedom of expression" he was witnessing. He wanted to understand it, to understand *them*, these men of action. When he wasn't listening to or fantasizing about baseball, he lost himself in books, the same urge drawing him to the pages of *Huckleberry Finn*: he was a spectator in search of a way to become a participant.

Later, Dorfman would earn a reputation for that rarest of qualities: wisdom. Those who knew him still talk about his talent for the pithy quip, the trenchant observation; he had a way of encapsulating an idea in a phrase that would often lead to an instant change in your thinking, a new way of seeing things. This was also handed down; without his father's homespun aphorisms, Harvey likely wouldn't have become the man he did.

Dorfman the psychologist was famous for being intolerant of players casting themselves in the role of victim. That too came from Mac. The elder Dorfman refused to let his son adopt that persona, even if it was warranted. "Suffering is good for you, kid, so long as you survive it," Mac would tell his son. Other times, Harvey would later recount, his father would point out that if everyone in the world gathered in a circle and put their problems in the center of it, a fellow would feel lucky to get his own back.

In dealing with professional ballplayers, Harvey sensed early on that they'd come to expect sympathy. They were raised to be "special," after all, and surrounded themselves with well-meaning people and sycophants who were loath to push them. Harvey had felt the power of tough love growing up. Once, at fifteen, he sullenly withdrew like most teenagers, as he recounted in *Each Branch, Each Needle*:

> *My father stopped me as I was headed out of our apartment. I was a high schooler at the time. "Are you feeling better today?" he*

*asked. I had been breathing pretty well and feeling—physically—
as well as I ever had.*

"Fine," I said, with confusion written on my face.

"Oh, then your rectumitis is improving?"

I asked him what he was talking about. "What's rectumitis?"

*"It's an inflammation of the nerve that runs from your asshole
to your eyeball and it gives you a [crappy] outlook on life. I pre-
sumed you were suffering from it."*

No wonder Harvey would go on to exhort scared pupils like
Moyer to be aggressive, to zealously defend their "f'ing circle."
At twelve, the tentative, sickly Dorfman had been told by his fa-
ther, "In life, you're going to be either the hunter or the prey.
Make up your mind which one it's going to be."

Mac Dorfman was not a wealthy man. He was a traveling
salesman for Van Heusen, hawking shirts, collars, and ties
throughout the metropolitan New York region. And yet his gen-
erosity knew no bounds. He died of a blood clot in the brain
when Harvey was in college. Shortly thereafter, money to the
Dorfmans started flowing in. Turned out, Mac had long made
loans to acquaintances who were down on their luck, sometimes
to the tune of $2,000. A World War I vet, he was stoic in the way
that men of that generation tended to be. Like Jim Moyer, he
wasn't given to public displays of affection. Also like Jim Moyer,
his love was to be inferred from his teachings—and from the
fact that he was always teaching. Every time he dropped a pearl
of wisdom on his impressionable son, it was as if he'd thrown
his arms around him. "Know what you're doing and you'll be a
confident boy," he told his son. "Know how to deal with what
happens to you and you'll be a confident man." The son later
came to tell *his* charges, "Believe it and you will become it."

When Harvey went off to college at Brockport State in

Rochester, he soon called home with stunning news that was worrisome to his mother. He was going to defy medical advice and play goalie for the school's soccer team. "You've got more guts than brains," his father told him, barely masking his pride. Harvey's adolescent path from spectator to participant was complete. In goal, he'd inhale epinephrine surreptitiously when the ball went down to the field's other end. In 1955, Brockport State would share the national title with Penn State. Later, Dorfman would be inducted into the school's hall of fame.

Harvey would eventually write about this period as the time in which he once and for all rejected comfort and security and started learning how to be mentally tough. "I determined to confront my difficulties—or any adverse situation—with a relentless attitude," he wrote. "I now know that once a will becomes truly strong, it becomes insistent. That being mentally tough requires us to develop the will to bear discomfort."

He'd go on to become a beloved English teacher at Burr and Burton Academy, a well-regarded prep school in Vermont. There he'd coach girls' basketball and perfect the approach to athletes he'd use for the rest of his life: the tough love, the wise-cracking ("Ladies," he once said, poking his head into a locker room of barely clad players with his eyes closed after a big win, "all I can say is, you've got a lot of balls!"), the inspirational quotes from great literary works.

He was ahead of his time, going so far as to turn a big, uncoordinated girl named Becky into a type of on-court enforcer. When an opposing player got overly aggressive, he'd approach hulking Becky on the bench: "You see that?"

She'd nod. "Take care of it," Coach Dorfman would say. Becky would enter the game and come out minutes later, after a succession of hard fouls that were sure to leave bruises.

The true teaching moments came during losses, though.

Once, the Bulldogs were getting blown out and Dorfman called a timeout late in the game; his girls couldn't wait to get off the court. "This is why we're here," he said. "To toughen up. To handle adversity with poise and determination. If you don't cave in—if you don't *quit*—under these conditions, no one in the state of Vermont will be able to handle you."

The next year, the girls won the state title, with Harvey quoting Aldous Huxley to them whenever they'd hit a rough patch: "Experience isn't what happens to you; it's what you *do* with what happens to you." Mac Dorfman—and, for that matter, Jim Moyer—couldn't have said it better themselves.

JUNE 1992

CHAPTER FOUR

When we fail to learn, we've learned to fail.
—Harvey Dorfman

Behind the wheel of his eggshell-white Lexus, Jamie Moyer fiddled with his car radio. Every song he settled upon seemed to offer an ominous commentary on his once again in-limbo future. On one station, Elton John and George Michael sang "Don't Let the Sun Go Down on Me." On another, some new R&B group named Boyz II Men crooned "End of the Road."

"There's gotta be some Zeppelin somewhere," Moyer, a classic rock devotee, muttered to himself as he surfed the dial. He smiled when the nasal twang of Tom Petty came through the speakers:

Gonna stand my ground / Won't be turned around...And I won't back down

That was more like it. Baseball season was already in full swing, only until now he hadn't been a part of it. It had been more than a year since his weekend with Harvey and there had been no panacea, no epiphany. He'd started last season with St. Louis, getting seven starts. That's when, with an 0–5 record, manager Joe Torre told him he was being sent down to Triple A: "We don't win when you pitch."

At Louisville, an underachieving team, he was 5–10 with a 3.80 ERA. Still, there were moments on the mound where he got out of his own way and got the sense that *this* was what Harvey was talking about in all those phone calls. In golf, they call it "intermittent reinforcement"—despite all the slices and shanks that came before, the feeling of that one solidly struck ball is enough to keep a golfer coming back, day after day. In Louisville, Moyer was up and down, but he had enough ups to keep with it, despite being released at season's end. He didn't feel like any corner had been turned, but he also wasn't ready to quit yet.

At the start of the 1992 season, he found himself in Mesa, Arizona, for spring training with his first team, the Chicago Cubs. He was happy with how he had pitched, but getting cut didn't really come as a surprise. He'd surveyed the field, was aware of the numbers game the big league club would be looking at— how many pitchers and how many spots they had—and knew he faced long odds. As the team readied to break camp, he was called into the Fitch Park office of Bill Hartford, the Cubs' minor league director.

"Jamie, we have to release you at this time," Hartford said. "The organization doesn't see you helping them as a starter and they don't see you as a relief pitcher at the big league level."

There was silence. Usually these meetings are perfunctory; when he got released by the Texas Rangers in 1990 (after a two-year record of 6–15 with an ERA just under 5.00), the phone call from general manager Tom Grieve was particularly terse: "We don't see you helping us." Now, however, Hartford had something else he wanted to say.

"You're almost thirty, Jamie," Hartford began. "We don't have room for you in the minors as a pitcher, but we think you'd make a good pitching coach, so we'd like to offer you a coaching job."

"I'm not interested," Moyer blurted out, almost before the words were out of Hartford's mouth.

Hartford shifted in his chair. Baseball men hate delivering this message; he wasn't just releasing Moyer, he was also telling him that, in the organization's opinion, his playing days were over. "Well, look," Hartford said. "We have your rights for three days, why don't you go home and think about it and get back to us?"

"My thoughts aren't going to change," Moyer said.

"Well, just go home and think about it."

So as the baseball season began, Jamie Moyer was once again a pitcher without a team, one with the most uncertain of futures. He was now twenty-nine years old and had been traded once and released by three teams—the Rangers, the Cardinals, and the Cubs. He was a career 34–54 journeyman, with a 4.56 ERA. Worse, this couldn't have happened at a more inopportune time. Jamie and Karen had bought a $380,000 house in Granger, Indiana, just outside of South Bend. Dillon was about to turn one year old. Plus, he'd made a commitment to his father-in-law, Digger Phelps—who as head basketball coach at Notre Dame had graduated *all* his players—that Jamie would complete his college degree. (He eventually would, at Indiana University.)

But with the news that his son-in-law had been released yet again, Phelps was no longer concerned about Moyer's academic credentials. He knew how hard it is for an elite athlete to face the end. That's why he took it upon himself to make a few phone calls on Jamie's behalf. His friend Art Decio was on the Notre Dame board of trustees and owned the Skyline Corporation, which sold RVs. He'd hire Jamie to be a salesman. "Maybe it's time to be a husband and a father," Phelps said when he told his son-in-law of the opportunity.

It was an instant replay of the conversation with Hartford. "This is not how it's going to end for me," Moyer said, cutting off his father-in-law.

"He kept his reaction inside, he didn't come back and challenge me," Phelps remembers today. "But obviously, he thought, 'Well, I'll prove him wrong.' Certain guys are that way. Don't get me wrong—I might not know baseball. But I can read athletes. And Jamie's a fighter."

Was Phelps playing some mind game with his son-in-law, trying to catalyze a breakthrough moment? Today, he'll only smile sheepishly at the thought. Likely, he was legitimately concerned for the security of his daughter and grandson, *and* he was testing the mettle of his son-in-law. Phelps is nothing if not practical, a trait his daughter did not always exhibit. Karen, who had been working part-time at a local department store to help make ends meet, was a romantic, and she was taken with her husband's never-say-quit attitude.

The couple was a study in opposites. They met when Moyer was on the Cubs and Karen, who had ambitious career plans in broadcasting, was an intern for WGN-TV. Cubs announcers Harry Carey and Steve Stone set the two up. She was polished and sophisticated, a wine drinker who had already traveled the globe at twenty-two; he wore cowboy boots with white jeans and took his meals at IHOP. Over the years, she made Jamie more worldly (he now owns a 2,000-bottle wine collection), while his work ethic rubbed off on her.

When they married in 1988, Karen didn't know she was in for a lengthy, nomadic adventure. Ultimately, she would pack boxes and move more than eighty times throughout her husband's career. After he was let go by the Cubs in late March 1992, what she saw as his inspiring refusal to give up even unleashed a burst of creativity in her; she started painting life-sized cartoon figures on the walls of Dillon's bedroom, Big Bird and Mickey Mouse peering down on the infant, while Jamie went off to work out with the Clay High School baseball team every day. When he'd get back home, he'd ask if his agent, Jim Bronner, had called. They both knew the clock was ticking: they had agreed to put the house up for sale on June 1 if he hadn't found a job by then.

Bronner was having a tough time, though. There was a lead in Japan, but even that went cold. Finally, in late May, Bronner had a bite: the Tigers' Triple A affiliate in Toledo needed a "mop-up man." That was the phrase: "mop-up man." Moyer wouldn't pitch much, and when he did, it probably wouldn't be meaningful innings. But at least he wouldn't be selling RVs or merely giving pointers on the field to other players only a few years his junior when he knew he could still get guys out. At least he'd still be in a uniform and on a mound, and he'd be doing what he'd done since he was eight years old. He signed for the remainder of the season. His salary: $12,000.

So here he was, rolling down the Ohio Turnpike, Tom Petty's lyrics getting him fired up, as he made his way to his last, best chance. It would be easy to think of this as his riskiest move to date, having turned down real paychecks in order to chase this unlikely dream for a mere pittance. But Moyer flicked off the radio and sat himself down for a talk, a talk that was an extension of the phone conversation he'd had with Harvey just days before.

"Think of this as an opportunity and have fun with it!" Harvey had said. He'd told Moyer of an old *New Yorker* cartoon. In it, an adult behind an outfield chain-link fence asks the boy centerfielder for the score. "Sixty-four to nothing, them," the boy responds.

"Oh, that's too bad," the adult says.

"Don't worry about it, mister. We ain't even been up yet," the boy replies.

Try to tap into that boy's sense of optimism and fun, Harvey said, "Like Willie Stargell said, 'The ump says play ball—not *work* ball!'"

Then Harvey posed a hypothetical: You're at a diner. The food you've ordered is brought to you cold. What do you do? Do you send it back or eat it anyway?

Moyer thought it over, mindful of Harvey's first rule: you can't feed him any bull. "I'd probably eat it," Moyer admitted.

"That's why you're not on a big league roster right now, kid," Dorfman said. We think of our athletes as tough, cocky even. But Harvey knew otherwise. He'd seen too many kids with talent fail because they were too invested in being nice guys. A gentleman is sensitive to the needs of others, Dorfman said, and that's precisely the instinct Moyer needed to shed in baseball. "You need to be *insensitive*," he told Moyer. "Insensitive to the crowd, the media, the manager, the opposing dugout. You need to be confrontational." In sports, nice-guyism was fatal. Dorfman reminded Moyer of what former big leaguer Enos Cabell had once said: "I don't want to be a star, they get blamed too much." There's safety in being unassuming and well thought of. To succeed, you need to be something of a narcissist. You need to send the food back.

Now, on Route 80, Moyer spoke to himself out loud, because he needed to hear himself say the words. Harvey had been talking to him for over a year about embracing who he was. And about knocking guys down.

And it wasn't only Harvey; pitching coaches had long told

him to establish the inside part of the plate. Dick Pole was the first; he was Moyer's pitching coach with the Cubs, first in Double A Pittsfield, Massachusetts, and then later with the big league club. Pole was brash and intimidating; some pitchers thought he was mean-spirited. Moyer, though, welcomed Pole's challenges; the coach's bellowing ways were just a sign of how committed he was to getting the best out of his charges. To this day, Moyer has Pole, whom Greg Maddux also credits as a major influence, on speed dial. Back then, Pole's message to Maddux and Moyer was the same: *Get inside. Be aggressive.*

Intellectually, Moyer knew Pole and other coaches were right, but he still hadn't been able to consistently get there, he still hadn't been able to just go for it and risk throwing into what he feared to be the wheelhouses of so many power hitters. So this was it, his last chance to get it done. His last chance to have the courage to be different.

"You're going to go there and be Jamie Moyer," he said. "You're going to hit some guys. If that means they pick the ball up and say, 'You dropped something,' that's fine. You're not going to give hitters too much credit. You're not going to be passive. You're going to throw what you want to throw, when you want to throw it. If you want to throw four changeups in a row, you'll throw four changeups in a row. No matter what anyone says. If you want to throw a 3–2 hook, you'll throw a 3–2 hook. No matter what the catcher calls."

Moyer had spent so long worrying about what others thought of him. Now, with his back against the wall, going over everything he had learned from Harvey, he was starting to feel liberated. Baseball, he was starting to realize, was full of rules born of conventional wisdom. He was going to disregard the rules. If he was going to go out, at least he'd go out *his* way. This was going to be fun. He turned the radio back on.

* * *

When you hear a major league pitcher talking about being "comfortable" on the mound, there's a tendency to dismiss it as mere jockspeak, another boilerplate cliché. But pitchers know what pitchers mean when they mention comfort level. They know the surreal feeling of being out there on that mound, with memories and thoughts and outside stimuli seeming to fly at you in waves. Getting comfortable in that frenetic mental milieu is, Moyer was learning, what pitching was truly about. Later, he'd conclude that it was the one thing the sabermetric revolution overlooked.

He'd become one of the game's ultimate Moneyball pitchers—as Michael Lewis would chronicle in his best-selling book, in a scene where a handful of Oakland A's hitters try to prepare before facing Moyer by watching video of him. Indeed, when the trend toward advanced analytics inspired by the likes of Bill James started to take hold, Moyer thought it contributed mightily to a greater understanding of the game and added important statistical touchstones to the sport. But there was one caveat: the movement's abiding allegiance to rationality can run counter to the experience of actually being on the mound. Success there is as much mystical and emotional as rational.

The great relief pitcher Tug McGraw wrote in his 1974 autobiography *Screwball* of his stream-of-consciousness thoughts on the mound. It was like a kaleidoscope in his mind's eye, a blur of images whizzing past: "I began flashing on when I was a kid in Vallejo...and said to myself: Look, this mound looks just like the one in Wilson Park," McGraw wrote. "Wilson Park is the place where we grew up playing ball in Vallejo twenty, maybe twenty five, years back....Sometimes I look at my dad when he's in the stands in San Francisco and many things flash back. But most of the guys don't talk about that kind of thing because it sounds so corny."

McGraw immersed himself in his distracting thoughts before narrowing his focus to just him and the batter. Sometimes, the images went away. Other times, they intruded on the task at hand. Moyer can relate; thoughts and memories come in waves. There are times when he'll hear a heckler and *want* to respond. It's as if the spectator has been plucked from the stands and is sitting right beside him. Later in his career, he'd silently thank that fan—if he could hear him, he knew it was a reminder that his focus wasn't intent enough. So he'd breathe deeply, find something to look at—a beer sign or a fan's shirt or an empty seat, anything to bore into—and he'd discard the distracting urge to call the heckler an idiot before returning his attention to the only thing that matters: his game of catch with his catcher.

But that discipline required a comfort level Moyer had found elusive early in his career. When things started going badly, he'd come to intimately understand the cliché about not being able to get out of his own way. It was as though there were a hologram of himself standing in front of him, blocking his view of the plate. "Get out of my way!" he wanted to shout at his own image.

When pitchers talk about "comfort," they're really talking about accessing what has come to be known as "the zone" or "the flow state," those moments of Zen on the field when mind and body blur into one and the athlete overcomes self-consciousness. When he was going good, "pitching was like being in the bubble," Jim Kaat, who had studied under Carlton's guru Gus Hoefling, once said. "When you're in that bubble, you're in a world of your own. I always knew that even when there were fifty, sixty thousand people screaming in the stands, the most peaceful place in the universe was right on the pitcher's mound."

The zone is where effortless concentration meets peak athletic performance, and its story is as old as our history. Twenty-five centuries ago, Chinese philosopher Lao-tzu declared that "the perfect runner leaves no track." In 1976, well before he became known for parenting someone who was famous for having a large rear end, Bruce Jenner was an Olympic decathlete who described feeling like he was "rising above myself, doing things I had no right to do." Surfer Kelly Slater put it this way: "You find the wave and the wave finds you, and you're so in tune with the ocean that you're both more *and* less aware than normal."

In baseball, Ted Williams famously claimed there were times he could see the seams of a fastball as it sped toward him. More recently, Jim Clancy, who spent most of his career pitching for the Toronto Blue Jays, would softly strum a guitar in the clubhouse prior to his starts, trying to get in the zone. Tigers reliever Willie Hernandez would cover his eyes with a towel while visualizing himself facing that night's potential batters.

When he got to Toledo, Moyer's job was to utilize many of the tools Harvey had given him to get comfortable. As he said to himself in the car on the way there, "You've been in the classroom for the last year. Now it's time to put it to practical use." After their first meeting a little over a year earlier, Moyer laminated two five-by-ten cards. On one he scribbled a series of notes and questions to review before every start, to make sure he was in the right problem-solving state of mind prior to taking the mound:

LEVEL OF CONCENTRATION: ALWAYS? OFTEN? USUALLY? RARELY? NEVER?

PACE OF WORK: SLUGGISH OR STEADY?

ADJUST IN TOUGH SITUATIONS: STEP OFF RUBBER, STEP
OFF MOUND

POSTURE, BODY LANGUAGE: AGGRESSIVE VERSUS
SLUGGISH?

FACIAL EXPRESSION: STRONG EYES VERSUS WEAK EYES

TELL YOURSELF WHAT TO DO ONE PITCH AT A TIME

RELAX BY EXHALING

BREATHING PATTERN: DEEP EXHALE BEFORE EVERY PITCH

The other card consisted of a grid of numbers arranged randomly from 00 to 99. Before starts, Moyer would find someplace
to hide—a broom closet or a corner of the trainer's room—and,
without pointing, he'd burrow into the chart, seeking out the
numbers in sequential order, searching for 1, then 2, then 3, and
onward, an exercise in optimum concentration. When he first
started, it took twenty-three minutes to get to 99. Now, on good
days, it took nine. Bad days, fifteen.

In Louisville, he would slink away to do this work, embarrassed by his Dorfman-inspired efforts, fearful of being razzed.
"Why hide?" Dorfman asked. "Are you committed to this or
not?" Part of the reason Detroit took a flyer on Moyer was
the hope that he could mentor a couple of young pitchers in
Toledo, Scott Aldred and Greg Gohr, who had big league stuff
but hadn't put it all together yet. Aldred was a 6´4˝, 195-pound
lefty with pop who had been up and down between the Tigers
and Toledo. Gohr threw in the low to mid-90s, and hadn't yet
made it to the Show. How was Moyer going to teach them anything if he was afraid to be who he was in front of them, a crafty
lefty seeking to figure this thing out?

The laminated cards were only part of the daily routine Dorfman had prescribed. Until now, Moyer had obsessed so hard on
his next start—visualizing a host of outcomes, including the bad
ones, for days—that he often felt exhausted come game time, as
though he'd already thrown nine innings. Dorfman slowed him
down. Everything between starts was scripted, building to the
ultimate mental outlook by the time the umpire called, "Play
ball."

It wasn't superstition; like many players, Moyer could be
superstitious, but Harvey had no time for that. No, Dorfman
believed that the best way to find the all-elusive zone was to
train the mind's muscle memory. "I'll put my spandex pitching
shorts on at the same time every day of every start," Moyer explains. "That's very purposeful. You're trying to re-create the
conditions that existed when you previously achieved mental focus. So when those shorts go on, it's like a signal that I'm starting
to raise my level of concentration. By the time I finish with the
concentration cards, I should be dialed in."

If Moyer's trek to Toledo was a Hail Mary intended to resur-
rect his career, he was in the right place. Toledo had a romantic
baseball past. Greats ranging from Jim Thorpe to Kirby Puckett
to Kirk Gibson had all played for the Mud Hens, to whom
the fan base was intensely loyal. Moyer was used to hearing
criticism from fans and media alike. But in Toledo, he sensed
support. More important, there was a simpler ethos in the air: it
was all just about the game. All the distractions that had weighed
on him at the major league level—the interviews with the media, the bottom-line machinations of the front office, the adult
autograph seekers who would turn around and make money off
his signature—all of it seemed to recede. It was easier to get to
that comfortable place when you didn't have a host of uncomfortable demands placed in your way.

It helped that upon his arrival in Toledo, Moyer met a young man who was also trying to find himself. Buddy Groom was a twenty-six-year-old lefthanded middle reliever from the one-stoplight Texas town of Red Oak, just south of Dallas. Moyer and Groom had both sensed a certain resigned attitude from their small towns back home: you'd given it your best shot, you'd made it this far; who ever *really* thought that Red Oak or Souderton would produce a baseball great? "We both had the same kind of mind-set," Groom, who went on to have a fourteen-year career in the big leagues, remembers today. "We kind of bonded, because we both wanted to prove people wrong."

Groom would go on to find himself as a bona fide big league pitcher in the mid-'90s after turning all his worries about his success—or lack thereof—over to the Lord. He'd post seven consecutive seasons of at least seventy relief appearances for the Oakland A's and Baltimore Orioles. Moyer would find himself through his devotion to Harvey Ball, digging ever deeper into the mental side of the game. Two vastly dissimilar approaches—with the same result.

It was Groom's example on the field that helped Moyer turn things around. Early in the season, Mud Hens pitching coach Ralph Treuel pulled Moyer aside. "You have a better fastball than you think, but you can't just live away with it and your changeup, because hitters are going to lean away and sit on the outside pitch," Treuel, now the minor league pitching coordinator for the Boston Red Sox, said.

Moyer knew Treuel was right, just as he knew Dick Pole had been. He was doing his best to be aggressive, but all the mental training in the world wouldn't give him the tool he most desperately needed: a pitch that could run into the righthanded batter. To date, he'd effectively been granting to righties permission to cheat "middle-away"—meaning any pitch directed to the middle of the plate, the outside corner, or just off the outer corner—because they didn't have to worry that he'd jam them inside. Groom, Moyer noticed, didn't have these problems. His friend was keeping righthanded hitters off balance because his cutter was keeping them honest.

As he would years later, when he first saw his idol Steve Carlton's slider up close, Moyer asked his new friend if he could teach him the pitch. This version differed greatly from the one that Moyer would throw in his forties. Groom's cutter was gripped on the side of the ball, with the middle finger hooking over the left seam and the index finger and thumb on the outside of the ball instead of underneath it. That made the middle finger dominant and created a cutting action that made a seeming fastball suddenly break into a righthander. (The Carlton pitch Moyer would throw nearly two decades later would have a more dominant grip, causing it to simultaneously break down and in to the righthanded batter.)

Moyer made his Mud Hens debut with an inning of scoreless relief in a game that wasn't close. A few days later, shorthanded, manager Joe Sparks needed a spot starter against the Richmond Braves. Moyer got the call, and the win, giving up one run on four hits in five innings. From then on, he was the team's most consistent starter. He'd end up going 10–8 with a 2.86 ERA.

Developing the new pitch was critical to Moyer's success, but so was exorcising the constant fear that came with pitching inside. The conventional wisdom is that for non–power pitchers, pitching inside carries a high amount of risk, because a hitter will see the pitch coming toward him more clearly and get a better rip at it. If a batter is looking for something middle-in, and if the pitch isn't located *just* right, the ball stands a good chance of being catapulted into the outfield seats. Toledo was where Moyer first started to question this conventional wisdom, and where he first started considering the notion of acceptable risk on the mound.

As Moyer started to jam more and more righties, he started to notice their frustration: *How come I can't get around on such a slow pitch?* He'd see them shaking their heads or tossing their bats away in disgust after yet one more pop-up. This was what Harvey was talking about when he first broached the idea of using their aggression against them. The more he thought about it, the more Jamie began to think it didn't make sense to consider pitching inside as particularly dangerous; on the contrary, conceding the inside of the plate seemed to be the true danger. He and Groom would watch ESPN nightly, where the parade of home run clips usually consisted of batters with their arms fully extended, crushing balls that were either out over the plate or on the outside part of the plate. Batters were being allowed to cheat owing to the fear and conservatism of pitchers.

"If I told you to chop a piece of wood, but you'd be bringing the ax down right by your foot, you'd be anxious about hitting your leg," Moyer explains. "As opposed to chopping the same piece of wood out in front of your body, with your arms extended. That's a much more comfortable way to chop wood."

This was one of Moyer's Eureka moments: pitching wasn't just about *him* getting comfortable, it was also about making the batter *un*comfortable. Many years later, he'd sit in the dugout with another teammate, Phillies ace-in-training Cole Hamels, and pass along the message it took him so long to find. "C'mon, let's count the number of uncomfortable at-bats," he'd say, and they'd catalog the number of times an opposing batter was forced to do something he didn't want to do—barely foul off an inside cutter, hit the deck to avoid high and tight heat, lunge at something off-speed away. More often than not, they'd see comfortable swings instead of the frustration Moyer learned to bring out in batters in Toledo.

That said, coming inside with 80-mile-per hour stuff is hardly risk-free. Make a mistake and you are more likely to pay a heavier price inside than out. "So change your thinking," Harvey would say: *accept your mistakes*. Baseball, Moyer was finally starting to realize, is a sport that's all about failure. The best hitters come up short 70 percent of the time, and it's the only game that, as part of its official statistics, actually recognizes and categorizes *errors*. So why not own your mistakes? Why not learn to risk, but risk smartly?

Moyer started accepting his mistakes, and moving on. Against Tidewater on July 9, he gave up early solo homers to Terry Hansen and Mitch Lyden, but rather than start pressing, he settled down and pitched a complete game, scattering six other hits. None other than his own father-in-law noticed it. He saw how Moyer would get tagged with a long ball early, but then shrug it off and end up pitching five or six scoreless innings after being on the ropes. "The kid's a survivor," Phelps told his friend George Steinbrenner, trying to—once again—get his son-in-law a big league job.

According to the surgeon and writer Atul Gawande, research in the medical field shows that complication rates after surgery are not that disparate from hospital to hospital. What sets surgeons and hospitals apart is their ability to "rescue after failure"—to prevent a failure from morphing into a catastrophe. The best surgeons, Gawande wrote in the *New Yorker*, "didn't fail less. They rescued more."

The stakes were higher in the operating room than on the

baseball diamond, of course, but the same principle applies: beginning in Toledo, Moyer was learning how to rescue.

It started when he began mulling over the notion of risk on the mound. Used to be, surrendering an early homer would send Moyer's confidence level on a torturous descent. You never want to give up a home run, but Moyer was now finding that sometimes it wasn't the worst thing. It was preferable to the big inning, where the opposing team litters the field with line drives, the lineup bats around and puts four or five runs on the board. Moyer was heeding Dorfman and changing his thinking when he realized that sometimes "a home run can be a rally killer."

After a homer, the man who would go on to give up more dingers than any pitcher in history would walk toward the catcher and ump, glove extended, urgently wanting that next ball in his grip. Instead of thinking, *I hope I don't give up another home run*, he'd silently say to his opposition, *Okay. That's it. You're done.* The slate was wiped clean and he was free, as Harvey would say, to "pay attention to the task in front of you, not to the runners behind you." Besides, giving up a home run but avoiding a big inning, he was finding, can give a pitcher as much momentum as striking out the side. The feeling that you've dodged a bullet, with its implication that this just might be your day, became a confidence booster.

Instead of being something to dread, adversity on the mound was an opportunity: something to overcome. On July 25, Moyer was stricken with a bad stomach flu. "When I went to bed, I wasn't feeling good," he told the *Toledo Blade*. "When I woke up I was throwing up and had diarrhea." He allowed at least one runner in every inning but one, winning a hard-fought seven-inning outing. He pitched out of four jams with runners in scoring position, thanks to 12 ground-ball outs and six strikeouts. He was starting to think deeply about the game. "I'd like to be able to get ground balls more consistently," he said after the gutty performance. "I'd rather have the ground balls, because then you can get the double plays. A strikeout is only one out."

Instead of cowering at its prospect, Moyer started to welcome moments of potential calamity. When on June 29 his team booted three balls behind him against Pawtucket, he realized he could do the natural thing and fall back on the gift of a ready-made excuse—*my teammates threw the game away!*—or he could embrace the challenge of overcoming the deficit his defense had put him in. He went seven innings, striking out six and spreading out seven hits—all dinky singles—for the win.

With the onset of fall came the certainty of a September call-up to the Tigers. But the phone call from manager Sparky Anderson never came. Instead, the parent club, in another display of baseball conventional wisdom run amok, called up the hard-throwing twenty-two-year-old Scott Aldred, who was 4–6 with a 5.13 ERA. Moyer's season ended. He was a free agent yet again. But more important was that he was finally thinking for himself, instead of blindly buying into the shibboleths of the game. He was once again without a team, but this time he *felt* like a major league pitcher. Now, this time, would any major league teams have interest in him?

NOVEMBER 2011

CHAPTER FIVE

> Physical pain is no match for us if our mental discipline is strong.
>
> —Harvey Dorfman

In 1974, actor Lee Majors appeared on America's TV screens, running in slow motion while a dramatic voice-over intoned, "Gentlemen, we can rebuild him. We have the technology. We can make him better than he was. Better, stronger, faster." It was the debut of the prime-time drama *The Six Million Dollar Man*, which quickly achieved pop culture icon status. The same year, life started imitating cheesy TV show when, not far from where Majors's slow-motion acrobatics were being filmed, Dr. Frank Jobe performed a radical new procedure on the marred left elbow of Los Angeles Dodgers pitcher Tommy John. It was a medical development that would change professional sports.

As pitchers age, the stress on the elbow accumulates. Tendons get inflamed, scar tissue develops. Tommy John was a thirty-one-year-old starting pitcher with a 13–3 record when all the strain culminated in the tearing of his ulnar collateral ligament—a career-ending injury. Or was it? Dr. Jobe was the Dodgers' team physician at the time, and he decided to take a gamble: he'd detach a tendon from John's right forearm (tendons in the hamstring or calf will also do) and implant it in place of the torn ligament. It was a long shot: the graft required removing muscle in order to drill holes into the arm's ulna and humerus bones, running the risk of infection or fracture. There was less than a 10 percent chance of success. John was likely looking at a future that would have him returning to his hometown of Terre Haute, Indiana, where he'd sell cars at his friend's dealership and regale customers with tales of a major league career cut short due to injury. Instead, John pitched fourteen more seasons, winning 164 games after the groundbreaking surgery. Today, some 11 percent of major league pitchers have had Tommy John surgery.

The same year that Lee Majors's character and Tommy John's arm were being rebuilt, a sports medicine prodigy graduated from Middletown High School in New York's Hudson River valley. Just as Jamie Moyer grew up on the baseball tutelage of his father, the man who would ultimately repair his arm came of age at his own father's knee. From the age of ten, David Altchek would follow his orthopedic surgeon father, Martin, on his rounds at Horton Hospital. He spent his high school years removing patients' casts.

After college at Columbia (where he played tennis) and medical school at Cornell, Altchek became an orthopedic surgeon in his own right at New York's Hospital for Special Surgery. That's where he invented something called the "Docking Procedure" for use in Tommy John surgeries—a less invasive way of getting to the bone. Altchek's method didn't require drilling as many holes or detaching any muscle. Suddenly the success rate of Tommy John surgery vastly improved.

But Altchek wasn't done yet. In recent years, he had noticed that more and more pitchers, particularly the older ones, were tearing their muscle tendon, known as the flexor pronator, in addition to the ulnar ligament. Typical Tommy John surgery had focused too much on reconstructing the ligament and hadn't devoted enough attention to repairing the torn tendon.

Outside of Dr. Jobe, a holy trinity of sports surgeons had gained notoriety in the last decade, their names appearing in sports pages almost as often as those of the athletes themselves. There was Dr. Lewis Yocum in Los Angeles, Dr. James Andrews in Alabama, and Altchek. Cases like Moyer's, where both the ligament and tendon had torn cleanly off the elbow's bone, were quickly becoming the province of Altchek. After that first injury while pitching for the Phillies in St. Louis in July 2010, Moyer went to Los Angeles for a consultation with Yocum, whom he already knew. When Yocum saw the extent of both tears, he referred the case to Altchek.

Now it has been a year since Altchek performed Moyer's surgery, and a mere two months since Moyer's return to the mound in Florida. Spring training starts in three months; within weeks, scouts from major league clubs will be coming to the tiny town of Poway, California, where they will approach an unassuming ranch house belonging to Dom Johnson, a kind of pitching whisperer, who has a mound and backstop in his backyard, and they'll determine if Jamie Moyer is ready to be a major league pitcher again. That is, if Altchek doesn't issue a verdict today that beats them to it.

Uh-oh. Is that a frown? David Altchek doesn't typically frown. The fiftysomething sports medicine all-star is known for his ebullient bedside manner. When Moyer first came to see him a year ago, not only did Altchek not laugh his new patient out of the examining room when the then forty-eight-year-old Moyer broached the subject of pitching in the major leagues again, but he encouraged Moyer's comeback dream. "Any other respectable, normal doctor might have had second thoughts, but I'm always overly optimistic," Altchek would later recall. "I had a strong feeling we could fix it. What I didn't know is how he'd heal."

Now, with his neatly coiffed coal-black hair that calls to mind a GQ model—he appeared in a Ralph Lauren ad campaign a decade ago—Altchek is turning Moyer's arm every which way and looking uncharacteristically grim. Or at least perplexed. He feels Moyer's other arm, the right one. Back now to the left. He has Moyer flex and stretch. He pokes around some more.

"Wow," he says, looking up at a wide-eyed Moyer. "Your body is reacting in ways I'm afraid we don't really understand."

There's a pause. Ever stoic, Moyer is expressionless. "What do you mean?"

Now Altchek smiles, for he's about to talk in a decidedly unclinical way. "I mean you're some kind of mutant," he says. "As players age, their cells need more time to recover. When I feel around here"—Altchek starts massaging the back of Moyer's elbow, where the reconstruction took place—"it feels soft, elastic, and normal. It's like we never did anything. It's bizarre. You're some kind of healing freak."

Moyer is relieved to hear this, but he has questions, of course. Few athletes have been as in charge of their own rehab as Moyer. Even before this surgery, he had been the least passive athlete in the clubhouse trainer's room. Through the years, he'd taken to half-jokingly telling his teams' trainers, *"I'll* decide," when discussing his course of treatment, an attitude he picked up from his Seattle teammate Jay Buhner, a clubhouse leader who was a veteran of countless sports injuries. In the Mariners' clubhouse, there was a diagram of a skeletal structure annotated with all of

Buhner's conditions; Jay had had no choice but to take charge of his care, lest he be a mere passenger in his own career.

Back home in San Diego, Moyer had been working out with a physical therapist recommended by his friend Trevor Hoffman, Yousef Ghandour. Ghandour had a way of making Moyer feel like he was a full partner in the rehab process. When Moyer threw recently in Dom Johnson's backyard, Ghandour noticed something.

"He said, 'At about pitch thirty-six or thirty-seven, I noticed that your hand speed slowed down,'" Moyer tells Altchek now.

"Does that surprise you?" Altchek says. "Being a freak of nature—which you are—doesn't help you as much with endurance. The painful part of physical gifts is, you know, you still have to build up your endurance."

"Well, my therapist said, at the end of my throwing session, it looked like I found it—"

"Ah, yes," Altchek says. "That's the phenomenon we don't understand that well—the famous 'second wind.'"

"Well, can I do strenuous elbow work now?"

"So now that you're out of the year, you can do elbow work, you just have to listen to it," Altchek says. "We have a lot of guys fail this. The flexor pronator is really slow to heal and what has screwed us is not the ligament, but the flexor pronator in the first year. So that's why we take a very cautious approach. So if you start to get any tendonitis, you have to back off."

"So pronations, supinations, manual resistance?"

"I'm totally good with that," Altchek says. "We're out of the danger zone."

As Moyer has aged, he's learned that recovery time is just as important as the time he's spent working out. He won't go hard every day, like he might have in his more macho (but, not coincidentally, less successful) youth. Now Altchek tells him the same principle applies in rehab. "Recovery is underestimated in our athletic world," he says. "We're always like, 'More is better, more is better.' Sometimes going slow or even doing nothing is best."

Altchek remembers something he's been meaning to ask. "You still using the steel balls?"

When last they met, Moyer told Altchek of his history with a couple of roughly one-inch steel bearing balls. Back in college, Moyer's coach, George Bennett, took him on a pilgrimage to Veterans Stadium, where he met Gus Hoefling and—gulp— Steve Carlton. The meeting with Carlton was perfunctory, except for the fact that Moyer noticed the presence of a couple of steel balls that, Hoefling explained, could help with a pitcher's dexterity. Ever since, Moyer has kept a pair in his locker. Every day, when opening mail or doing paperwork in the clubhouse, he'll absentmindedly conduct his own improvised dexterity drill, first rolling the balls around his fingers with his palm up, trying to keep them together. Then he'll flip his palm over, facing downward, and roll them without letting them drop. In the Philly clubhouse, Moyer turned young pitcher Cole Hamels on to the same drill.

When Moyer confirms that he's still using the bearing balls, Altchek shakes his head. "Do you even realize how brilliant that is?" he says. "The muscles in your forearm control the fingers, so you're really extending your workout of the forearm into the hand and fingers. I would have never thought of that. I'm telling all of my patients to do it—courtesy of Jamie Moyer."

Moyer laughs. Altchek is a man of science, and there's no clear scientific explanation for Moyer's weird healing talents. But he can make some guesses. Moyer's dedication to rehab is as good as Altchek has seen, but what sets Moyer apart is that, in effect, he's been preparing for this challenge his whole professional career. While with the Texas Rangers in 1989, he suffered a lat strain—an injury to the latissimus dorsi muscle, which stretches from the upper back to underneath the armpit. That off-season, he rehabbed the injury with a physical therapist in a program that worked his arm, shoulder, and core with light weights. By the time spring training rolled around, he had never felt stronger. "Why not do this *every* off-season?" he asked himself. From then on, even though he was no longer injured, he'd embark upon a prophylactic rehab regimen every off-season, strengthening key body parts—including the all-important serratus muscles—and steeling his body for the trauma to come. Years of preventive rehab may not only have staved off his injury until after he'd pitched 4,000 innings, it may also be stimulating a faster-than-normal recovery.

But there is another, less scientific key to Moyer's healing powers. In Dorfman's *The Mental Game of Baseball*, his guru prescribes an imaginative cure to pain—literally. "Begin to imagine and experience your injured part mending and becoming whole," Dorfman writes. "Experience it becoming stronger and healthier every day. Then imagine yourself performing exactly as you want to perform, well bodied and whole, without pain or weakness."

At Karen's prodding—"close your eyes and feel it healing," she'd implore her husband after his workouts—Moyer would visualize himself healthy and feeling stronger every day.

"Whatever you're doing, keep it up," Altchek says now, still shaking his head in wonder. Before officially releasing his patient, Altchek has two parting thoughts. The first, with a sardonic smile: "You really ought to think about donating your body to science." The second, shaking Moyer's hand: "See ya on *SportsCenter*."

* * *

Bounding out of the Hospital for Special Surgery on the Upper East Side of Manhattan, Jamie Moyer has been given the green light to defy all the smart money once again and make it back to a big league mound. For a year, all he's wanted is the chance to write his own ending to his career, as opposed to having an injury close the door for him.

Tonight, on the West Side, the Moyer Foundation will throw a gala celebration and fund-raiser, hosted by NBC's Stone Phillips. A few hundred well-heeled guests, including former Pennsylvania governor Ed Rendell, who lost his father when he was fourteen, will see video footage from Camp Erin, the nation's largest network of child bereavement camps, including one in each Major League Baseball city. They'll see kids who have lost loved ones, comforted by and bonding with other kids who have suffered loss. They'll hear from Karen and Jamie, whose throat will catch when he talks about how humbled he's been by the impact Camp Erin has had.

That's later. For now, as he's walking down Fifth Avenue, a car passes by and the driver leans on his horn. "Good luck, Moyer!" he shouts, roaring by. Moyer laughs. It feels like this comeback is really about to happen. "What an amazing journey you're on," I say to him.

"*Everyone's* journey is amazing," Jamie Moyer says. The next step on *his* journey is to get back to the big leagues. Again.

JUNE 1993

CHAPTER SIX

Control your thoughts, or your thoughts will
control you.

— Harvey Dorfman

It's a rite of passage: every pupil rebels at some point against a
mentor. Moyer's secret act of defiance against Harvey Dorfman
came early in the 1993 season, when he surreptitiously wore a
garter belt under his uniform.

Perhaps a bit of background is in order. After Moyer's 1992
season in Toledo he was once again looking for a job. One day
that off-season, he happened to be in his father-in-law's office
at Notre Dame when in walked former major league pitcher
Ed Farmer, a huge Notre Dame booster. Farmer was now an
advance scout for the Baltimore Orioles, and with him was his
boss, general manager Roland Hemond. Farmer's support for
all things Fighting Irish led him to the building that day —
he'd be addressing Notre Dame coach Pat Murphy's baseball
team — and Farmer invited Hemond to tag along because he
thought it would be an added bonus for the college kids to hear
from a big league executive. With time to kill, they stopped in

to say hello to Digger, who wasted no time selling his visiting son-in-law.

"I'm telling you, Moyer is a helluva pitcher, if only someone would just give him the ball," Digger, who always refers to his son-in-law by his last name, breathlessly lobbied Hemond. Digger, whose boisterous personality fills any room he's in, was in rare form: with his son-in-law sitting there, the coach was in full recruiting mode, as though Hemond was an on-the-fence parent of one of the high school seven-footers he was trying to lure to his program.

"What are you doing now, Jamie?" Hemond asked, put on the spot by Phelps's relentlessness.

"Looking for a job," Moyer replied.

"Let me see what I can do," Hemond said.

Within days, Hemond received a report on Moyer from his top scout, Gordon Goldsberry. "He's a bright guy," Goldsberry said. "His biggest problem is tempo. He's not going to blow the ball by anyone. He has to outthink hitters. But he takes too much time between pitches, which gives hitters too much time to think." That said, Goldsberry concluded that bad tempo was a correctable problem. "He's probably worth taking a chance on."

That March, Hemond invited Moyer to the Orioles' minor league spring training camp, where Moyer pitched well. He was signed to a $200,000 contract and assigned to the Orioles' Triple A affiliate in Rochester, New York. Karen, expecting the couple's second child, packed boxes once again, and the family rented an apartment in dreary Rochester, where Jamie and Karen promptly witnessed a mugging at gunpoint on the street.

Whatever was happening outside the stadium, it soon became clear that for Moyer, something on the mound had clicked: he was no longer a minor league pitcher. In eight starts, he compiled a 6–0 record, with a 1.67 ERA and a terrific WHIP (walks plus hits per innings pitched) of 1.019. Hemond attended a game in Rochester one frigid night, where he watched Moyer carve up the Richmond Braves and its can't-miss prospects Chipper Jones and Javier Lopez. In late May, the call finally came. Jamie was going back to the Show.

But there's a big gulf between Triple A and the majors. The Orioles, a team recently emerged from bankruptcy, were in their second year at their much-hyped new downtown stadium, Camden Yards. Moyer was bursting with confidence in Rochester, but, confronted by the pressure of yet one more last chance and surrounded by superstars like Cal Ripken Jr. and pitchers Mike Mussina and Ben McDonald, he quickly found the mound at Camden Yards an uncomfortable place. In his first ten days back in the majors, he lost all three of his starts, culminating in a shellacking at the hands of the California Angels on May 30, in which Moyer gave up seven earned runs and couldn't get out of the second inning.

Here we go again, he thought. With an 0–3 record and 5.74 ERA, how long would it be before manager Johnny Oates gave him a one-way ticket back to Rochester?

Yet Hemond, a three-time winner of baseball's Executive of the Year award, knew the degree to which conventional wisdom conspired against someone like Moyer. He knew that crafty pitchers had to overcome a stereotype—that their fortunes were dictated more by luck than skill, that it was only a matter of time until major league bats caught up with their junk. But Hemond had seen enough to know that cerebral pitchers possessed a skill themselves, albeit one that was a challenge to discern compared to fireballers. They used misdirection and trickery to get batters out. Moyer, Hemond thought, could be one of the those guys, like Eddie Lopat, who got by on guile and smarts. Lopat, nicknamed "Junk Man," pitched for the Yankees in the '40s and

'50s, and Hemond remembered how he used to frustrate hitters. Like Lopat, Moyer wasn't embarrassed by his lack of speed. Like Lopat, he worked with the tools he had and held his own.

Or so Hemond hoped. He'd seen how nerve-racking it could be to watch Moyer. Hemond remembers that he and his wife met another Orioles executive and his wife for dinner and a game that season. At dinner, the executive's wife asked who was pitching. "Moyer," Hemond said. The other couple frowned. "We're leaving," they said, explaining that they couldn't stomach watching Moyer: he just looked too damn easy to hit. Today, Hemond laughs at the memory. "I always relished that," he says.

But Moyer didn't know of Hemond's patience. He felt he had to turn his fortunes around quickly, and he'd try anything to get a win. Enter the garter belt.

Scooter Myers was the old childhood friend in Souderton who, growing up, had been like a little brother to Moyer. Through the years, they'd remained close. When he was still in high school, Scooter would trek down to St. Joseph's University in Philly to visit Moyer, where he was first introduced to beer and college girls. When Jamie got drafted, the two kept in touch by writing letters.

So when Scooter saw that his man was in a slump, he knew he had to act. He got inspiration from an unlikely church of psychic salvation: his favorite movie, *Bull Durham*, the Kevin Costner send-up of minor league baseball. Scooter had seen the movie so often that he'd work lines from it into casual conversation. When Jamie would answer his phone, he'd hear Scooter's voice on the other end with his usual greeting, the one he still hears to this day every time Scooter calls—"What's up, Meat?"—echoing Crash Davis's moniker for Nuke LaLoosh in the film.

For the six people in America who haven't seen the movie: in *Bull Durham*, the Susan Sarandon character, Annie, has

LaLoosh wear a garter belt underneath his uniform in order to reorient his head and get him pitching out of the proper "hemisphere" of his brain. Scooter thought Jamie needed some of the same medicine. So he sent a pinkish garter belt to Moyer. "You gotta wear it," Scooter said, daring his conservative friend. "Try something different!"

I can't believe I'm doing this, Moyer thought to himself as he deviated from his pregame routine in order to stealthily put the garter belt on under his uniform in a clubhouse bathroom stall. Harvey, if he'd known, would have been livid. He disdained the degree to which superstition ruled the game. Like Moyer, he'd seen slumping players empty the contents of their locker onto the field and set them aflame, and he'd had players who insisted on wearing the same ratty T-shirt when on a winning streak. In their phone conversations, Harvey railed against such magical thinking. He was trying to get players to take honest looks at themselves, to examine the root causes of their struggles— and to learn how to fix things themselves. "Attributing success or failure to powers outside of you is another way of denying responsibility," he told Moyer. "Don't be absurd. Trust your talent and preparation."

But trusting his talent and preparation didn't appear to be working. At this point, Moyer was willing to try anything. And besides, was the message from Harvey that dissimilar from Annie's? When she tells Nuke to "breathe through your eyelids like the Lava Lizards of the Galapagos Islands," was it all that different from Harvey's emphasis on focusing on your breathing as a relaxation technique on the mound? As for the garter, Annie is trying to get Nuke into the right frame of mind, and maybe by wearing the lacy underthing—by running the risk of making an ass out of himself *before* taking the mound—she is reducing the pressure and eradicating his fear. Same goal, different tactic.

And so it was that on June 10, 1993, Jamie Moyer, dressed in a tasteful pink garter belt—nothing too provocative—beat the Boston Red Sox, giving up one run on a solo shot to Mo Vaughn, in five and two-thirds innings. It was his first major league victory in three years. After the game, he called Scooter, who howled into the phone when his friend told him he'd worn the garter.

"Meat, you're full of it!" Scooter cried. To this day, he doesn't believe Moyer really went through with it. To this day, Moyer still carries the garter belt with him, in his shaving kit.

From the beginning of their relationship, there were many similarities between Jamie Moyer and Harvey Dorfman. Both were products of their respective fathers, both were staunch family men, both believed, on some level, that baseball was more than a game, that it provided object life lessons and guiding principles. Both also hated the Yankees; in Harvey's case, it was because his father—who always pulled for the underdog—would reply "whoever is playing the Yankees today" when asked for his favorite team. "I adopted his disdain for them," Harvey would later write in *Persuasion of My Days*. In Jamie's case, it was because, when he got to the big leagues, he felt like Steinbrenner's crew had too much power, that the team dictated league policy. Like Harvey, Moyer was contemptuous of bullies.

But perhaps their most salient similarity was their mutual enchantment with baseball's abiding mysteries. Both men decided early on to try and figure out the game, to ask questions and question answers, to somehow understand the strange turns baseball provided. By the time their paths had crossed, both had been humbled by the ever-surprising, unscripted nature of the game. "I've been doing it my whole life, and pitching is still a mystery to me," Moyer says. "Which is why I love it."

The 1993 version of Jamie Moyer was one of those mysteries. Who would have thought that after eight years of bouncing between the majors and minors, after being given up on by three teams, after countless shellings at the hands of overeager bats, Moyer would become a bona fide major league starter at age thirty-one, just as, only three years later, he'd take another startling leap and become an elite star? On one level, Moyer's success in 1993—he'd end up going 12–9 with a 3.43 ERA for the third-place Orioles—defied rationality; it flew in the face of the game's conventional wisdom, which holds that by the time a player has put in the years of service Moyer had, he is what he is.

Why now? Why did Moyer break through, when so many others whom he played with had failed? Manager Johnny Oates had confidence in him, which helped. But Dorfman didn't believe there was any single answer. He sure as hell didn't think that Moyer's 1993 season had anything to do with that damned garter belt. Or with the fact that he started eating the same meal before each start. (Karen, who had been putting together a celebrity cookbook for charity, one night cooked Joe Montana's shrimp and pasta recipe before one of Jamie's starts; after he won, Montana's dish became their every-fifth-day meal. "You and your shrimp and pasta," Harvey wailed when Jamie came clean.)

No, it more likely had something to do with the same instinct that led Moyer to Dorfman in the first place, his sense of wide-eyed exploration. Like the game itself, Moyer's career rewarded process. In his memoirs, Dorfman describes himself as a "seeker"; the same can be said about Moyer. No course of treatment—whether in the trainer's room or in Harvey's office, just as no new grip or pitch, is too out there for him. He is and has always been in an ongoing state of becoming.

In his striving eagerness to learn, Moyer started to set himself apart. Just as in Toledo, when he started thinking about risk and rescue, in Baltimore he committed to digging deep in search of lessons in his losses. After the garter belt game, he'd have to wait a while. He was 4–0 in his next five starts, with a stellar 2.45 ERA. He was to start the Orioles' final home game of the season's first half against the White Sox—just before Camden Yards hosted the All-Star Game, which would be accompanied by an Old-Timers' Game and a celebrity home run contest.

Moyer came into the start riding high, with a 5–3 record and a 3.13 ERA, having just thrown a complete-game four-hit shutout against Kansas City. But something felt off in the clubhouse before the game. Far more media buzzed around, as the national baseball press had descended for the weekend festivities. Sitting at his locker, every time Moyer looked up, he'd see another recognizable face. He chatted with Reggie Jackson about Reggie's dad, who had scouted Moyer out of high school for the California Angels, and about their upbringings in the exurbs of Philadelphia. Then Bob Gibson sauntered by—how could you not introduce yourself to Bob Gibson? And there was actor Tom Selleck—Magnum P.I.!—who would be playing in the celebrity home run contest.

At one point, it occurred to Moyer that he'd better find Tim amid all the tumult so he could prepare. Tim was his old high school teammate, Tim Bishop, who was now the Orioles' strength and conditioning coach. Upon reuniting, they had instantly fallen back into their friendship. Moyer was still skittish about broadcasting his pregame mental exercises—the visualization, the laminated concentration grid, the series of self-talk questions. So he'd taken to seeking out Tim, who would set him up in his office with the door shut, or in a utility closet, where he could narrow his focus by game time.

Only on this day, Moyer never got to Tim. He tried running

through the grid at his locker, but there was too much noise, too many cameras and conversations. He felt like his train of thought had been derailed. And then came his big mistake: *I'll find it when I get out there*, he thought. Yet when he set foot on the mound, he sensed it wouldn't be quite so easy. He'd so widely deviated from his pregame routine that he felt naked on the mound. "Warming up, it felt like I was out there without my glove on," he'd recall some nineteen years later, having frozen the feeling in time.

In the first inning, Frank Thomas turned on an inside pitch that didn't get inside enough and smacked a three-run homer. What followed was more of the same. It didn't help matters that in Moyer's head, Harvey's soothing voice was replaced by his own, berating himself for having been so weak-willed in his pregame preparation. He didn't survive the fifth inning and the White Sox beat him handily.

The next day, he, Karen, and the kids drove to Blakeslee, Pennsylvania, to spend the break with their friend Reverend Ray Deviney, who had officiated at their wedding. Moyer was pensive the whole trip; Karen knew he was beating himself up. *You were not mentally strong or mature enough to handle the moment*, he told himself over and over. *How could you let your teammates down?* he asked, more accusation than question.

When Jamie next spoke to Harvey, there was no sympathy to be had. Harvey would often rail against "multitasking"; in his view, proper preparation could never be done half-assed. When Moyer made the mistake of trying to rationalize his misstep in an effort to get past it — "It's one start, I'll bounce back" — Harvey exploded. "What are you going to do to get this *right*?" he demanded to know. Moyer would later be teammates with certain pitchers — Randy Johnson among them — who were so locked in from the moment they arrived at the ballpark on their starting days that they would not speak and refused to be spoken to. Teammates were warned. You approach them at your peril.

It didn't occur to Moyer to go quite that far. But this was a lesson that he needed some of that kind of resoluteness in his approach. He swore he'd never, ever let anything interrupt his pregame routine again. Harvey told him to remember what it felt like to be so unprepared. Moyer never wanted to feel that naked on the mound again.

Something happened in major league clubhouses in the new millennium: baseball entered a post-camaraderie era. To Moyer, it had always made sense that the game's communal square was called a clubhouse, as opposed to locker room. Given the game's meandering pace and marathon schedule, teams bonded, arguably more so than in other sports. That changed in the last ten to fifteen years. Now players clock out after games, like harried office workers looking to beat rush hour traffic.

When Moyer broke in with the Cubs, the team still played all home games during the day. That allowed teammates to go out en masse after the game. In Seattle, a large group of players, led by pitcher Jeff Fassero, would dine out on the road together. Fassero was something of a wine connoisseur, which is how Moyer—ever the student—got into collecting wine.

Used to be, after a game and the requisite interviews, players would gather around a keg in the middle of the clubhouse and dissect the night's events—a game wasn't truly complete until a group of guys analyzed it over a few cold ones. A few years ago, following the drunk-driving death of St. Louis Cardinal Josh Hancock, most teams banned alcohol from the clubhouse.

That dovetailed with other changes in the game. In recent years, as the contracts got ever fatter, players took relatives and friends from back home on their major league ride with them. The posse was born. Teammates became more insulated from one another; late in his career, Moyer would look around the clubhouse in amazement, for the landscape in front of him was filled with guys wearing iPods or texting or talking to their agents on their cell phones. (In Philly, he suggested banning cell phones in the clubhouse, to no avail.) The definition of teammate had morphed from blood brother (think Billy Martin and Mickey Mantle) to office-place coworker.

The Orioles of 1993 hadn't yet fallen prey to such a breakdown of team community, though. There, Moyer was welcomed into a culture that made going to the ballpark feel like he was attending pitching camp. On so many teams, there had long been a dividing line between hitters and pitchers. But on the Orioles, Moyer would regularly pick the brains of stars like Cal Ripken Jr. and Brady Anderson about how to attack opposing hitters, and they'd gain insight into a pitcher's mind-set by quizzing him.

Every day, Moyer found himself in extended conversations about the craft of pitching. He and thirty-three-year-old reliever Mark Williamson, thirty-year-old reliever Todd Frohwirth, and twenty-four-year-old Mike Mussina would talk shop for hours: in the bullpen, in the clubhouse, loitering around the batting cage during batting practice. "We'd talk about setting up hitters, about mechanics, about how to have a good bullpen," Moyer recalls. "I never tired of listening to those guys. I learned how to stay a step ahead of hitters from them. Pitchers don't talk like that anymore."

Mussina, who led the staff in 1993 with a 14–6 record, was like Moyer's mirror image. Both were from small Pennsylvania towns: Mussina was born in Williamsport, Moyer in Souderton. Both were high school prodigies: Mussina went 24–4 with a

0.87 ERA at Montoursville Area High School. And both were thinking man's pitchers.

Mussina had played three years at Stanford University before bursting into the majors in 1992 with an 18–5 record. "Mussina and Moyer were of the same mold," recalls GM Hemond. "Very analytical. They were always having deep discussions. Mussina was the player rep, so I had to sit on the other side of the table from him. He was an economics major at Stanford. I have to say, there were times I felt quite overmatched."

In a sport that sometimes seemed to shun deep thinking, both Mussina and Moyer were unabashed in the cerebral way they approached the game. Mussina essentially threw five pitches— fastball, sinker, knuckle-curve, changeup, and cutter—but, like Moyer, he didn't have a classic "out" pitch. Some might consider such an absence a weakness, but Mussina and Moyer saw it as an advantage. The hitter couldn't sit on one pitch at any given time; instead, location and speed change made all the difference. They'd compare notes on hitters and play long toss in the outfield, trying to outdo each other testing out new grips and delivery tweaks.

Between them, they won 26 games for the third-place Orioles, despite a long turn Mussina took on the disabled list with shoulder soreness. Not bad for a couple of small-town Pennsylvania boys.

Moyer had never been speechless during a hospital visit before, but this...this was different. The first image Jamie Moyer had of two-year-old Gregory Chaya, who was almost the exact same age as his eldest son, would stay in his mind's eye forever: a frail, sallow boy with no hair, tubes and wires crisscrossing his tiny body, sleeping yet shifting uneasily, clearly in discomfort. *Oh my God,* he thought, a lump instantly burning in his throat. *He looks just like Dillon*, his own two-year-old.

Luckily, Karen was by his side, because Jamie couldn't speak. It was just after Moyer had spent all of All-Star weekend flagellating himself over his last start. That weekend, his friend Father Deviney told him about this little boy from his congregation who was struggling for his life at Johns Hopkins in Baltimore. A visit could lift his spirits, not to mention those of his parents, Margie and Rob, who greeted the baseball player and his wife and walked them through their story.

Margie and Rob ran a family cement-mixing business back home in Blakeslee. In April, Gregory, the youngest of their three children, was diagnosed with leukemia AML, a form of cancer that usually targets adults. Now they were renting a Baltimore apartment to be near Gregory, who had just received a bone marrow transplant from Christopher, their eldest. Gregory's chances of survival were estimated to be 45 percent.

Karen, as emotive as her husband is cool, embraced Margie. This was supposed to be a one-off visit, something Moyer was a veteran of: you show up, bring some memorabilia, hopefully help comfort parents who are facing unimaginable challenges, and then you go home to your healthy, happy family. As they talked, Moyer said little, but he didn't want to leave. It wouldn't be *right* to leave. *It's so not fair*, he thought every time he looked over at Gregory, who, awake now, was shy and fragile and seemed so helpless.

That night, Moyer couldn't stop thinking about Gregory, and about Margie and Rob's dedication. Talking to them, he was struck by their determination and will. He'd visited sick kids before. As he moped around their Baltimore apartment, he and Karen wondered why he couldn't shake this one. Was it because Gregory looked so much like Dillon?

Or was it something deeper? Karen had never seen him so

shaken. "It's an unfair comparison to make, but do you think it has hit home because he's fighting for his life and you're fighting for your career?" Karen asked over dinner, while Dillon squirmed on his dad's lap.

Moyer thought about it for a moment. "Maybe," he said. "He's fighting for his life every second of every day. My job means nothing compared to that."

The next day was Moyer's first start since the loss to the White Sox before All-Star weekend. When he got to the ballpark, he called Gregory from a clubhouse phone. Gregory was in better spirits and he chattered on, mentioning something about Gummi Bears. Moyer made a mental note to bring him some. He told Margie he'd like to come around again. When he hung up, his eyes were glistening and the lump in his throat was back. He sat at his locker and wrote the initials "G.C." on the back of his cap and on his pair of spikes.

That night on the mound, Moyer was in easygoing command from pitch one. The Kansas City Royals managed just two hits and one run against him, en route to his sixth win of the season, lowering his ERA to 3.42. In the clubhouse after the game, the beat reporters wanted to know what "G.C." stood for. Uh-oh. Moyer hadn't wanted to talk about Gregory; he hadn't told anyone, not even Karen, about his little tribute. And he really *couldn't* talk about Gregory, not without getting visibly emotional. He hadn't thought this initial thing through, he realized. The media pack squeezed in around him and he announced he was dedicating his season to the young boy. "I really feel it's the least I can do," he was able to say through quivering lips. "He's fighting every day, whether he knows it or not."

From then on, Moyer would call or visit Gregory every day. Karen says she saw a spiritual bond develop. Gregory, who started referring to Moyer as "the guy on TV," would blow kisses to the TV screen when Moyer pitched. During visits, they'd throw a Nerf ball at one another, and Gregory would howl with laughter when Moyer would softly ricochet the ball off the wall and into the child's face.

Gregory was recovering; by August, he and his parents were down to two visits per week to the doctors at Johns Hopkins. By September, the cancer was in remission and the Chayas were able to return to Blakeslee. Then, around Christmastime, Gregory relapsed. He was taken to Children's Hospital of Philadelphia for chemotherapy, where the Chayas were greeted by a telegram from Moyer: WE ARE HERE FOR YOU. Soon, the doctors at Children's Hospital told the Chayas there was nothing else to be done. They recommended making Gregory as comfortable as possible for the next two or three months so they could all enjoy the time he had left.

That's when something remarkable happened. Margie Chaya simply said no: "This is not how it's going to be." Moyer called often, and found himself in awe of the Chayas' defiance. All those years of talking to Harvey about the power of will, and now here was this family telling their doctors that their belief was stronger than anything blood tests might show. The Chayas signed Gregory up for some experimental treatments at the Hutchinson Cancer Institute in Seattle; the family moved there, while Rob shuttled back and forth to Blakeslee to run the family business.

The Chayas had no transportation in Seattle, so the Moyers arranged for a van for the family, and Jamie called Mariners ace Randy Johnson and told him about his sick friend. Johnson befriended Gregory as well, presenting him with the ball from his first strikeout of the 1994 season. When the Orioles played Seattle, Gregory was doing well enough to make the game, where Johnson and Moyer posed for photos with him.

Three years later, Moyer was traded to Seattle—a move

Gregory called an act of "fate." Soon, his cancer would be gone. Today, he's back in Blakeslee, working for the family business. "The doctors can't tell you why he's alive," Moyer says, still welling up, all these years later. "Watching Gregory and his parents, you learn that a lot of this is belief. Here's a family with a little boy who was very sick and they believed they were going to find a cure for him. Well, I mean, he's a miracle. That's what I call him, my miracle friend."

Harvey Dorfman had long lectured his clients on the power of widening their lens. When they first met, he held a sheet of loose-leaf paper directly in front of Moyer's eyes.

"Describe for me what's in the room beyond this piece of paper," he demanded.

"I really can't," he said. "There's a desk and a chair. But I can't see the room."

"The piece of paper is your baseball career," Dorfman said. "Any large object held too close to you will block out everything around it. There's a world out beyond this paper. There's a world out there beyond baseball."

Dorfman would later contend it was no mere coincidence that Moyer started putting things together on the mound after he met Gregory. The high stakes of Gregory's struggle lowered those of his own. Suddenly, the game wasn't life-or-death anymore. Harvey, always trying to broaden his pupil's perspective, would say, "You've got a great life, a great wife, and great kids. If your career ended tomorrow, you wouldn't kill yourself. So what's the worst thing that can happen to you?"

Moyer always understood his point intellectually. But when he met Gregory, he finally *felt* it. For years, he would look upon 1993 as the year his career turned around. But it had nothing to do with superstition, and everything to do with inspiration. Turns out, Gregory Chaya was really his garter belt.

DECEMBER 2011

CHAPTER SEVEN

Think and talk the solution — not the problem.
— Harvey Dorfman

This is the part they don't see. The sportswriters and talking heads on ESPN often report in passing that an athlete has had "successful" surgery or has started rehab, and then — fast-forward two, three, six, or twelve months later — the fans see the finished product on the field. But in the months or years between injury and comeback lies this, the lonely hours of work in gyms and on obstacle courses and on treadmills immersed in tubs of water. It's tedious, repetitive, and all-consuming, and it's why so many older athletes ultimately hang it up: it's not that they no longer love the game, it's that they can no longer find the drive to push themselves back to their former level.

Those who do make it back tend to trick themselves into this otherworldly commitment. They imagine former rivals in the gym *at this very moment* in order to measure themselves against something, or they invent doubters in their own head that they can prove wrong.

And then there's Jamie Moyer.

For Moyer, rehab is not a means to an end. It's an end in it-self. He loves this part, in the same way that he loves his bullpen sessions. He loves it precisely *because* no one sees it, at least no one outside of Team Moyer, the quirky band of comrades he's gathered for the cause. He loves it for the camaraderie he feels with them, for the mission's sense of common purpose and shared adventure, and—just like in those bullpen sessions—for the trial and error and discovery that each day brings.

On this day, Moyer shuts his blaring alarm and bounces out of bed. It is 5:00 a.m. Karen, no stranger to working out her-self, she has an appointment with a spinning class in an hour. "Time to go to work," Jamie says, speaking for both of them. He needn't look far for evidence of what the work means to him; on the mantel in front of him, in the master bedroom of the family's home in the San Diego hills, sits the pitch-ing rubber from the mound of Philadelphia's Citizens Bank Park, which he excavated during the World Series celebration in 2008.

Today he'll be throwing for a handful of major league scouts in the backyard of his friend and pitching coach, Dom Johnson. He flicks on the light in his master bathroom and sizes himself up in the mirror. He starts to feel the familiar adrenaline rush: the challenge of all-consuming work is on the horizon. *Damn, I still love this,* he thinks. Most guys his age would dread the thought of what the day ahead would entail. Pain, exhaustion, drudgery. To Moyer, though, it is something else. One more op-portunity to get a little better. Evidence that he could do it— that he *would* do it. One more step on the way to showing every-one who had ever doubted him that he still had it.

* * *

When Moyer first approached physical therapist Yousef Ghandour to oversee getting his arm and body back into pitching form, Ghandour seemed skeptical. He asked the same thing that so many people did when they first encountered Moyer. "Why, with everything you've accomplished, would you want to go through this?"

"You know what?" Moyer responded. "I enjoy it. People don't normally do this, but that doesn't mean they *can't* do it."

Still, he had no illusions. "Look, I know the window is closing," he told Ghandour. "But I feel like I still have a pinkie in the window. If it closes completely, that's okay. At least I'll know."

Ghandour, a sucker for underdogs, was in.

So was Liba Placek, the fifty-eight-year-old mother of four whom the late NFL legend Junior Seau once dubbed "the Beast." Moyer wanted Placek, an unconventional strength and conditioning coach—Trevor Hoffman had suggested both her and Yousef to Jamie—to whip him into peak performance shape. She had treated many pitchers, which meant she knew firsthand what an unnatural and stressful act pitching was, that it required the two sides of the body to perform completely different tasks. It was a tough enough balancing act for healthy men in their twenties to pull off; she doubted this forty-nine-year-old could succeed. But she was taken by Moyer's commitment, enthusiasm, and courage. He was risking no small amount of pride—and a lifetime of achievement—to make it back. How could she, a woman approaching sixty who ended each group session at her Del Mar, California, LibaFit studio by standing upside down on one hand, not help the guy?

Then there was the mysterious Dom Johnson, a private pitching coach who, though known among the game's lifers, had never been one to call attention to himself. Johnson coached some forty minor league pitchers in the backyard of his Poway, California, ranch house. Fifty of his pupils were playing Division I baseball, and an average of thirteen were selected in the Major League Baseball draft in recent years.

When Moyer first appeared in Johnson's backyard, he did so with his parents, Jim and Joan, in tow. As Jamie explained the nature of his quest, peppering his speech with a string of Harveyisms, Johnson flashed back on his own education in the game. Like Jamie, he'd learned at the knee of *his* father, former major league slugger Deron Johnson. Through his dad, Dom had access to the game's great pitching minds. That's how he met Gus Hoefling and Steve Carlton. Hoefling asked him, "Can elephants walk across lily pads?"

"No," young Dom answered.

"That's why you'll never reach your potential," Hoefling barked. "Remember: what the mind believes, the body achieves."

Johnson took the question to Carlton: could elephants walk across lily pads? The All-Star pitcher smiled. "I haven't met that damn elephant yet, but he's out there."

Now here was Moyer, in his backyard, talking about coming back from Tommy John surgery and pitching in the major leagues again at nearly fifty years old. Dom Johnson had found his elephant.

Over the years, Yousef Ghandour had sat many professional athletes down in his San Diego Physiotherapy Associates rehab center for the talk. Your workouts, he'd tell them, will be a couple of hours, but they won't be of the macho "no pain, no gain" variety. They'll likely be tedious. Ghandour, a native of Jordan in his late forties, had studied at the legendary Ola Grimsby Institute. With a passion for the biomechanics of the human body, he'd spent years developing a philosophy that centered on more repetition but less weight than traditional approaches.

"Our goal is to increase your tissue tolerance to withstand more abuse," Ghandour told Moyer. "More repetition and less weight can be boring, but it's important."

Music to my ears, Moyer thought. During his time in Seattle, Moyer met Peter Shmock, a two-time Olympic shot-putter and the Seattle Mariners' former weight training coach, and became a devotee of the new science of recovery, which posits that the restful periods between workouts are actually the most important part of a fitness regimen.

Shmock had a holistic approach to training, incorporating t'ai chi ch'uan, yoga, and medicine balls into his workouts, and preached the importance of the mind-body relationship to athletes like Moyer and his catcher, Dan Wilson. Moyer learned to listen to his body, and he found that it seemed to grow stronger when he had the discipline to give it time to recover from Shmock's workouts.

Ghandour sounded a lot like Shmock. Both men were incrementalists and neither subscribed to the old-school attitude that "pain is just weakness leaving the body." Ghandour's program began with an assessment of Moyer's range of motion and exercises to restore basic mobility. Next came the coordination phase, in which Ghandour would sleuth out which muscles were relying on which muscles to compensate for their own weaknesses.

Then came the endurance phase, where the focus is on building up the tolerance of the muscles in question. When under tension, muscles either lengthen, shorten, or remain the same. Moyer would be put through a series of low-weight exercises, such as ever so slowly lowering a three-pound dumbbell from the curl position twenty-five times in sets of three, which provides resistance while lengthening the muscle.

After a few weeks of building up Moyer's tissues and ligaments, only then would it be time for strength training. And that's when Moyer's regimen would shift to fewer reps with higher weight on Ghandour's pulley system. Ghandour was an evangelist when it came to working out with pulleys, which provide optimum resistance and help guard against tendonitis flareups compared to traditional weight training. He'd presented his pulley theories to the Professional Baseball Athletic Trainers Society Baseball Medicine Conference, sharing billing with Dr. Lewis Yocum, and had started marketing specially designed pulleys for travel and at-home use. As soon as the strength training phase began, Moyer was sent home with one that he'd hook on a door to work his shoulder muscles on days he wasn't in Ghandour's gym.

In working with pitchers, Ghandour often found weak neck muscles. Knowing that the job called for quick neck movements—checking the runner at first, spinning to make a throw—Ghandour devised neck rotation exercises for the pulley. "Most people don't know how to strengthen the neck," he says. "For Jamie to do this at forty-nine, we had to not only get his shoulder and arm built up, we had to get other areas, like the neck, strengthened too, so over the course of a season there'd be no compensation."

Three mornings a week, Moyer would follow Ghandour's protocol faithfully. He'd do the exercises, get proprioceptive neuromuscular facilitation, or PNF, stretching—basically a stretch with manual resistance to help with flexibility, coordination, and timing—and receive some soft tissue massage. Most important, however, was Ghandour's calming presence. Just as Harvey Dorfman's voice in his head made him feel not so alone when on the mound years earlier, so too did Ghandour's as he tried to battle the comeback odds. "Yousef has a way of making you feel like you're his only client," Moyer would say.

Liba Placek could tell Jamie Moyer was a pitcher just by looking at him. His left shoulder was lower than his right and his left foot rolled in—two telltale signs of someone who had spent the last four decades in the unnatural act of throwing a baseball. Moyer had thrown so many pitches that his hip flexors were misaligned and his left foot was, in her words, "angry," which basically meant he had trained it to angle inward.

"This is all reversible," Liba told Moyer after her initial evaluation of his posture. Placek has the soothing Czech accent of her homeland, which is juxtaposed against the hard-core nature of her workouts. She uses an amalgam of corrective exercises, borrowing principles from Pilates and yoga, to enhance body alignment, stressing balance. Workouts in her unassuming studio, with its mirrored walls and floor strewn with yoga mats, tend to break even the toughest of athletes, because she targets the weak spots of otherwise strong men. After each in-studio session, she leads her charges on "The Patch"—a nearby Navy SEALs–like obstacle course with giant running logs she leaps over, under, and around, before sprinting some 200 yards up what has come to be known as Puke Hill. The workout is what led Seau to call her the Beast. "Liba is such a stud," Seau told *Sports Illustrated* in 2005. "I'd rather face a 350-pound lineman than face Liba and one of her workouts."

Placek is a onetime volleyball player who subscribes to something called the Egoscue Method, which emphasizes a series of intense stretch and flexibility movements. Placek took photos of Moyer and showed him how the years of throwing had created an imbalance between his left- and right-side muscles. That corrodes the posture, which sets off a chain reaction of problems—the shoulder might rotate in response, or the hips might sway, or the ankle might turn in—all of which can lead to injury.

Three times a week, Moyer took Liba's regimen, often bringing sons Dillon and Hutton, or daughter Timoney, along. He even conquered Puke Hill without having the dry heaves. Within weeks, Liba had overcome her doubts about Moyer reaching his goal and had become a believer. She'd had clients who found excuses for their bodies; here was a client who had an excuse—recovering from what others might have considered a career-ending injury—but refused to use it. "Let's get to work," Moyer would say upon arrival at LibaFit each morning.

"In no time, I started to see a truly great athlete," Liba recalls.

Dom Johnson first considered the phenomenon of Jamie Moyer in 2008, the year Moyer led the Phillies to a World Series championship. Johnson had known of Moyer forever, of course; but he hadn't really *thought* of Moyer. Not until slugger David Justice talked about Moyer in a way Johnson had never entertained. One day, Justice visited Johnson's Poway, California, backyard to address "Dom's kids"—a group of highly touted high school, Division I, and minor league pitchers who all shared an ambition to one day make the major leagues and the wherewithal to find Johnson, a guy whose sole form of advertising was word of mouth. Justice's message was the baseball equivalent of a "Scared Straight" lecture.

"I can tell just by looking at you all that you're not tough," he said. "Hitters know who's tentative, who's pitching scared, and, I gotta tell ya, most pitchers are 'in for show and away for dough,'" he said. "That's what we hitters say about you. That you won't pitch inside, except for show. So I can train my eyes low and away 'cause none of you guys will throw inside."

After a few more minutes of Justice's ranting, a young pitcher asked, well, who *does* pitch inside? "That Moyer guy," said Justice.

Justice had a history of being flummoxed by Moyer: in 40 career at-bats, Justice had hit just .225 against the lefty, with a meager OPS (on-base plus slugging) of .673, more than 200 points below his career average. "I can't just sit there and look away, 'cause he keeps coming in on me. And it's not just that he comes in once to set up outside. He pounds away at your hands, and it messes you up, 'cause he's got no fear."

Indeed, Moyer had messed with Justice's head for years. In 1998, Justice hit the only home run off Moyer of his career when, after Justice fouled off five straight pitches, an exasperated Moyer walked off the mound toward him. "What do you want?" Moyer asked.

"Huh?" Justice responded.

"Tell me what to throw and I'll throw it," Moyer said.

Could this be serious?

"A fastball," Justice said, motioning with his bat to indicate the preferred spot. Moyer was true to his word. Justice lined the ball out of the park. For Moyer, breaking down baseball's version of the fourth wall that existed between pitcher and hitter was an occasional calculated risk. Michael Lewis's *Moneyball* contains a scene in which Moyer uses the same tactic against Scott Hatteberg to induce a line out. Ever playing mental ball, Moyer reasoned that the sudden intrusion into the at-bat can throw off the hitter as effectively as any off-speed pitch.

Moyer wanted to goad hitters into carrying on an inner dialogue about *his* intentions, instead of thinking about theirs. In a game that requires ultimate concentration, he wanted his voice reverberating in his opponent's head. After the gift of that one homer, Justice never tagged Moyer again, and he'd subsequently dreaded facing him.

Listening to Justice, it was the first time Johnson had ever thought of the soft-throwing Moyer as an intimidator. But then he started watching closely. So when Jamie Moyer appeared one day, recommended by a mutual friend in the Phillies organization, Johnson leapt at the chance to work with him.

Johnson, a beefy, imposing presence, was something of a local sports legend himself. He'd starred on Poway High School's three-time championship basketball teams in the mid-'80s that included future NBA player Jud Buechler. When Dom led Poway to a 1986 upset over Pasadena Muir High School and future NBA star Stacey Augmon, his dad attended the game from Anaheim, where he was a coach with the California Angels. Deron Johnson's presence at the game created a stir, because he was one of Poway's original local legends, having turned down a Notre Dame football scholarship in the 1950s to sign with the Yankees and going on to have a sixteen-year big league career that included a World Series championship in 1973 with the Oakland A's.

Deron's son, forsaking basketball, followed his father's footsteps into the game. Dom signed with the San Francisco Giants and advanced to Double A in the Angels system. When Dom first told his father he wanted to align himself with the enemy—pitchers—Deron told him he'd introduce him to a who's who of pitching greats. "You'll talk to them," Deron said, "and when a common theme emerges, pay attention." That led him to Gus Hoefling and Steve Carlton, not to mention greats like Howie Gershberg (who counted among his protégés Frank Viola, John

Franco, and Chuck Finley), Darren Balsley, Dave Duncan, and Claude Osteen.

But perhaps his greatest teacher was Deron, who schooled him to think like a hitter. Deron showed Dominick how hitters try to pick up the pitcher's grip on the baseball through the "back window"—the farthest point from the batter in the delivery. Ideally, when rearing back to throw, the lefthanded pitcher's left hip should obscure the hitter's view of the ball; if not, if the arm swings too far toward third base, the hitter can spy the grip and have a leg up. "Every time the hitter sees the ball, he has the advantage," Dom explains. "The more you can keep the ball out of his sight, the later he has to react to the pitch."

Johnson has spent years developing his pitching philosophy. It's built around four fundamentals. The first two dovetail perfectly with Liba's fitness emphasis on proper balance: Dom argues that, first, the lower and upper half of the body should always face the same direction—square to the plate—and, second, that after the leg kick, both feet should remain on the ground through the motion. "You're never stronger on one leg than you are on two," he says.

Principle number three is what is commonly known as "arm path," which holds that the arm should follow the same linear direction to the target each time, on a downward plane with the same forty-five-degree release point, or arm slot. Johnson's fourth and final precept he calls "sighting." When starting out, most pitchers don't know where the ball is going, outside of aiming for the catcher's glove. But to really get it to the catcher's glove, often you have to pick a different spot to throw to. For instance, a lefty throwing a slider to a lefty may train his eyes on the catcher's left shin guard.

When Moyer first started throwing to Johnson in the backyard, the pitching coach was amazed by Moyer's sighting skills. "Okay, this one is up and in to a lefty, in the window between your ear and shoulder," Moyer would say, before delivering the ball right there, with stunning, as Johnson would say, "repeatability."

Johnson knew Moyer didn't need his rudimentary philosophies; his role was to dissect the nuances of Moyer's mechanics, to pay attention to the slightest of details, in order to, as he says, "make sure the ball is coming out good every time."

He was struck by Moyer's openness to every critique, no matter how minor. Once, as the catcher, Johnson noted that he could see the ball through Moyer's back window when Moyer threw from the windup, though not from the stretch.

"That's because I'm coiling more from the windup," Moyer said.

"Well, if you're not coiling out of the stretch, why coil out of the windup?" Dom asked.

Moyer paused. "That makes sense." He smiled. "I'm not going to coil anymore."

Days in Dom's backyard in late 2011 and early 2012 felt happily familiar to Moyer. They were like those lazy days at Camden Yards years ago, when he and Mussina and the others would toss a ball back and forth and talk pitching for hours. He'd spend hours at Dom's, talking mechanics and mind-set with wide-eyed kids. He'd long ago dedicated himself to the cause of continual improvement, becoming something like baseball's living embodiment of *kaizen*, the Japanese business philosophy that seeks to repeatedly upgrade all functions. Well into his thirties, famed Japanese slugger Sadaharu Oh once explained his legendary work ethic by observing that one's potential is endless. In the States, Moyer knew, potential was thought to come with an expiration date. Like Oh, Moyer saw self-improvement as a process, not a destination. That's what Dom's backyard represented to Moyer: it was the laboratory for his ongoing experiments.

At times the scene verged on the comic. One of the first times he was about to throw, not three feet from the mound, up popped a gopher through the ground; pitcher and rodent froze, staring each other down, until the pitcher shrugged and assumed the varmint was a baseball fan. From then on, the minor league kids who were always in attendance would begin each session by asking, "Hey Jamie, is your gopher coming today?"

Those same kids made Moyer's twice-weekly bullpen sessions even more special. Each day would turn into impromptu teaching sessions; once, Dom had about forty kids over to hear the veteran. Moyer walked them through the ins and outs of the game, explaining, for example, the complicated "touch signs" he'd developed in Seattle with his catcher, Tom Lampkin. Instead of going through countless signs to indicate the next pitch's location, Moyer would signal that he wanted to throw to the right side of the plate on the next pitch by catching the ball back from Lampkin with his right foot forward.

"Now," he said to the rapt youngsters, "what if, once I'm back on the mound and looking in for the sign, I want to change where the pitch is going? Tell me how I'm doing that now." He peered in to Dom, who was crouching behind home plate, nodded yes to Dom's call, and then entered his windup and threw before turning back to the kids. "How'd I just change the location of that pitch?"

They had no clue. He did it again. Still nothing. Finally a hint: "Watch my pearly whites." And there it was: after nodding yes to Dom's call and while making the first move of his windup, Moyer briefly smiled, showing the whites of his teeth. That tells his catcher to change the location to its opposite side:

if the call had been for a fastball away, this subtlest of grins would mean Moyer wants to come inside with it instead. It's a way to speed up tempo on the mound and hide location from runners on base. It also requires a very observant batterymate.

Of course, Moyer couldn't help but impart to the youngsters some Harveyisms as well. He told them how he'll go for a walk behind the mound and bend over to tie his shoe. "That's when I lose it on myself," he said. "'C'mon Moyer, get it together—execute!' Then I stand and take a series of deep breaths"—Moyer, courtesy of Dorfman, believed that deep breathing in tense situations slowed down the body's fight-or-flight responses and increased the chances that one can find that ever-elusive zone state—"and I put the last pitch behind me and return my focus to this pitch. Because that's all you have, your next pitch."

Johnson chuckled, knowing that Moyer had just unleashed on the minors and Division I a group of kids who would all be tying their shoes behind the mound while cursing themselves sotto voce.

By the end of 2011, Moyer had gone through Ghandour's strength training, he'd become a veteran of getting up and down Liba's Puke Hill, and, with Dom's help, he'd tweaked his mechanics to the point that he could put his mind on autopilot and trust them. In the months after his Tommy John surgery, he'd put on fifteen pounds, so he spent a weekend eating nothing but a concoction of maple syrup and lemon juice, cleaning out his body's toxins, before switching over to a steady diet of salads and grains, getting down to his 185-pound playing weight in no time. It was time. Now, with spring training roughly three months away, Moyer's agent, Jim Bronner, extended invitations to major league teams to make the trek to Johnson's backyard to see Moyer throw.

* * *

"My God, does this guy miss?"

That's what Dom Johnson hears one scout whisper to another while Moyer, time and again, hits Johnson's targets. It's a December 2011 weekday and some ten major league scouts—mostly pro scouts, with a couple who are more used to evaluating minor leaguers also in attendance—take notes while Moyer runs through his bullpen session for them, sixty throws to a variety of spots.

Ghandour is standing nearby. He's watching the mechanics closely, making sure that the stress of the moment and of multiple throws doesn't tire Moyer and alter the delivery. Muscle compensation is the enemy—particularly over the course of a long big league season.

After Moyer's last pitch, he looks at his visitors. "Anything you guys want to see?"

One scout—no doubt one of the minor league guys—speaks up: "Can you throw a two-seamer inside to a righthander?"

Dom wants to blurt out, *What do you think he's been doing?*

But Moyer beats him to it: "I've only been doing that for twenty-six years."

He winds up and—*thwack*—the ball sizzles right over the inside corner, calf high. "Put that in your pipe and smoke it," Moyer says, smiling.

The scouts are effusive, as are the reports that major league general managers share with Bronner. "He's Jamie Moyer," one says incredulously. Another observes, echoing Rollie DeArmas from so many months ago, that watching him felt like "2008 all over again." Another writes that Moyer can still "hit a gnat's ass."

Yet there is no barrage of offers. Moyer had long been aware of baseball's risk-averse culture, and to how GMs throughout the game found comfort in subscribing to the conventional wisdom.

He'd even seen it in managers, in their groupthink rush to embrace pitch-count mania or the allegiance to the three-out save.
(When Moyer was coming up, closers sometimes pitched two
or three innings to preserve a win.) It made him miss managers
like Don Zimmer, who was a gambler by habit and in nature,
and would make moves on hunches.

Getting a team to take a chance on a forty-nine-year-old
starter is going to require someone willing to roll the dice.
Plenty of teams are willing to have him come to spring training,
but these are invitations born of polite formality. He doesn't
mind paying his own way, but he wants a real opportunity. Pitts-
burgh is interested, but Moyer had always hated the Pirates'
mound: it was harder than most, less forgiving, and the dirt was
dry and choppy. The list of serious suitors quickly comes down
to the Baltimore Orioles or Colorado Rockies; the Orioles say
they'll be making a big league offer, but a minor league one
comes instead. Moyer thinks it's no coincidence that their interest seems to cool after the Orioles hire Dan Duquette as general
manager. Duquette, who had been out of baseball for a decade,
had been Moyer's general manager in Boston in the mid-'90s
and had traded him to Seattle when Moyer had a 7–1 record.

Meantime, Dan O'Dowd of the Colorado Rockies tells Bronner that Moyer would have the opportunity to compete for his
team's fifth starting spot. The Rockies don't figure to be that
good a team, and though Moyer had pitched well there in the
2007 National League Division Series, he doesn't know how
he'll do in the altitude over the course of a season. But someone
is willing to give him a chance, which was all he ever wanted.
He signs a contract for $1.1 million, provided he makes the
team coming out of spring training.

* * *

It's two weeks before he packs up the Yukon SUV for spring training in Scottsdale, Arizona, and Jamie Moyer has just made his farewell visit to Dom's backyard, where he watches some high schoolers throw for some scouts, at one point stopping the proceedings to show an eighteen-year-old that the way he's taking the ball out of his glove is tipping his pitches to the batter.

This process, which began a little less than a year ago with some backyard soft-tossing with his sons Dillon and Hutton, has now come to this: like a rookie, he'll be going to spring training to make a team. Unlike a rookie, though, his excitement is tinged with bittersweetness. For the last year, for the first time in his adult life, he has been able to be present in the daily life of his family. He's gone to Dillon's games at the University of California at Irvine, and he's been in the stands for Hutton's baseball, Duffy's soccer, Grady's tennis, Mac's golf, and Timoney's basketball games. Every day, he has cuddled up with Yeni and Kati—the two "littles" who were adopted from Guatemala—and worked with them on their Kumon, an at-home math and reading program.

Karen has made sure the kids share her enthusiasm for this latest project of their dad's, referring to it often in grandiose, historic terms. She sees her husband's quest as a lesson *for* them, an eloquent example for them to follow. But Moyer knows it means their father won't be around, that he'll be away playing a child's game.

"Believe me, there have been times I've asked myself, 'Am I putting myself before my family?'" he says now, cruising down State Route 56, otherwise known, appropriately enough, as the Ted Williams Freeway, named for San Diego's favorite baseball son. "Or have I my whole career? Maybe I have. Maybe it's wrong."

There's a pause. "But, you know, this is what I know, this is what I do, and this is what I'm good at," he says. Moyer looks into his rearview mirror and then, double-taking, looks again. "Did you see that?" he asks, perking up. "Did you see that granny back there?"

He slows down. Coming up on our right is a beat-up pickup, windows down, with a woman who has to be in her late seventies, blaring the song "Holiday" by Madonna. Her left arm is flapping out the window to the beat as she sings along full throttle, almost drowning out her truck's belches as well as Madonna's lyrics:

If we took a holiday / Took some time to celebrate

Moyer waits until she's alongside him in the right-hand lane, and then his passenger window is down and he's laughing and honking and screaming:

"Yeah!!! Sing it, sister!"

She gives a thumbs-up and then they're singing together, the SUV and pickup side by side at low speed on the Ted Williams Freeway, Moyer at the top of his lungs: *"Holiday!"*

After the song, the elderly woman shouts, "I always do this! People should be more joyous! You only live once!" before she peels off onto an exit ramp and is gone.

"What a great spirit," he says. His mood has brightened considerably; the doubts about putting himself ahead of his family have been tabled. It's a beautiful February day in Southern California. He's heading back to spring training, he's just spent ninety minutes talking about the nuances of pitching with Dom and his kids, and he's just received an impromptu object lesson in how to embrace aging with a never-dying sense of passion — the same example his wife is convinced he is providing for his kids. As Jamie Moyer often says, "It's all good."

JUNE 1997

CHAPTER EIGHT

> Good learners risk doing things badly in or-
> der to find out how to do things well.
>   —Harvey Dorfman

On June 15, 1997, Jamie Moyer stood on the mound of the
Seattle Kingdome and told himself to summon a voice. Only
this time it wasn't the raspy sound of Harvey Dorfman he was
yearning to hear. It was the next best thing: the gruff growl of
skipper Lou Piniella.

It was Moyer's first full season with the Mariners, having been
traded by the Red Sox to Seattle the previous July. He'd been
7–1 in Boston, and finished the 1996 season 6–2 for Seattle.
That made him 13–3, the best winning percentage in the majors, with a 3.98 ERA.

This season, however, had been another story; he was 5–2
with a 4.53 ERA. But something wasn't right. In the month of
May, he'd given up seven home runs, including two in consecutive losses to the Royals and Rangers. That's what led him into
his manager's office just days before. Piniella wasn't all that popular among his pitchers—he'd been a hitter himself and didn't

have a lot of patience for them. His reputation was well known: his intolerance for what he thought of as mental mistakes on the mound—particularly walks—chipped away at pitchers' confidence. But Moyer had felt a developing bond with his manager, whose palpable will to win matched Moyer's own.

"I'm not feeling comfortable, Skip," Moyer said. "Are you seeing anything?"

Piniella, head buried in scouting reports on his desk, looked up. "You're not throwing your change enough," he said. And then he looked back down.

There was a pause. Moyer was tempted to argue. Not throwing the change enough? *The change was what got me to the big leagues in the first place.*

"Really?" he said.

"You're not throwing enough of them," Piniella said. "And the ones you are throwing, you're not *committed* to. Don't just show it. The changeup is who you are, for Chrissakes."

Moyer was stunned. The conversation lasted all of a couple of minutes; back at his locker, Moyer realized the exchange had prompted a familiar feeling. Moyer's two great mentors—Jim Moyer and Harvey Dorfman—were both, like Piniella, straight shooters. They wouldn't seek to comfort him; they'd challenge him. No matter how critical they were, he always knew they just wanted him to push himself and get better.

Moyer had grown accustomed to his big league managers conveying all types of no-confidence votes in him. When he was struggling, they'd avoid eye contact in the clubhouse or get someone up in the bullpen at the earliest hint of trouble during a game. Yet ever since he arrived in Seattle, he'd sensed that Piniella was different: he could be critical and demanding and in-your-face, but it all came with a sense of belief, as though he were saying, *I don't think you're a piece of crap, so why do you?*

On the question of the changeup, moreover, Piniella took a page from Harvey and made their brief interaction about something bigger than that one pitch: he suggested it was really about Moyer's self-*identity*. It's like he was saying what Harvey always said: *You're different. Don't be afraid to be who you are.*

Still, Piniella was a hitter—what did he know about pitch selection? Moyer left Piniella's office with some lingering doubts about his manager's prescription. But then he caught himself: *Are you really going to ask him a question and then dismiss the answer?* That led Moyer to check the pitching charts. So far this season, he'd thrown the changeup roughly 15 percent of the time. And maybe only half of those were being thrown for strikes or near-strikes. *What do you know?* he thought. Maybe Skipper Lou was on to something.

Now here he was on the mound, L.A. slugger Mike Piazza approaching the plate, conjuring Lou's voice: be *committed* to the change. He knew what that word meant: you've got to be committed to the location, committed to the pitch. Hitters sense doubt. Harvey used to quote pitcher Frank Viola. "When you doubt your pitch selection, you don't have anything," Viola said. "You end up throwing the 'other' pitch, and you don't give your all because you're not really committed to it."

It was time to recommit to the changeup. Pitching is about deception, and the changeup is the ultimate trick pitch. It requires that you sell it with the same arm speed and arm path with which you present the fastball. If you just throw it for show—simply to let the hitter know you have it—you're actually eliminating it as a weapon.

In their pregame meeting, Moyer told catcher Dan Wilson he was going to be more aggressive with the change. With one down in the first, Todd Zeile grounded out weakly on an away change, after fouling off the exact same pitch. Now, with two outs, here was Piazza, hitting .367, coming off a 4-for-4 day that included his 12th home run. Moyer started him with three high and tight fastballs—two at 84 miles per hour, one actually hitting 86. Piazza fouled the first two off and looked at the third for a ball.

Mouse meet cat. Moyer had busted Piazza inside three straight times. Now he followed with a 76-mile-per-hour changeup away, on the outside corner. Piazza lunged forward and barely nubbed it foul. *An uncomfortable swing.* What next? Another change, also at 76, only this time it was over the middle of the plate—but dipping below the zone. With two strikes, Piazza was looking to protect the outside part of the plate, so this pitch—even though it was white on white—had the effect of jamming him. Again, Piazza barely made contact. *Another uncomfortable swing.*

He'll be looking inside and hard, Moyer thought to himself. In other words: Piazza would assume the two straight changeups were simply meant to set up something similar to the pitches that started the at-bat. But Moyer was actually doing the precise opposite. He considered the first three pitches as the setup to this series of arrhythmic changes in speed. He dropped a 75-mile-per-hour changeup an inch or two off the outside corner, too close for Piazza to take; the hitter lurched forward off his front foot and whiffed wildly to end the inning. The last two batters: two outs on five changeups.

In the second inning, second baseman Wilton Guerrero came up. Guerrero had made some dubious news just two weeks before: in a game against the Cardinals, he had grounded out, shattering his bat. Rather than run out the play, he'd frantically scrambled to pick up the scattered pieces, raising the umpires' suspicions. Indeed, Guerrero had been corking his bat, ultimately leading to a suspension and fine.

Now Moyer started the young utility infielder with a 75-mile-per-hour changeup, low and away. Off his front foot, Guerrero flailed at the ball, swinging well in front of it. And then came the inexperienced hitter's big mistake. He broke into a wide grin and shook his head.

That's what I like to see, Moyer thought to himself. In the never-ending poker game between hitter and pitcher, every re-action from a batter offers some piece of information to his opponent. When a hitter complains to the ump about a call, for example, he's inadvertently providing the pitcher with data about his state of mind, pinpointing which location makes him most uncomfortable. Now Guerrero's awkward, off-balance swing and his sheepish reaction said to Moyer, *I can't hit that pitch*.

Moyer expected Guerrero to make an adjustment, to look to protect against something soft and low again. Moyer toyed with going even farther out—trying to entice a chase—but decided instead to come back with another changeup, this one at 74 miles per hour, over the plate but well below the hitting zone. It turned out that Guerrero was guessing changeup, but the de-viation in location still kept the fat part of the bat off the ball. Guerrero topped it routinely to third base for an out.

And so it went. Moyer faced Piazza twice more, and got him both times on changeups. When rightfielder Raul Mondesi came up in the fourth, Moyer toyed with the dead-fastball power hitter. The first pitch: a changeup outside for a ball. Then Mondesi, expecting fastball, swung well in front of a 75-mile-per-hour changeup. Moyer then went to his slowest pitch—a 70-mile-per-hour curveball on the outside corner: 1–2. Now a high and tight fastball that was fouled off, followed by a high and tight cutter for a ball: 2–2. A 74-mile-per-hour changeup was low for a full count.

Moyer peered in and shook off Wilson's sign for a fastball.

Hell if he's getting a fastball for a strike. This was what Moyer would become known for over the ensuing ten years in Seattle: his utter unwillingness to give in. It's what Piniella would mean when, a couple of years later, he'd say that the best way to hit against Moyer was to "think backwards." Roughly three-quarters of the time throughout the major leagues, pitchers will throw fastballs on 3–0, 3–1, and 3–2 counts.

Not Moyer. Against Mondesi, he pulled the string on a changeup, causing Mondesi to get out in front of it and pull it foul. Certainly a fastball would be next, right? Nope. The same pitch that got Guerrero, a 75-mile-per-hour changeup below the strike zone, induced a weak pop-up to third.

Piniella took Moyer out after six innings. He gave up two runs for his sixth win. How aggressive was he? Of his 103 pitches, 36 were changeups. But more important than the raw number was the type of pitches he made. Of the 18 outs he recorded, an astonishing 11 came on the changeup.

After the game, Piniella approached him in the clubhouse. There was no gloating, no reference to their conversation just days before. Just, "Way to go," with the hint of a smile. At his locker Moyer smiled. *That son of a gun knows this game,* he thought.

On July 30, 1996, when Moyer was traded by the Boston Red Sox to Seattle for light-hitting outfielder Darren Bragg, he was not optimistic. He was going to play for a manager who was not known to be pitcher-friendly, and nor was the Seattle Kingdome known as a pitcher's ballpark. It was hard to see how this was going to be a good fit.

In three years in Baltimore, Jamie had established himself as a legit major league pitcher, going a combined 25–22 with a

4.41 ERA. But he could never nail down a consistent spot in the starting rotation. In 1995 he was in his option year as an Oriole, earning $1.1 million. He started the season in the bullpen, clawing his way back to starter by midseason, and ended up starting 18 games and relieving in nine others.

He signed with the Red Sox as a free agent that off-season, a one-year deal for $825,000 with a $225,000 signing bonus. Yet it was more of the same. Moyer started five games in April— going 2–1 with a 6.10 ERA—before manager Kevin Kennedy relegated him to the bullpen. In July, he got a chance to prove himself again, going 3–0 in four consecutive starts. After pitching seven innings to beat the Royals, Moyer's record stood at 7–1, with a 4.50 ERA. Good numbers, but Moyer was still the sixth man in a five-man rotation.

Hadn't he proven his worth as a starter? The pattern kept repeating: he'd get the odd start, but never felt secure. He was always looking over his shoulder to see if someone was up in the pen, always anticipating the manager's hook. All he wanted was a job description. Instead, he got media reports that he was about to be traded to Texas.

Karen pointed out that maybe a trade wouldn't be the worst thing. They knew Texas and liked the Rangers as an organization. Moreover, Moyer didn't like the ethos of the Red Sox clubhouse. The team was led by some big, famously undisciplined personalities, including Jose Canseco and Roger Clemens. They were great talents, but chaos seemed to reign around them. Cell phones and pagers were just finding their way into major league clubhouses, and phones were ringing—and being answered!—during team meetings.

Weeks earlier, Moyer had decided to make his case. He made an appointment to meet with general manager Dan Duquette. *You brought me here to contribute*, he planned on saying, *and I've done my share, winning seven of eight deci-sions. I've earned a regular starting job.* Only he never got the chance. Duquette was a no-show. Then, after Moyer's win over the Royals, he got word: he'd been traded. But not to Texas. To Seattle.

Karen was shocked. *Seattle?* That was clear across the coun-try. Moyer quickly caught a flight to meet up with his new team in Milwaukee. Though he was happy to escape the lax club-house atmosphere of the Red Sox, yet another move made him feel like a perennial journeyman, a player who might never truly find a home.

And then he met Lou. When Moyer entered the Mariners clubhouse in Milwaukee, Piniella came waddling over, hand outstretched. "We brought you here to pitch," the manager said. "We need pitching. We think you can help us. We didn't bring you here to fail."

Piniella's clipped words washed over him, bathing him in comfort, not unlike when he'd hear Harvey. But it wasn't just the voice. Like Harvey, Piniella instantly made Moyer feel like someone was in his corner. For the first time, he felt like his manager was truly an ally, not an antagonist.

"You're in the rotation and starting the day after tomorrow," Piniella said, walking away. On Thursday, August 1, 1996, Moyer went seven innings against the Brewers, giving up one earned run on four hits, raising his record to 8–1. Maybe he'd found a home after all.

Lou Piniella was one of baseball's old souls, a fiery leader who had little compunction when it came to getting in umpires' or players' faces. Regarding the former, he'd lumber out onto the field, face burning red, veins bulging from his neck, and…*com-municate.* He may have been hot-tempered, but he was never misunderstood.

For all his showmanship, though, his antics always had a purpose. When you saw him charge an umpire from the dugout, reversing his cap en route so he could literally get nose to nose with his combatant, there was a method behind the histrionics. Even when, in 2002, he yanked a base from the ground and tossed it into rightfield—only to chase it down and, apparently unhappy with his first effort, toss it *farther*—there was a calculation, an intention to fire up his guys. Once, he purposely threw his cap down on his way to the umpire, planning to pick it up after his tantrum and throw it to the crowd; when he was tossed from the game, however, the bat boy dutifully picked up his cap and delivered it to him as he started back to the dugout. "Gimme my damn prop!" he barked to the startled kid.

"Lou was very smart and a lot of what you saw with him on the field was deliberate," says Hall of Famer Pat Gillick, general manager in Seattle from 2000 through 2003. "He'd think his team needed to be awakened and he'd do something to stir it awake."

No wonder he and Moyer hit it off. Even in his playing days, Piniella was constantly looking for a mental edge. "I was no home run hitter, so if I came up with two outs in the early innings, I'd maybe get a slider and I'd roll over on it, bounce out, and let the pitcher and catcher think they could get me out that way," Piniella, a .291 lifetime hitter, told the *Seattle Times* in 1995. "Then later in the game, maybe the score is close, maybe we need a runner, maybe with runners on, I'd be thinking they'd go slider when they had to make an out pitch. If I got a fastball up and in, I could tell for sure a slider was coming next, down and away."

As a manager over twenty-three seasons, Piniella and his will to win not only infected his teams, it imbued his charges with his personality—combative, cunning, intense. "Playing for Lou was like having another teammate, he wanted to win so badly," Moyer recalls.

But Piniella's famous fire had a downside too, particularly for pitchers. He'd throw tirades when his pitchers walked batters. In the dugout, he'd berate pitching coaches in front of the team. "WHY ARE WE NIBBLING?" he'd roar. Moyer saw how some pitchers would allow Piniella to impede their focus, so put off were they by his second-guessing. Moyer, however, welcomed Piniella's feedback, even if it was harsh. You always knew where you stood with Lou. Moyer was similarly candid with Piniella. In fact, when Lou visited the mound, Moyer would do something few pitchers ever do: tell the truth.

"How you feeling?" Piniella asked one time.

"Well, Skip, I've got half a tank," Moyer replied.

Piniella eyeballed him. "What the hell does that mean?"

Moyer didn't want to come out, but he felt obligated to level with his manager. "It means I'm half full and half empty," he said. Piniella smirked and put his hand out for the ball.

Moyer was receptive to Piniella's coaching because, in his experiences with his father and Harvey, he had learned to tell the difference between criticism and coaching. He wanted to be challenged. And ever since his first day in a Seattle uniform, when Piniella signaled that he believed in him, Moyer didn't want to let his manager down.

Now, in his first full season with Seattle, he had taken Piniella's advice and flummoxed the Dodgers with 36 change-ups, 11 for outs. It would be the turning point of his career.

Moyer would go 17–5 in 1997, with an ERA of 3.86. His combined winning percentage of .789 in 1996 and 1997 was among the league leaders. Until he reinvented himself yet again with a revamped cutter in Philadelphia, he'd never again throw the changeup less than 28 percent of the time. Thanks to Skipper Lou, he'd made himself into an elite pitcher.

Unlike his relationship with, say, the curveball, Moyer's courtship of the changeup was long and complicated, characterized by fits and starts and disappointments, before culminating in wedded bliss after Piniella's 1997 intervention.

In the early '80s, Moyer was a dominant collegiate pitcher with essentially two pitches: a roughly 84-mile-per-hour fastball and the looping curve he could throw over the plate for strikes. At St. Joseph's University, that was enough; he rewrote the school's record book, setting a single-season mark for strikeouts (90), and winning 16 games (fourth all-time) with a 1.99 ERA. His ERA of 1.82 in 1984 was the twelfth best nationally.

But he knew his limited repertoire of pitches wouldn't be enough to get him drafted. Enter Kevin Quirk. Quirk had been a dominant St. Joe's righthander who had graduated from the school in 1981, Moyer's freshman year. Quirk was drafted by the Yankees, but never made it out of the minors. He returned to campus after two minor league seasons to help out the baseball team, his unique changeup in tow.

Befitting the name, Quirk was a free spirit, a hard partier who as a student had doubled as the St. Joe's Hawk, the mascot at basketball games who ceaselessly flaps his arms. (ESPN once applied a "flap-o-meter" to the Hawk during a telecast and concluded that the bird flapped its wings an average of 3,500 times per game.)

Quirk showed Moyer his changeup. Even to this day, there's no one way to throw a change. Some pitchers palm the ball, others throw a "circle change," their fingers encircling the ball. Quirk's grip was particularly unusual. With the open horseshoe facing first base, his middle, ring, and pinkie fingers would grip the top of the ball. The index finger and thumb would rest off the ball, underneath it. It was almost as if he were making an "OK" sign with his fingers and wrapping it around the ball. The removal of the dominant index finger creates a looser grip and more backspin, slowing the ball down in flight.

Moyer must have thrown thousands of changeups before ever working up the courage to attempt it in a game. When he first tried it, the ball would either sail clear over the catcher's head or bounce well in front of the plate. But gradually he came to see the pitch for what it was: the ultimate deception. To this day, he calls it the most important pitch in baseball, other than the fastball. The grip allows you to throw the changeup with the same arm speed, and from the same release point, as the fastball, but it's far slower. Once he could master control of it, he knew he'd have something to counteract the lack of velocity on his fastball, something to regularly keep hitters off balance with.

By the time he was in the minors in the Cubs system, the changeup had become Jamie's best pitch. It was utterly emasculating to hitters; their eyes would widen as it approached the plate, so slow, so hittable, and yet they'd swing at it well in front of their bodies. And as more and more hitters trudged back to the dugout, unable to make contact with such a seemingly powder-puff pitch, Moyer began to understand for the first time what it was like to use the hitter's ego to his advantage.

But then something happened once he made it to the major leagues. He started to lose confidence in the pitch that had gotten him to that level. He started nibbling and being cautious with it, which led him to get behind in counts, which led him to throw fastballs when they were most expected. All of which eventually led him to Harvey Dorfman.

But it wasn't until, of all people, a consummate hitter—Piniella—gave him permission to have confidence in the changeup, to throw it with aggression, that he fully turned things around. Seattle GM Pat Gillick saw the transformation in real time.

"Nowadays, you watch a game, and all the announcers talk about is this guy throws 94, this guy touches 96," Gillick says. "You never hear the word 'deception.' But that's what pitching is. As video got more and more popular, hitters started to pretty much know what pitchers will throw on certain counts. But Jamie and guys like Jimmy Key, Greg Maddux, and Tom Glavine always had a knack for throwing the unexpected pitch in an unexpected location when the hitter least expected it."

In baseball, there's a difference between throwers and pitchers, a distinction that is often predicated on mastery of the changeup. In the late '90s, Moyer became one of the best changeup pitchers in the game, right up there with his friend Trevor Hoffman. There are still great changeup pitchers today—Johan Santana and Cole Hamels come to mind—but not as many. And the ones who do remain tend to be guys who also have the option of rearing back and blowing the ball by hitters, like Justin Verlander.

Moyer and contemporaries like Key, Maddux, and Glavine had to rely on their guile and craft. And Moyer ended up outlasting them all. "You could almost say Jamie was the last pitcher," Gillick says, laughing. "I know this: if he were coming out of college today throwing 83 or 84, he wouldn't get much of a look. Best case, he'd be a guy who you keep in the minors a long time, see if he can develop."

As Moyer developed, so did the Mariners. For the next six years, he found himself on an immensely talented team, one that shared his work ethic and hunger to get better. There was no longer any reason to be shy about his Dorfman-prescribed pregame mental rituals; turned out that every Mariner had some form of idiosyncratic routine.

Randy Johnson, who went 20–4 in Moyer's first full year in Seattle, was a perfectly pleasantly fellow four days a week. But on the day of a start he wore a scowl and no one spoke to him. Designated hitter Edgar Martinez would spend hours every day in the batting cage—but not hitting baseballs. Instead, he'd fill the hitting machine with tennis balls, on which he would have written numbers with a black felt-tip pen. He'd hit each ball while simultaneously yelling out the number on it—a daily exercise in concentration and focus.

Then there was Ken Griffey Jr., probably the most talented player Moyer had ever seen. Moyer marveled at Junior's raw ability. In 1997, Griffey was the American League MVP, with 56 home runs, 147 runs batted in, a .304 average, and a league-high .646 slugging percentage. Yet Moyer never once saw him so much as stretch before a game. His sole form of preparation was to take batting practice early, sending balls rocketing into the seats to the delight of the legions of fans who would arrive in time to see Junior's pregame show.

As talented as Griffey was, he was also one of the guys. The Mariners in the late '90s and early 2000s often socialized off the field, and, unlike many superstars, Griffey was part of the mix. Not so a young Alex Rodriguez, whose talents rivaled Junior's. He led the AL in hitting with a .358 average in 1996, hit 23 home runs in 1997, and then hit over 40 per season for his remaining three years in Seattle. His teammates always sensed that he was destined for a bigger-market club, somewhere like New York or Los Angeles. "There's nothing wrong with that," Moyer says, thinking back. "Someone's gotta play in those places."

Moyer came to learn that, as important as superstars like Griffey and Rodriguez were to the team's success, just as important were teammates like Jay Buhner and John Marzano, guys who were hardly destined for Cooperstown but whose leadership qualities and fun-loving personalities contributed mightily to the "we're all in this together" mind-set that characterized the Mariners for Moyer's first six years in Seattle.

Rightfielder Buhner was a born leader, someone who knew when to joke around with a teammate and when to get in his face. He also had an innate way of reaching out to the fans. One promotion was Buhner Buzz Night, which found the follically challenged outfielder in front of the stadium before a game, shaving fans' heads and giving away free tickets to his victims. By then, the Mariners and their fans had fallen into a full-blown love affair, and Buhner was one of its catalysts.

Moyer took note. The more he was accepted, the more he and Karen grew to love Seattle, and the more secure he grew to be in his role on the team. The Mariners debuted a series of funny, self-deprecating TV commercials featuring Moyer. One, called "The Change-Up," showed a pitch heading for home plate in slow motion, while the catcher and batter have time to chat about a new seafood restaurant downtown — before the pitch is called a strike and Moyer deadpans, "I put a little something extra on that one."

Just as important to team chemistry was backup catcher Marzano, who hailed from South Philly and who would later die in a tragic 2008 fall down the steps at his home. Marzano called everybody "Cuz" and was always running his mouth — loosening up Griffey, which helped make the superstar one of the guys.

"Nice game today," Griffey might say to Marzano — who *hadn't* played. Marzano would come back with a crack about

Griffey's silk shirt and leather pants, a decidedly un-Seattle style of dress.

Buhner was the first judge of the Mariners' Kangaroo Court, a player-created system with the power to levy fines, designed to spur morale and establish subtle codes of conduct. Buhner would carry around a shoebox and players could bring a claim by writing their grievance against a teammate on a piece of paper, naming their witness, and placing it in the shoebox. Claims couldn't be brought for on-field missteps; rather, the court adjudicated baseball's mores, the unwritten rules that govern the game, like how long a teammate could fraternize with an opposing player before a game. A Mariner would time how long others spent shooting the breeze at the opposition's dugout. If a teammate yapped away for more than two minutes, there'd be a case filed against him in the shoebox kept in the Seattle dugout. When the case was tried—when Edgar Martinez succeeded Buhner, he actually wore a robe and carried a gavel when court was in session—fines would be assessed. At the end of the year, the total of fines collected would be given to charity, or, more often, used for a team party.

It was all coming together. Moyer was on the type of team he had always fantasized about, a team with a shared sense of purpose. And with his newfound confidence in the changeup, he was an integral member of it. Moyer followed his breakout 1997 year with two solid seasons, going 15–9 with a 3.53 ERA in 1998, followed by a 14–8 record and a 3.87 ERA in 1999.

He sustained some injuries in 2000, starting the year with a shoulder injury and ending it by suffering a hairline fracture of the left kneecap in a simulated game before the American League Championship Series that kept him from facing the Yankees, the eventual World Series champion. His record was 13–10 with a high 5.49 ERA, but it was all good. He'd use his first taste of inconsistency in three seasons to fuel his off-season workouts, a furious regimen designed to prepare for 2001, where magic awaited. But first there would be a different kind of magic.

Michele and Jerry Metcalf figured the meeting would follow a familiar script. It was 1998 and their fifteen-year-old daughter, Erin, was a rabid Mariners fan. She was also battling liver cancer. Through the Make-A-Wish Foundation, the nonprofit organization that grants wishes to patients facing life-threatening illness, Erin's wish was about to come true: dinner with a couple of Mariners during spring training.

Many times, Michele and Jerry knew, such meetings are very brief. And that was fine: Erin would meet her idols, they'd talk baseball, the ballplayers would pass on some compassionate words of wisdom about the battle in front of her, and she'd be left with an inspiring memory.

But a strange thing happened that night in Scottsdale, Arizona, at the upscale restaurant Michael's at the Citadel. In walked Jeff Fassero and his wife, Cathy, along with Jamie and Karen Moyer and their six-month-old infant, Duffy. And the Moyers then proceeded to go off script.

At the time, Erin was not feeling well. She'd been undergoing grueling chemotherapy and had developed neuropathy—nerve pain in her toes—as a result. She'd been having a tough time digesting bland pieces of chicken, let alone the five-course meal chef Michael DeMaria had prepared for the group.

Much of the talk revolved around baseball. The Metcalfs had lived in Philly, so they and Jamie bonded over tales of Steve Carlton and Mike Schmidt. Karen asked Erin about her medical odyssey, and what followed was a plainspoken litany of invasive treatments, surgeries, and weekly chemo sessions. Erin was sluggish, but Karen noticed that she was nonetheless eyeing Duffy. "Would you like to hold her?" Karen offered.

Erin was an athlete on the fast-pitch softball field, with a hard-hitting, imposing plate presence. But now, with a baby cooing in her arms, she was just a teenage girl, falling in love. It wasn't just that here she was cradling a new life when hers was in such jeopardy that touched the Metcalfs so; it was also that the Moyers seemed to immediately welcome Erin into their family. Duffy stayed with Erin throughout the dinner, even when Chef DeMaria sent over a pizza from his nearby pizzeria for Erin, who was able to get down a couple of slices.

At the end of dinner, Karen asked for the Metcalfs' contact information. "We'd like to stay in touch with you," she told Michele. The Metcalfs hadn't thought the night would involve anything beyond a pleasant dinner. On the way back to their hotel, Michele asked Jerry, "Do you think we'll ever hear from them again?"

The next morning, there was a package waiting for Erin at the front desk. Karen had dropped off a box of Mariners gear. More packages, home visits, and phone calls followed. Early that season, the Mariners played the Yankees and Erin watched as Jamie plunked Paul O'Neill with a pitch. The next day, Jamie stopped by for a visit—with that very game ball for her. "I'm so glad you hit Paul O'Neill," she said. "He's such a crybaby."

Every time Erin would get down, it seemed like the phone would ring and Karen Moyer would be offering tickets to a baseball game or just stopping by for a visit. "It was like Karen would sense when Erin was low," Michele remembers.

The Moyers were touched by Erin's spirit. "Mom, it's not fair that these one-year-old and two-year-old kids have cancer," she'd say of the infants in her ward.

"Well, honey," Michele replied, "I don't think it's fair that you have cancer."

"But I've lived fifteen years," Erin said. "These babies haven't had a chance to live a life yet."

On June 3, 2000, Karen and Erin planned to take part in a three-hour walk in support of organ donation. Erin was failing, but she insisted on going in her wheelchair, attached to an IV filling her with pain meds. She and Karen talked the whole time. Erin told Karen something she hadn't told her family: that she was worried how her older sisters, Maria and Megan—who had taken a semester off from college to help care for Erin— would cope with her death.

"Can you imagine?" Karen said to Jamie, tearing up later when recounting the conversation. "Her biggest fear is how her dying will affect her sisters?"

Two weeks later, after telling her mother, "I'm ready to go," Erin Metcalf passed away.

Karen Moyer doesn't let an emotion fade; she acts. She became determined to address Erin's concern about her sisters and decided to create a grief camp for kids. Now the mother who asked her children each morning, "What is your purpose to-day?" and the pitcher who considered every pitch to have one as well, had found a bigger purpose: after Erin's passing in 2000, and with the blessing of Michele and Jerry Metcalf, Camp Erin was born.

Today, Camp Erin is the largest network of child bereave-ment camps in the country. The Moyer Foundation has raised in excess of $22 million to serve kids in distress.

"We put kids with other kids who have gone through what they've gone through, and with counselors who tell them that what they're feeling is what they should be feeling," Karen explains. "We've provided a safe place for kids to talk about their loss and achieve closure, while honoring their loved one and having fun with other kids all at the same time."

In the process of establishing Camp Erin, the Moyer Foundation became a nationwide model for athlete philanthropy. Much of its success is due to the Moyers' hands-on style. In 2000, when they started with just a couple of part-time employees (there are now two offices, one in Seattle and one in Philadelphia), Jamie would pick up the office's trash every other day in his pickup and take it to a nearby Dumpster.

At the first camp, just outside Seattle, Jamie stopped by after a day game. He walked into the cafeteria, where stood a chalkboard filled with photos of the campers' loved ones who had died. A little boy approached and grabbed his hand, pointing with his other hand to a photo on the board. "My uncle took me to my first baseball game," the little boy said.

"That's really cool that you remember him this way," Moyer said, kneeling down. "He'd really like that."

Later, his voice would quiver when he related the story. "That was his connection to me," Moyer would recall. "It was bold of him to do that, and you kind of felt like he was healing."

Moyer paused, still thinking of that long-ago little boy, his first real taste of the difference Camp Erin could make. "Sometimes in life, you have these moments, and they change you forever," he said. "Baseball has given me many things I'll always be thankful for. That moment was one of them."

Just as Moyer's relationship with Gregory in Baltimore coincided with his becoming a bona fide big league pitcher, so too did the interaction with Erin track with his emergence as an elite starter in the game. Coincidence? Harvey Dorfman would say not. Moyer, he knew, was someone who sought inspiration from the everyday. Having a front-row seat to bravery—

particularly as performed by children—couldn't help but be motivating and perspective-broadening.

In 2000, the year Erin died, Moyer had his first disappointing season in years. It's not as if he consciously thought of Erin, or of the kids who courageously told their stories of loss at camp, or of Gregory's continued good health, as he trained that off-season. But all of those object lessons were with him, on some level. Harvey had long ago predicted it: he'd turn his career around when he became aware that there was life *beyond* it.

As the 2001 season dawned, Moyer once again had something to prove, and so did his team. Not a lot was expected of the Seattle Mariners. Griffey was gone; one year before, his numbers in decline, he had been sent to the Cincinnati Reds. He'd requested a trade after the Mariners wouldn't move in the fences of their new state-of-the-art ballpark, Safeco Field. Rodriguez was history too. After the 2000 season, in which he hit 41 home runs and drove in 132 runs, A-Rod did what many of his teammates long thought he'd do: he took the money and ran, signing with Texas for a record ten-year deal worth a quarter of a billion dollars.

The oft-injured Jay Buhner would miss most of the season. To fill the power gap, the Mariners signed Ichiro Suzuki, Japan's leading hitter, and free agent Bret Boone. Since taking over in 1999, Pat Gillick had said goodbye to Randy Johnson, Griffey, and A-Rod; 2001 looked to be a rebuilding year.

But the Mariners opened the season winning 20 of their first 24 games and never looked back, leading their division by 19 games with a 63–24 mark at the All-Star break. Ichiro became an international sensation, a rookie who would lead the league in batting average (.350) and hits and stolen bases en route to winning MVP and Rookie of the Year honors. Boone had one of the best seasons for a second baseman in history: 37 home runs, 141 runs knocked in, a .331 batting average, an OPS of .950.

And Moyer emerged as an ace, going 20–6 with an ERA of 3.43 and a WHIP of 1.102, finishing fourth in the Cy Young Award voting. When he pitched seven innings on October 5 to beat the Rangers 6–2 (holding A-Rod hitless in four at-bats), it was his ninth win in his last eleven starts. It made him a 20-game winner for the first time, but, more important, it marked his team's 115th win of the season, surpassing the 1998 Yankees for the second best regular-season record ever. A win the next day tied the Mariners with the 1906 Cubs for the single-season record in victories.

It was a magical, mystical season. The catchphrase in the clubhouse became, "Two outs, so what?" because no deficit was too daunting to overcome. "It's an amazing feeling," Moyer recalls. "It's a feeling like you're going to win every day. And everybody knew it—our team, and the other team. You could feel it. Guys would be in the dugout, saying, 'Okay, what do we need, four runs? No problem. We'll get 'em.'"

How'd they do it? To hear Moyer and Gillick tell it, it was all about character. The 2001 Mariners had no superstars, just a collection of close-knit, fundamentally sound ballplayers who adopted their manager's persona on the field. They were an old-school bunch; if an opposing pitcher threw high and tight, nothing needed to be said: high and tight it was, in pointed re-ply. They went into bases hard, spikes up, and performed the selfless acts of winning baseball: throwing to cutoff men, hitting behind runners, bunting base runners over. Over four million fans flocked to Safeco, because the Mariners were winning, yes, but also because of *how* they were winning. It was as if Safeco were a time machine and, entering it, you could catch some great 1950s baseball.

"I used to think ability was 80 percent of the game and things like character and mastering the mental aspect accounted for 20 percent," Gillick says. "Now I think it's much more even. That Seattle team proved the difference that character and baseball smarts can make."

In the postseason, Moyer continued his storybook year, going 3–0 with a 1.89 ERA, outdueling Cleveland ace Chuck Finley twice in the divisional series. But the Mariners couldn't beat the Yankees when they needed to the most, and the magical season ended bitterly with a loss to New York in the American League Championship Series.

It was a swift, unforeseen end. Still, after the dust had settled and the years had passed, and even after Moyer had realized the boyhood dream of every major leaguer and won a World Series, he'd look back on 2001 with more fondness than any other year, and on the 116 wins with more pride than any other accomplishment. Part of it was the sheer constant adrenaline rush of stepping onto the field night in and night out with the absolute certainty you were going to win—they lost a mere seven games per month. And part of it was because he and his teammates had done it together, right up until that final out in the Bronx.

* * *

Like Piniella, Moyer is a baseball traditionalist, someone who's aware of the game's unique position among American sports. History, and agreed-upon yardsticks to judge that history, matter in baseball in a way they don't in, say, football and basketball.

During Moyer's decade in Seattle, however, the sport underwent two game-changing trends. In a relatively short span of time, these two developments—the rise in use of steroids and the sabermetric revolution—upended the most traditional of sports.

Pinpointing the precise dawning of the steroid era is a fool's game, but somewhere in the early to mid-'90s is a good starting point. Jose Canseco, Mark McGwire, Rafael Palmeiro, Alex Rodriguez, and Lenny Dykstra have all been implicated in the use of performance-enhancing drugs in the early '90s. By the middle of the decade, it was impossible to deny that something had fundamentally altered the game. In the thirty-two seasons following 1961, when Roger Maris and Mickey Mantle both hit over 50 home runs, the game had seen only three seasons of 50 or more home runs: Cecil Fielder's 51 in 1990, George Foster's 52 in 1977, and Willie Mays's 52 in 1965. But, starting in 1995, there would be sixteen 50-home-run seasons over the next seven seasons.

By the time Moyer became a top-flight pitcher in 1997, there was a widespread assumption that the game's inflated power statistics were attributable to causes beyond the effects of lowered pitching mounds or juiced balls. In 1998, the celebrated "Chase" season, McGwire and Sammy Sosa both set their sights on the single-season home run mark, with McGwire eventually hitting 70 and Sosa 66. Just a step behind them was Moyer's teammate Junior, with 56. Barry Bonds broke McGwire's season-single record in 2001 with 73 homers, despite never having hit as many as 50 in any prior season.

All this time, Moyer never saw evidence that anyone was taking anything—nothing in teammates' lockers or in the trainer's room. Nor were there any admissions in the clubhouse of any performance-enhancing drug use. But common sense told Moyer and his teammates that widespread cheating was going on, and that baseball was turning a blind eye. During games,

Picture day in the Moyer household, early '70s.
L to R: Jamie, mom Joan, sister Jill, Jim.

The Little League All-Star in the early '70s.

As a Chicago
Cubs rookie in
1986, Moyer
beat his boy-
hood idol Steve
Carlton in his
first-ever start.

Cal Ripken Jr. and
Moyer on the field
at Camden Yards.
Ripken holds Dillon
Moyer and Jamie
has Hutton.

Celebrating
making the
1997 playoffs
with Seattle
teammate Ken
Griffey Jr.

Celebrating
making the 1997
playoffs with
Seattle teammate
Randy Johnson.

With cancer patient Gregory Chaya in 1998: "He's my miracle friend," Moyer says.

With Erin Metcalf, the inspiration for the Moyer Foundation's Camp Erin, along with Seattle Mariners teammate Jeff Fassero.

In Seattle, Moyer became an elite pitcher, winning 145 games between the ages of thirty-three and forty-three. (Courtesy Ben VanHouten)

With wife, Karen, and father-in-law, Digger Phelps.

Dinner at Philadelphia's Saloon Restaurant with Digger and the rest of the Phelps crew on the eve of Moyer's first-ever World Series start.

The Moyer clan after Jamie excavated the pitching rubber from the mound during the World Series celebration in 2008.

A long time coming: Jamie and Karen kiss on the field after the Phillies beat the Dodgers to make it to the World Series in 2008.

In 2009, St. Joseph's University recognized the work of the Moyer Foundation and granted Karen and Jamie honorary degrees as Doctors of Public Service.

Celebrating on the field with (L to R) Katilina, sister Jill, Timoney, and Duffy.

With eight kids at home, Moyer, pictured here as a Seattle Mariner on Literacy Day in the late '90s, is a veteran when it comes to reading Dr. Seuss.

The Family Moyer, Summer 2013. L to R, front: Yenifer, Katilina, Grady, and McCabe. L to R, back: Timoney, Duffy, Dillon, Karen, Jamie, and Hutton.

At forty-nine, Moyer came back from Tommy John surgery to pitch for the Colorado Rockies early in the 2012 season. (Courtesy Colorado Rockies)

Thanking the fans after becoming the oldest pitcher to ever win a major league game. (Courtesy Colorado Rockies)

At Moyer's fiftieth birthday bash benefiting the Moyer Foundation, his former teammate Cliff Lee (left), pictured here with fellow Phillie Chase Utley, bid $20,000 for a collection of autographed Moyer game balls. (Courtesy the Moyer Foundation)

Moyer can still hear the voice of his late mentor Harvey Dorfman: "What are you going to do about it, kid?" (Courtesy Anita Dorfman)

Moyer and teammates would sit on the bench and point at opposing players and vote on who was using.

"Yes, yes, no," they'd say, singling out players, sometimes arguing. Some were no-brainers. A reliever who ended the previous season throwing at 92 would show up to spring training clocked at 97 or 98. A slight leadoff hitter five years earlier had now become a bulky power hitter. They'd page through old media guides, comparing the size of players' heads now to earlier in their careers.

Moyer was angry about what steroid use had done to the game, and he faulted baseball for its laissez-faire reaction to the trend. He considered the numbers of anyone who had tested positive to be tainted and argued that such players shouldn't be voted into the Hall of Fame: "Who in their right mind would vote for anyone who got caught taking that stuff?"

In January of 2010, Commissioner Bud Selig proclaimed that steroids were "virtually nonexistent" in the game. By spring training 2012, baseball's powers-that-be would have had fans believe that the era of tainted numbers was over. But is it? In short order, Ryan Braun, Bartolo Colon, and Melky Cabrera all tested positive for elevated testosterone levels (although Braun was later cleared on appeal). When he heard about Cabrera, Moyer made a beeline for his iPad. *Didn't I face him this year?* he wondered.

Sure enough, early in 2012, Moyer, pitching for Colorado, faced Cabrera, who got a big hit and RBI against him. "Interesting," Moyer mumbled to himself, staring at the screen. Ever competitive, Moyer is rankled by the possibility that the playing field wasn't always level. Like other first-time offenders, Cabrera faced a fifty-game suspension..

"Why not have a real zero tolerance policy?" Moyer asks. "If guys know that the first time they test positive for something, their careers will be over, they won't cheat. It will take making an example of one or two people, but you'd end the madness. But baseball hasn't shown the guts to do that."

Cabrera notwithstanding, the irony behind Moyer's ire is that he feels more cheated as a fan than as a pitcher. It's not lost on him that his career took off as the steroid era dawned. That wasn't a coincidence. He feasted on a generation of juiced-up, overeager hitters who were all convinced they could take him deep. For a pitcher who took advantage of batters' egos, it was a grand moment in the game: he was David, they were Goliaths, and the changeup was his slingshot.

At the same time that pitchers like Moyer were having to adjust to a generation of hitters who were bigger, stronger, and quicker to recover than ever before, a new way of evaluating performance took hold. The sabermetric revolution had at its root an age-old schoolyard conflict: it grew out of a battle between jocks and nerds. (The name is derived from the acronym SABR: Society for American Baseball Research.)

The nerds, led by Bill James, challenged much of the game's conventional wisdom and introduced objective formulas for gauging player value. They said that metrics like batting average were overrated, because that statistic's relation to run scoring—the ultimate purpose of the game, after all—was tenuous at best. On-base and slugging percentages, they found, were actually better yardsticks with which to measure a hitter's worth.

As for evaluating pitchers, a statistic like WHIP—walks plus hits per innings pitched—was seen as a better way to gauge effectiveness than, say, ERA, in that it quantifies a pitcher's ability to prevent batters from reaching base, just as strikeout-to-walk ratio best revealed a pitcher's control. And fielding-independent pitching (FIP) statistics were devised to measure a pitcher based on plays that don't involve fielders: home runs allowed, strike-outs, walks, hit batsmen.

The jocks scoffed at the nerds. What did these spreadsheet-bearing geeks know about playing baseball? A lot, it turns out. They may not have played the game, but there could be no doubt that the statheads were on to something in terms of how to evaluate it. When Michael Lewis published *Moneyball* in 2003, the story of Billy Beane's sabermetric-informed running of the Oakland A's, a long-simmering squabble was brought into the mainstream.

"*Moneyball* told a neat story that made for good reading," says legendary manager Tony La Russa, who retired in 2011 with the third most wins in major league history. In the latter stages of his career, he saw many teams create front-office positions for the generation of numbers-crunching geeks Lewis's book gave rise to. "But it's been exaggerated to take credit for things it can't substantiate. It's become a fraud. That Oakland A's team had great starting pitching and its closer saved almost 50 games. Those players were all developed through the team's farm system, the way we've always done it in baseball. Analytics have a place, yes. But there's no replacement for judging things like leadership and competitiveness, which is what coaches have always done."

There can be no doubt that the new metrics have identified the right *statistical* categories to measure when judging baseball prowess. What it didn't do is quantify how players attain their level of performance. The argument against sabermetrics too often conflates sabermetrics itself with Lewis's book—with the story of Billy Beane himself, whose evangelizing for analytics bordered on ideology for the precise reason La Russa pinpoints: it was accompanied by a rejection of the importance of the *mental* game.

There's a backstory here. Beane was once a can't-miss phenom who had all the physical skills but perhaps not the requisite mental ones. He'd shatter bats in frustration, destroy dugouts, get in fistfights. When he was in the Oakland A's system in the late '80s, such behavior brought him to the attention of none other than Harvey Dorfman. Dorfman worked with Beane, who was never able to grow into the player scouts thought he'd be.

In *Moneyball*, Dorfman tells Lewis that Beane was typical: a precocious talent who lacked a coping mechanism when he confronted failure for the first time. Lewis recounts Beane's response: "He thought it was [B.S.] to say that his character— or more exactly, his emotional predisposition—might be changed....All these attempts to manipulate his psyche he regarded as so much crap."

Beane tells Lewis, "Sports psychologists are a crutch. An excuse for why you are doing it rather than a solution. If somebody needs them, there is a weakness in them that will prevent them from succeeding. It's not a character flaw; it's just a character flaw when it comes to baseball. It wasn't anyone's fault. I just didn't have it in me."

In his final memoir, *Each Branch, Each Needle*, Dorfman— never one to back down from a fight—throws high and tight at Beane in response. "'A crutch'?" he asks. "Billy employed what is called in semantic circles a dysphemism, which *suggested* the most disagreeable aspect of a point he wished to establish, rather than using the word itself. That word is 'dependency'— and Billy knew damn well, or should have, that a healthy independence is what I ask each athlete to strive for as a goal....The courage of honest introspection is a required first step toward changing of negative, ingrained habits....Awareness is the first step to change."

When slighted, Dorfman tended to respond with the same sort of aggressiveness he urged his pitchers to demonstrate on the mound. This was a man, after all, who, when Barry Bonds showed up to his hotel room for a 2 p.m. appointment at 4 p.m. with his posse in tow, told the slugger to "lose my number and never contact me again." Now, dissed by Beane, Harvey was in full-throated Harvey mode: "As for his comments about 'weak guys'?...The strongest people I know face up to their issues; the weakest I know run away from them—or deny them....Not ever addressed is that the mental game is intellectual, as well as psychological. Much of my work has little, if anything, to do with the 'psyche.' How to think, what to think, and when to think—rationality—is about mental preparation, strategies and approaches to the game. And, oh, yes, responses. Such as throwing equipment. Still unacceptable, after all these years."

According to Lewis, Beane saw "no point in trying to get inside players' heads, for instance, to reshape their approach to the game." He quotes Beane, perhaps thinking of his own career: "You don't change guys; they are who they are." Presumably this means that if a hitter is an overeager free-swinging collegian who rarely walks, he'll never quiet his approach and learn to be more selective.

It is, of course, an ahistorical argument masked as a rational one. Countless players grew into All-Stars by tweaking their mental modus operandi. In the '70s, Mike Schmidt made himself into the best third baseman ever by overcoming the paralyzing effects of pressure. In the late '80s, Dave Stewart, pushing thirty, finally put it all together. In the early '90s, Randy Johnson, a mediocre pitcher at age twenty-eight, got out of his own way and joined the game's elite. The entire 2001 Seattle Mariners team, as Pat Gillick learned, stands as a testament to the difference attitude and approach can make.

And then, of course, there's Moyer, who—through years of study—managed to turn himself into an aggressive, inside-pitching master of deception. Had Beane been right, wouldn't Moyer have been run out of the league in the early '90s?

Meantime, Moyer had become the face of the Seattle franchise. After his 20–6 season in 2001, he went 13–8 in 2002. Despite the drop-off in wins, he arguably pitched better than the previous year. His ERA was 3.32, he logged 230 innings, and his WHIP was a career-best 1.075, among the league leaders.

The following year, with a 12–5 record and 3.02 ERA at midseason, Moyer was an All-Star for the first time, at all of forty years old. The game was held at U.S. Cellular Field in Chicago, the city where his professional career began. Karen was pregnant with Mac and couldn't travel, so Moyer took his boys with him. Twelve-year-old Dillon and ten-year-old Hutton were about to have the weekend of their dreams. Because he had no one to watch the boys in the stands, Dillon and Hutton were with their dad in the clubhouse and dugout.

Come gametime, Moyer sat in the dugout, taking in the sheer firepower around him. *How cool would it be to play on a team with all this talent?* he wondered. When he got the call in the bullpen to start warming up—he'd pitch the fourth inning, replacing Roger Clemens—his heart started pounding. As he threw, he couldn't find the plate. Everything was up, up, up. *You're too keyed up,* he told himself. He knew he had to stop and collect his thoughts. He stepped off the rubber and had a private Harvey moment with himself.

Throw as slow as you can, he told himself—the first and only time he'd ever have to offer such self-advice. *Focus on down, down, down.* Once on the mound, he settled down quickly and made short work of the National League's two, three, and four hitters: he struck out the Cardinals' Jim Edmonds and induced Pujols and Bonds into flyouts.

But the best part of All-Star weekend came next. Walking into the dugout, his teammates lined up to high-five him; among them were the beaming faces and outstretched hands of Dillon and Hutton, who were more excited than anyone. "What a privilege to have my boys with me," he'd remember later.

After the break, Moyer picked right up where he left off. He ended up a 20-game winner for the second time, going 21–7 with a 3.27 ERA and a WHIP of 1.233 for a Mariners team that won 93 games but barely missed the playoffs.

But that year would mark the end of Seattle's winning ways for some time, and the end of a stellar run for Moyer. He went 7–13 in 2004, giving up a career-high 44 home runs. The Mariners finished 63–99 in what Moyer called a "disastrous" season. Late in it, Moyer phoned Harvey.

"I just can't get comfortable," Moyer said.

"*Can't*? Why *can't* you?" Harvey barked through his perpetual cough, calling attention to Moyer's negative self-talk. Moyer had held off on calling him, figuring that by now in his career, he could right his own ship. But he was now zero for July, August, and part of September: 0–8 in his last 15 starts.

"I don't know what it is," he told Harvey.

"Are you doing anything different? Are you paying attention to your routine?"

"I am, but it feels like I'm just going through the motions," Moyer said. Dorfman considered the bigger picture: after all his struggle, after all the years of being cut and disrespected, of being shuttled back and forth between the minors and majors, of being ridiculed for his soft-tossing ways, Moyer had finally broken through and become an elite pitcher. He'd won 20 games in two of the last three seasons and could have easily won 20 in 2002 had his team scored runs for him. He had, in other words, made it. Harvey had seen it before: players expend so much psychic energy to succeed that they misplace the mental edge that got them ahead. "I think you need to put something on the line," Dorfman said.

"Put something on the line?"

"You've always needed something to prove, something to fight for," Dorfman said. "You've made it. So what's left to fight for? You need to come up with something to put on the line. Any ideas?"

Moyer was at a loss.

"What about your kids? What about telling yourself that you're doing this for them, that if you fail, they'll feel it?"

After talking with Dorfman, Moyer told himself he was pitching for his kids' future, and he then went out and beat the Angels, giving up three runs in six innings, his first win in two months. He carried Dorfman's advice into the following season, the final one of his three-year, $15.5 million deal, and reversed his record: 13–7 with a 4.28 ERA and a solid WHIP of 1.385. But the Mariners finished 69–93; the glory days were long gone and Moyer was now about to turn forty-three.

At the close of the 2005 season, Moyer got his own taste of how sabermetrics were being used—some might say abused— by tepid front offices. The Mariners had just hired Bart Waldman, a Harvard- and Georgetown-educated lawyer, as their new vice president, baseball counsel, and associate general counsel. He'd be taking over the handling of the team's free agent player contracts, which included Moyer, from general manager Bill Bavasi, who had replaced Gillick in 2003.

Moyer had represented himself ever since Jim Bronner and his partner Bob Gilhooley had sold their agency to SFX Entertainment in 2000. Bronner had been in Moyer's corner since the early journeyman years. He'd been more than an agent; he'd become a close friend and trusted confidant. For the first time, Moyer faced a contract negotiation without him. It was tricky terrain. In sports contract negotiations, teams, in trying to make the best deal for themselves, have to argue that their asset—the player—is not as valuable as he thinks he is. That's particularly awkward when the team's representative is talking directly to the player.

Most such negotiations are conducted by phone, but Moyer wanted a face-to-face meeting. "I'm ten minutes away," he explained. He eventually got his meeting, but it was anything but satisfactory. Moyer was the Mariners' all-time winningest pitcher. Perhaps naively, he thought that, given what he'd accomplished for the organization, it would be a pretty simple deal.

Waldman thought so too—but their definition of "simple" differed. Waldman referenced sabermetric calculations as an argument for his take-it-or-leave-it $5.5 million offer for one year. Moyer wasn't complaining about the money. He still felt fortunate to make millions playing the game of his youth. But there was something about being treated as just another free agent that left a bad taste in his mouth; the whole transaction felt cold and antiseptic. And, he suspected, it was not unrelated to the game's newfound idolatry of data.

Rather than engage on whatever data Waldman had come up with, Moyer pointed out what his career had always shown: you can't gauge heart or professionalism or being a good teammate or performing under pressure by running a computer program. There isn't a software program able to discern baseball smarts.

"The computer doesn't judge personality or heart, and any good organization is going to take that into consideration—what kind of person do we have?" Moyer said, subtly identifying a problem in the Seattle clubhouse the last two years, in stark contrast to the close-knit, winning teams of the Gillick era. "If that's overlooked, all it takes is having a couple of bad players personality-wise who are destructive or distracting to remind you how important it is to have good people."

In the end, he took the contract, but Jamie wasn't sure how much longer he'd be in Seattle, where there no longer seemed to be as much of a desire to excel.

By 2006, Moyer knew the end was near for him in Seattle. He had grown tired of the me-first mind-set of the Mariners' clubhouse. He was now forty-three years old and he found himself thinking often about that 2001 team, its work ethic and camaraderie. This team, a much younger one, didn't exude a passion to win, and it was wearing on him. In mid-August, the Mariners had lost seven in a row and were already well out of postseason contention. Before his start against the Angels in Anaheim, Moyer had had enough. He sensed that some teammates were just going through the motions. When things didn't go well, they'd hide from the media in the trainer's room. If you're eager to stand before the beat reporters and the TV cameras when you've done something good, he felt, you have to take the heat when you've done something bad. He decided to call a team meeting, something rarely done by pitchers.

"Think back to when you were eight, nine, ten years old," Moyer told his teammates. "You weren't playing to get paid then. You were playing for the fun of the game. You enjoyed it. We need to recapture that spirit. We need to go out and play as a team. Instead of having twenty-five players and twenty-five cabs, let's have twenty-five players and one bus, with everyone on it, going in one direction. Let's try and make something of this season. Let's be a spoiler."

Only Raul Ibanez spoke up in agreement. Most looked back at Moyer, expressionless. One teammate didn't even turn to face Moyer while he spoke. That night, Jamie called Karen. They spoke for an hour and a half. Moyer explained that too many in the clubhouse seemed to be comfortable with losing. "I can't do this anymore," Moyer told his wife. "It's too draining. I'm going to retire at the end of the year." The decision was made. His mind was made up.

Until the next day, that is, when general manager Bavasi asked if, in keeping with the provisions of his contract, he'd sign off on being traded to the Phillies.

MARCH 2012

CHAPTER NINE

Hoping you will do something means you don't believe you can.

—Harvey Dorfman

He's been on a steady diet of salads and electrolytes, so on this, the eve of his return to a big league mound for something other than tossing some pain-in-the-ass batting practice, Jamie Moyer is treating himself: a burger and a beer, on a deck overlooking a serene lake in Scottsdale, Arizona.

He takes a gulp and looks both ways before speaking. He's got to talk softly, because he doesn't want to broadcast a hint of vulnerability. He leans forward to make his admission: "I'm *terrified*."

Of what? His eyes widen at the thought. "That I just can't do it anymore, after all this." He sighs. "That this is it. Or that I'm going to be seen as some type of damned novelty act. I am so outta here if I think that's happening."

It's a week into his twenty-fifth spring training with his eighth team, the Colorado Rockies. Everything he does, he senses coaches and trainers and media looking at this gray-haired guy with the wispy stubble of a beard, and they're searching for signs. How's his arm? Is he limping? He feels like he's always being evaluated, whether it's during pitchers' fielding practice, or the distance run he opts to take with the rest of the staff, even though he gave up running outside years ago in favor of the Hy-droWorx 2000, an underwater treadmill.

In the field, clubhouse, or bullpen, coaches approach and, with a concerned look and soothing tone, gently touch his arm. "How you feeling today?"

Moyer issues his standard response: "I'm good, how are you?" as though he were misinterpreting the question for polite chit-chat.

They tell him not to push himself, to take it easy. Eat well. "I don't know about this place," he tells Karen in their nightly call. He's staying in the guesthouse of Jeff Fassero, his Seattle team-mate in the late '90s, now a minor league pitching coach. His accommodations contain everything he needs: a bed, a wash-ing machine, and a color TV set that gets the MLB Network. "Everyone is really nice. Almost too nice. The good teams I've been on, there's an edge to them. You don't want to say a mean-ness, but at least a hardness. They weren't so concerned with how everybody is *feeling*."

He's pitched two batting practice sessions. "I stunk," he says. Nothing new there; Moyer's never been a good batting practice pitcher. He tries to keep the ball off the fat part of the bat; the batting practice hitter expects all moon balls into the sweet spot. The more Moyer tried to comply, the more he had no idea where the ball was going. In the clubhouse, when asked about his batting practice stint, Moyer quipped, "I kind of look at my whole career as live batting practice."

Tomorrow, though, comes an intra-squad scrimmage. Team-mates Jason Giambi and Todd Helton are managing the two respective squads. Jeremy Guthrie, a newcomer who went 9–17 for the Orioles last season but is an innings eater and is expected to be the staff ace, will be one starter, Moyer the other. He seems more nervous for this than he did for his 2008 World Series start.

When it's time to leave, Moyer slaps down some bills. "What's the worst that can happen?" he asks, getting up to go. "I can't find the plate? I hit a couple of guys? Big deal. I can jump in the car and be home in five hours."

At first, you think: bravado. Then you realize: it's just Jamie channeling Harvey, lowering the stakes, minimizing the pressure. It's what Tug McGraw was getting at years ago when he said, "Ten million years from now, when the sun burns out and the earth is just a frozen iceball hurtling through space, nobody's going to care whether or not I got this guy out." If you're okay not attaining your goal, you're more likely to get it.

Baseball aficionados fall into two groups: the craftsmen and the poets. Players tend to be the former; they're often too busy trying to get better at the game—and too distracted by their frustrations in it—to spend a lot of time waxing sentimental about its bigger meaning. The hardest-core fans tend toward the latter; they're the ones for whom the movie *Field of Dreams* is more spiritual road map than it is the story of a guy who built a baseball field in his backyard.

But such is baseball's allure that the two groups are seldom mutually exclusive. Moyer is the consummate craftsman, a pitcher who has thought about the act of throwing a baseball literally every day of his adult life—indeed, for most days of his *entire* life. Yet for all his professional stoicism, and for all the countless hours of working out, the mental preparations, the tweaks in the bullpen sessions, the sheer number of pitches thrown—58,485, fifth all-time—he is not *just* a baseball craftsman, especially at this time of year. Moyer, like so many of baseball's lifers, quietly attends to his craft with the soul of a poet.

How else to explain the rush of awe he felt when, after eighteen months away from the game, he first set foot on the baseball diamond at Salt River Fields, the Colorado Rockies' state-of-the-art facility in Scottsdale? It was so green and so familiar; the sound of bat on ball filled the air—the true harbinger of spring, as Bill Veeck once said. Through the years, Moyer often felt this way on day one, humbled that he was but a tiny part of an epic history—the history of a game, but also, corny as it sounds, of a country. But it was particularly poignant now, because a part of him had wondered if he'd ever feel this way again. Day one of spring training 2012 found him meeting new teammates, being handed a uniform, running with his pitching brethren. In a larger sense, it found him feeling like a rookie again, breathlessly wondering what the future holds.

The Colorado Rockies of 2012 are in need of Moyer's experience. Last year's version lost 89 games, but it was the way they lost that led general manager Dan O'Dowd to want to change the team's culture. The 2011 Rockies were young, cocky, and complacent—a toxic combination. Now O'Dowd has stocked up on veterans, seeking to import the type of work ethic and pride that goes into winning baseball. The Rockies very well could open the Cactus League season starting six players born in the 1970s—and one, Moyer, from the '60s. There's Jason Giambi, forty-one; Todd Helton, thirty-eight; Casey Blake, thirty-eight; Marco Scutaro, thirty-six; Ramon Hernandez, thirty-five; Wil Nieves, thirty-four; Jeremy Guthrie, thirty-three; and Michael Cuddyer, also thirty-three.

It's no accident, then, that Moyer is assigned a locker in the clubhouse between pitching prospects Drew Pomeranz and Tyler Chatwood. Pomeranz is a 6´5˝, twenty-three-year-old lefty with a gun for an arm. Chatwood, twenty-two, is 5´11˝ but can hit the mid-90s with his fastball. Some scouts had likened him to a young Roy Oswalt. Manager Jim Tracy, only seven years older than Moyer, pairs Moyer and Pomeranz as long-toss partners. The movement on Moyer's ball takes Pomeranz aback, but it's the seriousness with which Moyer approaches his craft that Tracy and O'Dowd are hoping rubs off on the younger pitchers.

But change isn't coming to the Rockies solely in the form of new personnel. Tracy talks about a new attitude, one based on better team chemistry and "authentic relationships." To that end, early in camp, each player is given an assignment: to research a teammate—without using the team's media guide—and stand in the middle of the clubhouse and introduce him to the rest of the squad.

Most of the players simply google the teammate they've randomly chosen from a hat, then get up and deliver the predictable: where the subject went to school, what his stats were in the minors, in a hesitant monotone that lasts all of a minute.

Moyer picks Guthrie's name from the hat. Rather than do a simple Internet search, that night he procures the phone number for Guthrie's wife and mother and contacts both. The next day, when it's his turn to speak about Guthrie, Moyer does a five-minute tour de force. "Jeremy was the state chess champion in Oregon," he tells the Rockies. "But he wasn't always so well behaved. When he was a little boy, he once strayed from his mother and the police had to find him. He also drove his Big Wheel very fast down hills. He also used to sell candy bars from his locker at school, until the authorities found out about it and shut him down. He was kind of an outlaw."

Not one of the Rockies put as much preparation into the exercise as Moyer, which was entirely purposeful. "If I'm given an assignment, I'm going to prepare to the fullest," he says. "That's something the young guys have to learn."

Moyer is right to fear becoming a sideshow. That's what happened to Satchel Paige, who at fifty-nine started a game for the Kansas City Athletics in 1965. Paige, the legendary Negro League player, was signed for one day by A's owner Charlie Finley as a marketing ploy. Paige pitched three innings; between them, he sat in the bullpen in a rocking chair being tended to by an attractive young woman dressed as a nurse. When he was taken out, the lights dimmed and the crowd serenaded him with the song "The Old Grey Mare."

Moyer doesn't want the sentimental treatment. He wants a chance and he wants to be taken seriously. As spring training dawned, he was already getting a sense of just how easily this quest could turn into punch line. When it was announced that the Rockies had invited him to camp, a blog headline blared, "Rockies Offer Jamie Moyer Chance for Career-Ending Injury." Not a day goes by without someone—announcer, writer, coach, or fan—referencing his age. The media coverage seems intent on unearthing every conceivable factoid in order to underscore the same conclusion: the dude is *old*.

To wit: He qualifies for his AARP card come November. He is older than eight of the game's managers and sixteen general managers. His team's best player, Troy Tulowitzki, was all of twenty months old when Moyer made his major league debut, and four of the pitchers he is competing against for a spot in the starting rotation weren't even born yet.

As for the rotation, Guthrie and twenty-four-year-old Jhoulys Chacin are locks for two of the Rockies' five starting spots. Chatwood, Pomeranz, twenty-eight-year-old Guillermo Moscoso, twenty-three-year-old Alex White, twenty-seven-year-old Josh Outman, and twenty-five-year-old Juan Nicasio—making a major comeback himself, from a broken neck—are all competing with Moyer for the remaining three slots.

But Moyer doesn't consider the kids—to Moyer, the father of a twenty-one-year-old, they're *all* kids—his competitors. No, his yardstick is his health—can his body hold up? And his true competition is time itself.

He'd been told he'd have a chance to make the rotation, but what did that mean? At forty-nine and not having thrown a big league pitch in nearly eighteen months, how long would the Rockies give him? As he made his way to the mound on a practice field for the intra-squad game, Moyer wondered, *Will I be cleaning out my locker in a couple of hours?*

Likely part of his anxiety stemmed from the fact that he was going to war short on ammo. He'd decided to not throw the cutter early in spring, because it was coming out flat from his hand. He was convinced he didn't yet have the arm strength necessary to give the ball its bite, that sudden dipping motion down toward the righthanded hitter's back ankle. So the pitch he'd come to rely on so heavily late in his career was on the shelf.

Rather than feel ill-prepared, though, Moyer completed his warm-up tosses and felt his inner Harvey kicking in, just like old times. *Task. At. Hand.* The first hitter was outfielder Eric Young Jr. Moyer held back a smile, for he remembered that nearly two decades ago, Eric Young Sr. had been 0 for 12 against him. Like his father, Junior hit a Moyer changeup lazily into the outfield for an easy out.

In two innings, Moyer threw 42 pitches, 27 for strikes. Not his usual command, but he thought, *I'll take it.* Between the nerves and the absence of the cutter, he felt relieved to give up only three hits, one run, and no walks while striking out one. Late in his second inning of work, utility infielder Jordan Pacheco, on the bubble to make the team, fielded a ground ball on the foul side of third base and was about to toss it to some kids in the bleachers.

"Hey!" Moyer barked. "That's my ball!"

Pacheco froze as his pitcher came off the mound toward him.

"I don't take your bat away after you foul one off, do I?" Moyer asked, holding his glove up.

"Sorry, sorry," Pacheco stammered, while both dugouts exploded in nervous laughter.

Afterwards, Moyer apologized to the kid, who had no idea this kindly old gentleman in the clubhouse could be such a hardass between the lines. Manager Tracy and pitching coach Bob Apodaca both congratulated Moyer, remarking that he'd shown a little rust, but the test would be how his body would feel tomorrow. That night, he felt relieved. The next morning, he felt ecstatic, because his arm felt like it could go another few innings already.

On the night before his first start of the spring, Jamie Moyer has a hankering for a cheesesteak, that artery-clogging Philadelphia delicacy. When it comes to gustatory cravings, he is as stubborn as he is on the mound. In some ways, though, finding a credible cheesesteak in the Arizona desert is a taller order than facing Pujols with runners on.

Jeff Fassero comes to the rescue, however. He alerts his boarder to Corleone's in Scottsdale. "It's a little place in a strip mall," Fassero says. "But the guy is from Philly."

That's all Moyer needs to hear. We're off in search of Moyer's "cheese wit," Philly shorthand for a steak sandwich with cheese (provolone, in Moyer's case) and fried onions.

When he walks into Corleone's, Moyer is transported back to his roots. On the wall is a framed copy of the *Philadelphia Daily News* front page when the Phillies—his Phillies—won the World Series in 1980. "We Win!" it reads in big bold black letters. It's the front page Moyer saw Tug McGraw hold aloft during his remarks in the parade celebration, giving voice to years of baseball frustration. "All through baseball history, Philadelphia has had to take a backseat to New York City," McGraw said. "Well, New York City can take this world championship and stick it, 'cause we're number one!"

Next to the *Daily News* cover is a framed Pat Burrell number 5 Phillies jersey, signed by Pat the Bat himself. Moyer is standing at the counter, taking in the memorabilia that line the walls and looking at the menu board, when rushing out of the open kitchen comes a wild-eyed, well-built young man.

"I gotta thank you! I just gotta thank you!" Giovanni Caranci is saying, coming out from behind the counter, arm extended for what turns out to be part handshake, part South Philly hug. "I gotta thank you for the World Series!"

Caranci, who relocated to Arizona a few years ago and opened a chain of Philly-themed sandwich and pizza shops, had season tickets to the magical 2008 season. "I think I remember you," Moyer says. "Didn't I get you and your son some stuff?"

Caranci is stunned—one day, Moyer tossed some T-shirts from the bullpen to him. They reconnect like old war vets; Caranci wishes Moyer were back with the Phils this season. They talk about this year's Phillies team. "A lot is going to depend on Roy," Moyer says of ace pitcher Roy Halladay. "He didn't look good the other night."

In fact, Moyer watched Halladay, his friend and fellow Dorfman pupil, and immediately texted him: "Looks like you're drifting to the plate."

On this night, though, he can waste little time worrying about Halladay's mechanics; he spent today looking at his. Tomorrow will be his first start, but four days ago he made his first appearance of the season (not counting the intra-squad exhibition), and he spent this morning looking at video from the outing.

Moyer pitched two innings in relief against San Francisco at Scottsdale Stadium. The Rockies had shelled starter Tim Lincecum for five runs in two innings by the time Moyer came in. His command was much improved; in the fourth inning, his mix of fastball and changeup led to three straight soft groundouts to second base. In the fifth, he gave up a single, the only one he'd surrender. He stepped off the mound and turned to second base umpire Dana DeMuth.

"I was absent last year," Moyer said. "Can I still bring my hand to my mouth on the mound?"

DeMuth laughed. "Yes, you can."

"Okay. Just checking."

In two scoreless innings, he threw only 22 pitches; Giants catcher Chris Stewart was seen muttering to himself on his way back to the dugout after flailing at a two-strike changeup.

"I was terrible," Giants ace Lincecum said after the game, before being asked to comment on Moyer. "Wow! He's forty-nine. He's going back out there."

While Moyer was happy with his command, something felt off. The cutter still isn't ready. More importantly, every pitch should ideally come from the same release point, lest the pitcher tip the batter off to the forthcoming pitch, and Moyer was not in the same arm slot on every throw.

In the last decade, watching video had become all the rage in the major leagues. Every team has a video coordinator, and players and coaches spend countless hours "breaking down tape," deconstructing at-bats and pitching sequences into intricate frame-by-frame parts. During games, hitters will leave the dugout to view their last at-bat, and pitchers will sneak looks between innings.

Moyer is not a video devotee. Part of that is generational—he's more comfortable with his own hand-scrawled notes from his decades of confrontations on the mound; beyond those, he relies on what, as he puts it, each at-bat is telling him in real time, what he's gleaning from a hitter's body language or expression, not unlike a poker player looking to identify and exploit the opposition's tell.

Which isn't to say he never watches video—Moyer is too open-minded to dismiss it out of hand. He just doesn't rely on it as much as other players. He doesn't trust the centerfield camera angle, so he can never be sure where a pitch actually *is*, and for Moyer, where the pitch is, its exact placement, is the whole ball game.

He watches himself on video when he's trying to solve a particular mechanical mystery, but even to his keen eye, the nuanced differences in pitch-by-pitch arm slot positioning evade him. He's searching for a *feeling* when he throws, the familiar sensation of muscle memory at work, and he's found that watching tape of himself in pursuit of that can actually distract him from finding it.

Moyer does watch hitters' at-bats. He subscribes to a major league service that makes available on his iPad every at-bat in the league. He'll watch and search for what he calls hitters' "jam spots," the farthest location inside that a hitter will offer at and be unable to keep in fair play. Once he has the jam spot, he'll work it time and again, until the batter proves he can get around on it.

This morning he looked at tape to see if he could discern his arm slot, but instead he noticed something else. "My right hip was leaning too far to the plate on my leg kick," he says now, taking a bite of his cheesesteak and waving a thumbs-up in the air to the nervous proprietor keeping an eye on him from the kitchen.

Now he puts the sandwich down and rises in the middle of Corleone's, starting his pitching motion from the stretch right next to the condiments stand while other customers look on. He shows what he's been doing—the right hip is out front, leaning toward home perhaps an inch and a nanosecond ahead of where it should be—compared to the motion he practiced this morning. "So, okay, now this is something I have to work on," he says. A lefty leading too much with the right hip runs the risk of opening up too soon. That's when balls get up in the zone and when pitches targeted inside to righthanded batters can catch too much of the plate.

He sits down and returns his attention to the cheesesteak. Tomorrow, he'll start against the White Sox in a three-inning stint. For now, though, he's just a Phillies fan, the memorabilia and the food taking him back to another time. "Remember Big Bull Luzinski?" he says, referring to the Phillies team of his youth. "Now there was a tough out."

Luzinski was preceded in the lineup by the majestically talented Mike Schmidt, though for most of Moyer's adolescence Schmidt was an underachiever who was a target of the Philly boo-birds. It wasn't lost on Moyer that Schmidt turned an underachieving career into a Hall of Fame one through work ethic and by figuring out the game.

"Very few in the game worked as hard as I did, and I never got credit for that," Schmidt said in 1995, sounding as old-school as Moyer. "I'm talking about being consumed by the sport. Players today come to the park, watch some TV, read a newspaper, make a sandwich, have a few laughs, break out the cards, ease into their uniforms, and then it's time for batting practice. When I got to the park, I started preparing immediately. I was all business."

It was long before Harvey and the era of the sports shrink, but Schmidt got better because—not in spite of—his cerebral nature. "I went from ducking every time they threw a breaking ball to being the best righthanded breaking ball hitter in the league, because I had the patience and the drive to learn the game," Schmidt recalled. It's true—it was arguably Schmidt's analytical nature, not his natural talent, that turned him into a Hall of Famer. When his career started to wane in the mid-'80s, it was his studied approach to the craft of hitting that resurrected him. He changed his approach, started hitting down on the ball, and began using the whole field instead of trying to pull everything.

"At this level," Moyer says now, "everyone is talented, or they wouldn't be here. What separates the best from the rest is this." He taps his head.

This waltz down memory lane concludes with Moyer's last bite of his cheesesteak. "You can't get good cheesesteaks outside of Philly," he says, noting that a shop in, of all places, Bradenton, Florida, also makes a mean one. He wipes his mouth. "This is a very good one."

As their son completes his warm-up tosses, Jim and Joan Moyer are a study in contrasts. They have just arrived, along with daughter Jill, on a flight from Philly.

"You didn't think we'd miss his first start in nearly two years?" Joan says. Her legs bob nervously as she grabs scoopful after scoopful of popcorn. Jim, on the other hand, is placid, holding the game program open in his lap, pen poised to score each play as he's done for decades. This was what it was like when

Jamie pitched for the Phillies, and Jill would drive their parents an hour each way to every home game he pitched. Before that, during his time in Seattle, the Moyers would stay up late to watch on the satellite dish, Jim scoring silently, Joan fidgeting nervously.

Karen and a bunch of the kids are here too. Fourteen-year-old Duffy helps watch "the littles," Kati and Yeni, while eighteen-year-old Hutton and eight-year-old Mac look forward to going into the clubhouse after their dad pitches.

They won't have long to wait. On the field, Moyer looks sharp in the first. He retires the side on just seven pitches, all strikes. It's more of the same in the second, when a two-seam fastball below the zone induces an inning-ending grounder to Tulowitzki at short for a double play. That's thirteen pitches through two innings today, and four scoreless innings thus far. Karen looks relieved enough to chat with some of the other wives in the stands.

In the third, Moyer gives up his first run of the spring on an RBI base hit by Eduardo Escobar. With a runner on and two outs, up comes White Sox catcher A. J. Pierzynski, a 6´3˝, 240-pound lefty who struck out all of 33 times last season and has never seen a fastball he didn't want to crush. Moyer starts him with a 72-mile-per-hour changeup that breaks down and in, right over the inside part of the plate. Strike one.

After getting something soft and in, most hitters will look for something hard and outside. Moyer toys with busting him inside again, but decides to mess with Pierzynski's rhythm even more. He throws a 65-mile-per-hour looping curveball that starts out heading for Pierzynski's right hip and quickly drops out of the zone and away from the hitter; Pierzynski lurches for it, swinging well in front *and* well over it. Strike two.

Pierzynski is something of a hothead, with a reputation as

an emotional—some say dirty—player. Now he steps outside of the batter's box, clearly frustrated. This is the part of the game Moyer loves. *Will he? Won't he?* At 0–2, having just seen two slow pitches, Pierzynski is likely looking off-speed again or expecting a waste pitch—something well out of the strike zone in the hope that he'll chase a bad ball.

Moyer doesn't like the phrase "waste pitch," because he considers every pitch to have a purpose. Besides, why give the hitter what he expects, even if it's well outside of the zone? No, having caught Pierzynski off guard by a slow pitch followed by an even slower one, Moyer now has the batter out of sync. Uncomfortable. Better to keep attacking. He comes back with a two-seam fastball at 79 miles per hour—79 following 65 and 72 is really equivalent to a pitch in the 90s—and it freezes Pierzynski, who takes it on the inside black for a called third strike.

Moyer comes off the field to loud applause, and manager Jim Tracy's outstretched hand greets him at the top of the dugout steps. Within minutes, Karen's cell phone rings. "Send Hutton and Mac down," Moyer says, and they're off like base runners given the double steal sign.

After the game, Karen and the kids wait outside the clubhouse. Moyer comes out with a stat sheet, showing him credited with the win. Karen smiles. "It's been a long time since one of those," she says. Three innings, three hits, one run, two strikeouts. And that's having thrown only two cutters; one for a ball and the other, up in the zone, for a base hit.

"Today's a good day," Moyer says, Kati and Yeni both grabbing a leg. Moyer hasn't seen the kids in a couple of weeks, and dinner with the brood awaits. As he leads the pack toward the parking lot, he wants to know something. "How was my velocity?" he asks. Seventy-nine, he's told. He winces, partly because he wants to get a 10-mile-per-hour differential between his fastball and his changeup, instead of the six or seven miles he's now averaging. But the pained facial expression may also be because he's got some discomfort in his groin. Probably nothing, he thinks. *It's all good.*

Jamie Moyer has been in a conversation with his body as long as he can remember. He'd learned to trust it; trust, after all, is the cornerstone of any such intimate relationship. He'd listened to its aches, pains, tweaks and dings, and, most of all, its weariness. When his legs felt like logs, he knew that it was the midseason blahs—and he knew as sure as he knew anything that it was just something to "gut out." He recognized "dead arm," that tranquilized feeling in the dog days when his left arm seemed to have had the life drained from it, as something to slog through. Through it all, Moyer had taken comfort in the knowledge that, as he'd often explain, his body clock knew how to recover just enough to get him to his next start.

Now, just days after his triumph over the White Sox, what he'd thought was a minor tweak of the groin has flared up into full-on pain every time he plants to throw. At first he thought it was something he could once again gut out. He'd come to camp with his own supply of anti-inflammatory pills; knowing how sensitive management would be to having a forty-nine-year-old trying to make the roster—rightfully so—he didn't want to ask the trainers for anything and thereby reinforce any doubts the front office might have about his physical state.

But now the pain hasn't subsided, so Moyer makes his way to the trainer's room. In 2009, his season in Philadelphia ended when he required surgery for a torn groin; the speculation is that this latest episode is the inflammation of some scar tissue from that procedure. The team announces that he'll miss his next start and undergo treatment. He'll get a cortisone shot, which will help quiet things. He also calls Liba, and she e-mails him a series of stretching exercises.

A couple of other pitchers are banged up as well. Pomeranz's next start is postponed due to a strained glute, and Chacin has a blister on his right index finger that limited him to 44 pitches in his last outing. But they're not forty-nine years old. Moyer worries that any malady, no matter how minor, will scare management off from making a commitment to him.

He knows he has no control over that. So he decides to control what he can, to live in the training room and to do Liba's exercises. Day by day, the tightness and soreness begin to dissipate.

Finally, eight days after his win over the White Sox, Moyer is given the go-ahead to try it out and pitch a couple of innings against the Diamondbacks' Triple A squad on a practice field. He gets banged around—four runs on six hits in less than two full innings—so the beat reporters can't figure out why he's positively joyous afterwards.

The groin feels much better, that's why. That is the real test. As for the results, Moyer felt too strong, having not pitched in over a week. When he's not a little fatigued, his ball tends to elevate. By the second inning, he was rediscovering his rhythm and the lower part of the zone, and he punched out the last two batters he faced.

"I think it was a step forward," he says to the press.

Manager Jim Tracy seems to agree. "What I'm looking for over the course of the next couple of weeks is the question, 'How does he bounce back?'" Tracy says. "More important, as we get in a position of stretching him out, how does his body respond from one outing to the next?"

Meantime, the other pitchers vying for a spot in the rotation haven't used Moyer's downtime to pull away. Chatwood has a start in which he records only 14 outs on 61 pitches. Pomeranz comes back from the glute injury and gives up three runs on six hits in four innings against the Angels' Triple A team. Righthander Guillermo Moscoso gives up five runs on seven hits in three innings against the Padres. Moyer is scheduled to start against the Giants on Thursday night, March 23. Karen flies in. A good start will help to ease any fears about his body's ability to recover and likely make him a frontrunner for the rotation. A bad start probably means retirement finally looms.

He sees the text when he wakes up. I've been immersed in Harvey Dorfman research, and I've sent Moyer a Dorfman quote: "To aspire to great achievement is to risk failure." He reads it over and over again. Karen walks into the bedroom; her husband, on the verge of tears, looks up at her.

"What is it?"

He holds out the phone. "It's like I just heard from Harvey," Moyer says wistfully, suddenly reminded of the impact Harvey had, and continues to have, on his life, even though Dorfman is gone.

Later, at the ballpark, Moyer has a very comfortable bullpen session. His mechanics are free and easy, his mind strangely clear and calm. The first batter of the game, Angel Pagan, smokes a sinker to centerfield, where Dexter Fowler, retreating, snares it. It turns out it will be the one and only time a Giant will get solid wood on the ball.

Four days ago, Moyer wondered if the pain in his groin would permit him to return to this spot. And he worried that even if it did, the setback would have spooked Rockies management. Now here he is, easily mowing down the Giants lineup. But that's baseball. And that's Moyer's career. Every time onlookers think he's done—every time *he* wonders if he's done—there seems to be a surprise waiting. Part of the answer to the question "Why does he do it?" has to do with the game's wonderfully unscripted nature. You just never know.

Moyer pitches four perfect innings. Twelve up, twelve down, including four strikeouts. Only twice does he go to three-ball counts. Of 45 pitches, 30 are strikes. The *Denver Post* calls it a "mini-masterpiece." He added the cutter tonight, and, true to Harvey's quote, he was extra aggressive with the changeup.

The media wants to know if his performance stakes his claim to a starting spot. "You'll have to ask the guy down the hall [manager Tracy] about that," he replies.

The pack dutifully goes to Tracy, who is effusive. "As I have said many times this spring, he looks like Jamie Moyer," he says. "It certainly doesn't look like he missed any time last year."

Before meeting Karen outside the clubhouse, Moyer texts me: "I achieved & took the risk tonight. I love these quotes. Keep 'em coming. Ur motivating me even more."

It isn't exactly Moyermania, but the story of his comeback has become national news. After the win over the Giants, *The Today Show* calls. Moyer gets to the ballpark at 5 a.m. so Matt Lauer can interview him via satellite. The *New York Times* comes in and *MLB Tonight* sends a camera crew for a feature.

The White Sox are also back for one more shot at him. Moyer battles through four innings, after lobbying Tracy to send him out for the fourth. He accumulates his highest pitch count of the spring: 92, 53 for strikes. He gives up three runs, striking out four, and keeps his team in the ball game. He is 2–0 with a staff-leading 2.77 ERA through 13 innings.

After the game, Moyer heads back to Fassero's guesthouse. He is stretching out on the floor when the MLB Network feature on him airs. There's footage of him running in the outfield, playing long toss, fielding bunts.

"Is that what I look like?" he mutters to himself, a surprised lilt to his voice. "Holy crap. That guy looks pretty stiff."

Moyer laughs when, on air, MLB Network analyst Mitch Williams, who is two years younger than Moyer but has been out of baseball since 1997, marvels at Moyer's comeback. "I like Mitch," Moyer says. "We have a history." It's a dubious history from Williams's perspective: in 1988, Moyer and Rafael Palmeiro were traded by the Cubs to Texas for Williams, thereby giving up 544 future home runs and 239 future wins from Moyer in exchange for 52 saves and five wins from Williams.

Meantime, the phone won't stop ringing. Rockies PR reminds him of an ESPN radio call-in tomorrow morning, where they'll play audio of his father-in-law's maniacal laugh for him.

Dillon calls to talk over his at-bats at Cal-Irvine. "Just concentrate on hitting the fastball," his father says. "Don't worry about anything but making solid contact with the fastball."

Jill returns her brother's earlier call. Jim and Joan are visiting with Karen in San Diego, and Jim got dehydrated and was taken to the hospital for fluids. "At some point, we're going to have to talk about Mom and Dad coming out and living with us," Moyer says.

As he absentmindedly flicks channels while on the phone, Moyer's eyes widen when he sees that one of his favorite movies is on. When he's done talking to Jill, he turns up the volume. "I must have seen this twelve times," he says.

It's called *Despicable Me*, and it's animated. "Wait till I tell Yeni, Kati, Mac, and Grady I watched this," he says.

It's a safe bet that few other major leaguers are spending this evening talking to a college-aged son about hitting, a sibling about how to handle the aging of their parents, and watching—and loving—an animated children's film on cable.

"I've never been in this position before, Jamie," general manager Dan O'Dowd begins. Moyer has called him to find out where his head is at—if the Rockies aren't going to make him part of the rotation, he wants to be released in time to hook on with another team.

"I've never had to make a decision on a forty-nine-year-old before," O'Dowd says. "This is totally new territory."

"Well, I was forty-nine when you brought me here," Moyer says.

"You've done great, which is why I'm really struggling with this," O'Dowd says. "We're thinking of signing you to a forty-five-day contract, to see how this goes, how your body holds up."

"That wasn't the deal," Moyer says. The deal was a one-year contract for $1.1 million if he makes the team.

They agree to meet in person the next morning. A flurry of phone calls ensues, Moyer to Karen, Moyer to his agent, Jim Bronner. It's going to be a stressful night. Meantime, Tracy is telling the media horde that Moyer in the rotation "feels like the right thing to do," but that the front office was still deliberating over the pitcher's ability to recover every five days. Tracy goes so far as to speculate that Moyer would start the second game of the season, at Houston. That way, he'd be sandwiched between Guthrie and Nicasio in the rotation, two hard throwers and two innings eaters.

The next morning, prepared to ask for his outright release rather than accept a provisional forty-five-day contract, Moyer finds a contrite O'Dowd. "I prayed on this all night," O'Dowd, a spiritual man, says. "You've done everything we've asked. You made this team. It's the right thing to do. If for some reason it doesn't work out, I want you to know that we'll find something for you in the organization."

They shake hands. Moyer is a big leaguer again, though it's something of a bittersweet feeling. O'Dowd means well, but hearing him talk about it not working out is like a dagger, an announcement of the team's lack of confidence in him. It reminds him of when Don Zimmer came out to the mound that time in the '80s. "Get this guy out or you're going back to the minors," he said. Zimmer may have been aiming for tough love, but the message Moyer took from him was, *I'm not on your side.* Now, over two decades later, Moyer has made the team, but he hears a similar—even if unintended—vote of no confidence.

In the clubhouse, Moyer approaches Tracy.

"I want to thank you for this opportunity," he says.

"No need to thank me," Tracy says. "You earned this. This isn't some handout, which is what I'm going to say to the press."

On March 30, Tracy announces that forty-nine-year-old Jamie Moyer has made the team and will start the second game of the season against Houston. It's the twentieth anniversary of Moyer's release from the Chicago Cubs, when the offer to become a pitching coach was made.

Now it's two decades later and Moyer has one more start in the Cactus League, going five innings and giving up one earned run against Seattle. He finishes the spring with a 2.50 ERA in 18 innings. But, in a harbinger of things to come, the Rockies boot two ground balls behind him, leading to two runs and the loss.

Karen makes arrangements to look at rentals in Denver. Jamie Moyer starts thinking about the Astros' lineup.

OCTOBER 2008

CHAPTER TEN

The ego must get out of the body's way.
—Harvey Dorfman

On the day before his first ever World Series start, Jamie Moyer awoke in his penthouse apartment on Philly's posh Washington Square and made his usual trek up Walnut Street to Starbucks. On the street, despite what was being said on the radio call-in shows about his 0–2 record and 13.50 ERA thus far in the postseason, there was nothing but good vibes being sent his way. "We love you, Jamie!" yelled a college-aged girl walking a yellow Lab. "Don't take no crap, Moyer!" the driver of a plumber's van spat out his window, thumbs-up, the audio of one of those radio stations blaring through the window.

On those shows, fans fearful that yet another inevitable Phillies collapse was on deck were already preemptively lining up their scapegoats. "Moyer's great, but he's done," one caller lamented. Another wasn't so diplomatic. "Put a fork in him!" he wailed.

The irony behind all the panic was that, though young Cole Hamels was commonly thought of as the Phils' ace—given the combination of his fastball in the mid-90s with a world-class changeup—Moyer had been the team's most consistent starter all year. He compiled a team-high 16 wins (against only seven losses) and a 3.71 ERA. Not only that, he'd been the Phillies' ace down the stretch, going 9–1 the last three months of the season with a 3.28 ERA, and winning the pennant-clinching game against the Nationals.

But the playoffs thus far hadn't gone nearly as well. In the first round, against wild card Milwaukee, Moyer ran into his kryptonite, something that seems to derail him a couple of times each year and send his ERA skyward: a shrunken strike zone. In those instances, when his precision on the corners goes unrewarded, Moyer finds himself consistently behind in counts, and ultimately has no choice but to throw fastballs over the meat of the plate. Against Milwaukee, home plate umpire Brian Runge consistently squeezed him, seeming to call every close pitch a ball.

Moyer keeps mental notes on the umpires in the same way that he logs his experiences with hitters (though he doesn't like to know who the ump will be until he gets on the mound, lest that information detract from his focus). He knew he had always done well with Runge behind the plate.

Always looking for an edge, Moyer would ride the umps in a good-natured way—it was his way of being friendly *and*, ever cognizant of the mental game, of taking up space in their heads. Runge would give as good as he got. They'd jokingly tell each other to "F off" before games; sometimes, Runge would write "F" and "U" on two baseballs and have the bat boy deliver them to Moyer in the dugout prior to a game. On this night, though, Runge wasn't giving his partner-in-joking any calls—and when Moyer peered at him, as if to say, *What the hell?* the ump removed his mask and made a subtle shoulder-shrugging motion.

Moyer took the gesture to mean that things were out of Runge's control, that he'd been told to tighten the strike zone. Moyer wasn't surprised. Through the years, he'd had umps essentially apologize to him, explaining that they'd been warned or put on probation by the league and were under orders not to expand the plate. Consistently pitching behind in the count, Moyer lasted four innings and took the loss. Then, in the National League Championship Series, the Dodgers teed off on Moyer, chasing him in the second inning.

After that game, a reporter asked manager Charlie Manuel if Moyer was going to get another start. "I think he deserves it," Manuel had said.

Walking back from Starbucks, Moyer's thoughts turned to his only other World Series experience: as a fan, in 1980. His idolization of Carlton culminated in that triumphant 1980 season, which followed so many heartbreaks, so many times the Phillies had come tantalizingly close to winning it all, only to fail.

The day after Tug McGraw struck out Willie Wilson to bring the hometown team its first ever Series win, Moyer and two buddies ditched school for the big city, taking a subway for the first time and joining the throng of crazed fans celebrating the big win at JFK Stadium, where the day's parade would culminate in a series of speeches.

When the team started making its way into the stadium on a procession of flatbed trucks, the loudspeaker blared the Philly Sound song "Ain't No Stopping Us Now" by McFadden and Whitehead, and Moyer was overcome by the emotional outpouring all around him.

Not only had Philly never won before, it had also suffered one of the worst collapses in pro sports history when in 1964 the Phils were up six and one-half games with 12 to play—only to blow the pennant. It was a crushing civic scar, as if the baseball gods had confirmed for a city that lived in New York's shadow that, indeed, it would never be quite good enough.

But now here were McFadden and Whitehead blaring and grown men crying and strangers hugging, hundreds of thousands lining the city streets and packed together in an ancient stadium, united in a common cause. Down on the field, Moyer saw Carlton, famous for his long-standing refusal to speak to the press, smiling and waving to the ecstatic crowd.

Amid all the emotion, Moyer felt the pull of his own World Series dream. *I want this someday*, he thought. And here he was, twenty-eight years later. He'd be facing the upstart Tampa Bay Rays, winners of 97 regular-season games, led by slugger Evan Longoria (or Eva, as the Phillies fans would derisively chant) and speedy centerfielder B. J. Upton. The teams had split the first two games in Tampa; game three just might determine the momentum, and ultimately the outcome, of the Series.

A few hours later, it dawned on Moyer that although the dream was becoming reality, it wasn't exactly as he'd fantasized.

Because he'd never imagined the diarrhea.

The Moyers are nothing if not clan-oriented; Karen's favorite phrase is "the Moyer, the Merrier." So on the eve of Jamie's World Series debut a full eighteen of them dined at the Saloon in South Philly, a dark, wood-paneled Old World Italian restaurant. Talk about baseball karma: the Saloon used to be Steve Carlton's favorite haunt. While the adults drank red wine and dined on tender osso buco, Moyer, his stomach rumbling ominously, nibbled on some bland pasta. "I've got to get home," he told Karen, before leaving the group and walking back to their condo.

Those in attendance suspected he may have been nervous, given that tomorrow would be the realization of a lifelong dream. The pressure was indeed on, but Moyer knew his new-found stomach woes had nothing to do with that. By the time he got undressed and was about to get into bed, the diarrhea started. Then the chills and fever came.

By morning, he'd sweated through his sweats. When he wasn't struggling to get to the bathroom, he lay motionless and weak-limbed. Karen forced him to take a few spoonfuls of soup and a bite of a peanut butter and banana sandwich.

"You better call Charlie and tell him you can't pitch," Karen said at around 11 a.m., referring to manager Charlie Manuel, thinking that the manager might switch him and Blanton in the rotation.

Moyer was stunned. He'd always referred to baseball as his job—and he'd never called in sick. Karen didn't know it, but her expression of doubt was precisely what he needed to hear. After all, when Moyer hears someone say he can't do something, it's like he's been given a gift: now there was a goal, and it was to prove his wife wrong. "That ain't happening," he said. "This is the biggest game of my life." Ever since he first hooked up with Harvey, he'd been practicing problem solving; now here was the mother of all problems. He decided to shower and get back in bed for a couple more hours of sleep. And then he was going to work, where he'd, in his words, "gut it out."

After his nap, Karen tried once more, telling her husband that he might be dehydrated and needed to go to the hospital. He burst out the door without a word, though, and was off into an overcast day with a forecast of rain. It was close to two o'clock, which, even though the game wasn't scheduled to begin until 8:30 p.m., meant he was late. Not by any standard other than his own; the Phillies didn't prescribe a certain time of arrival. No, Moyer had his own timetable for his elaborate set of pregame rituals.

On his way to the ballpark, he mapped out his gutting-through strategy. It was to focus on the minute-by-minute detail of his routine. He remembered Harvey telling him that so many—fans, media, even coaches—erroneously view an athlete's game-day routine as merely the manifestation of superstition. In the same way that athletes repeat physical acts so as to burn motion into their muscle memory—each ground ball scooped or high heater bunted a subtle signal to the body to get used to performing the function *by rote*—Harvey taught him that the same principle applied to the athletic *psyche*. You had to practice focus and being in the present tense so that on game day, you just *are*.

Everything Moyer does on game day is timed and planned to achieve laserlike focus by the time the umpire yells "Play ball." Now here he was, confronting a potential mammoth distraction: a stomach in revolt, a fever, the cold sweats. What to do? Nothing but what he'd done since that Old-Timers' Game experience at Camden Yards in 1993, when the presence of Tom Selleck distracted him from his job. (*Really? Tom Freakin' Selleck?* he'll say now, years later, tragedy plus time amounting to comedy.) When Moyer steps out of his routine, as he did on that day in Baltimore, he feels like something is missing, like he's playing without his glove or without a shoe. He feels incomplete, and it takes him away from the task at hand. When that happens, he consciously returns to his routine, in the same way a Zen Buddhist blots all else out by returning to his own breathing, hoping that all the years of working on his concentration and focus will kick in, like muscle memory.

After scoring some Imodium from the team trainer, Moyer changed into shorts and made his way to the team's hydro room, which is filled with whirlpools and a hot tub. Moyer jogged on the underwater treadmill to get his muscles loose.

Every pitching coach and team doctor will tell you the same thing: for someone who has thrown as many pitches and logged as many innings as Moyer, his ability to recover in time to make his next start is astounding. Many mornings after a start, he says, his left shoulder feels as raw as a piece of meat hanging in a butcher shop. The layperson might take that as a sign to be still, to rest, to heal. Moyer learned early on that the best response to bone-crushing soreness is to get the blood flowing through the stiff spots. He devised a different running program for each day between starts (long-distance the morning after; foul-pole-to-foul-pole sprints on day two), and combined that with lightweight arm exercises to promote healing.

After fracturing his kneecap in Seattle, however, the running led to chronic knee soreness. So he looked for other cardio outlets; with Karen, he became a devotee of spinning. But then he met the HydroWorx 2000 and he was smitten. There was no pounding on his back, hips, knees, or ankle joints. Exiting the tub the morning after the most hellacious of starts, he'd feel the soothing, calming sensation of his body recovering.

Now, emerging from the water, the farthest thing from his mind was his growling stomach. Next came a visit to the weight room, which is always fun for a starting pitcher on game day, because that's where he gets treated like a kid on his birthday; it's considered *his* day, so he gets to select the radio station. Moyer's teammate, big ol' boy Joe Blanton, likes to blare honky-tonk music. Moyer, the game's last baby boomer, opts for classic rock— usually prompting his hip-hop shortstop Jimmy Rollins to mutter something under his breath along the lines of, "Led *who?*"

While younger teammates no doubt cringed to "Stairway to Heaven," Moyer punched at the air, using three-pound dumbbells, working and stretching the serratus and rotator cuff muscles. A good twenty-minute stretch followed.

As he worked out, teammates would come in, chat, wish him well. Moyer is happy to be spoken to on the day of his start, unlike Roy Halladay and Randy Johnson, two of his most successful teammates over the years. "I want to be part of the group, I don't want to be excluded," Moyer explains. "But Roy and Randy do things a little differently, and it works for them. You create who you want to be, and your teammates respect who you are."

Next, at 5 p.m., Moyer changed into his Lycra pitching shorts and "sleeves," the undershirt of his uniform. Because he's beginning to don the clothes he will wear on the mound, the adrenaline starts to pump—just a little. Meantime, he gathered his mental cards from his shaving kit—the concentration grid, the Dorfman-inspired problem-solving tips—and made his way to the same back storage closet as so many times before. Behind its closed door, he studied his cards, literally concentrating on his concentration, making sure to breathe deeply. Earlier, in the HydroWorx 2000 or the weight room, he was getting comfortable, clearing his mind and stretching his limbs. Now it was getting real. By the time he was saying the numbers on his concentration grid aloud (without pointing to them), he was beginning the process of narrowing his focus to the point that when on the mound he won't actually hear 46,000 screaming fans.

By 6:30, Moyer was hearing rumblings in the clubhouse that there would be a delay due to weather. He ignored the chatter, again concentrating on what he could control. So he sat at his locker and reviewed his many notes hand-scrawled throughout the years on every batter in the opposing lineup. Before the Series, the Phils' scouts had distributed their scouting report on the opposition. Moyer read the report, as did catcher Carlos Ruiz. But Moyer always trusted his own notes, and his own experiences, more. So, stack of old lineup cards on his lap, he went back in time, discovering the sequence and location of pitches that had worked for him in the past against the guys he'd need to get out tonight. Then he sought out Ruiz, and the two huddled over the lineup card and compared notes on every hitter.

When Moyer came to Philadelphia from Seattle in August of 2006, Carlos Ruiz was recalled from the minor leagues just two weeks later. They'd been teammates and batterymates ever since. Ruiz arrived in the major leagues speaking broken English and lacking confidence, and has since matured into a .300 hitter and one of the best catchers in the game. Moyer played no small role in the catcher's development, sharing insights and anecdotes with the impressionable Latino in hotel lobbies, dugouts, and luncheonettes for years. Early on in their relationship, he talked to Ruiz about taking charge behind the plate, sharing with him an interaction he'd had with one of his first catchers, Jim Sundberg.

One afternoon in 1986, long before he'd found his zonelike comfort level in his pregame rituals, rookie Jamie Moyer was nervous as hell. He'd be facing Houston's Nolan Ryan on NBC's Game of the Week in a matter of hours. In the trainer's room, Moyer was on the table while a trainer stretched his arm every which way. Sundberg, a veteran, ambled in and, without a word, placed his hand firmly on the young pitcher's chest. "Hey, kid," he said. "You just pitch today. I'll call the game."

Instantly, Moyer felt a wave of relief. Suddenly, his gruff catcher had made him feel not so alone. All he had to do was throw the ball—something he'd been doing his whole life. Sharing this with Ruiz was as if to say, *You have no idea the impact you can have.*

Once, during an intra-squad spring training game, Moyer

found himself facing Sundberg. In the middle of the count, Moyer's catcher called a fastball in. Sundberg saw his usual batterymate shake his head yes, and then no. When the pitch came, Sundberg timed it flawlessly, as if he knew what was coming, and parked it deep in the outfield bleachers.

As he ran around the bases Sundberg laughed at his friend. After the game, he caught up to Moyer. "Look, I knew what was coming," he said.

How? Moyer wanted to know. When Sundberg saw the young pitcher shake his head yes and then no, he knew Moyer was saying yes to the type of pitch, followed by no to its location. He also knew that usually a pitcher doesn't shake off a breaking ball's location. So it was simple deduction: a fastball was on its way. Since he was so familiar with Moyer's fastball—he knew it would be around 84 miles per hour, and that it would probably be low in the zone—he sat back, awaiting his big fat gift.

Leaving the ballpark that day, Moyer realized: *Catchers know all.* The game always takes place in front of them and they don't have the luxury of relaxing and being mentally out of a single play.

So it was that seeking out Ruiz's take on the opposing team's lineup had become a critical part of Moyer's game-day prep. By now in his career, he had become much more in control on the mound. He decided what pitches to throw and when, but he was always mining his catcher for information.

Now, going over the Rays' lineup, Moyer told Ruiz how he'd want to approach certain guys, while peppering his teammate with questions: Has so-and-so changed anything at the plate? Does he shorten up with two strikes?

Rookie power hitter Evan Longoria posed a challenge. "He's one of those guys who can do a lot of damage if I elevate the ball," Moyer told Ruiz, affectionately nicknamed "Chooch" by his teammates and the entire city of Philadelphia, almost all of whom were unaware that the moniker referred to a woman's private parts. "Longoria gets those arms extended and he's tough. But if you make a mistake on the inner part of the plate, he can hurt you, too."

They spent a lot of time discussing outfielder Carl Crawford. Moyer had long said that if he were a general manager, he'd build a team around Crawford because of his versatility. He could change the game in so many ways. "Carl's a down and away guy," Moyer said. "If I don't get it away, he'll pull it. If it's away and not down, he'll hit it to leftfield. And if it's outer third and slightly elevated, he'll kill it."

"You gotta get in on him," Ruiz said.

"Either that or challenge him by making a *good* pitch down and away," Moyer said, meaning make a pitch that led Crawford to *think* he was getting his pitch—only to find out after it was too late that the pitch was just slightly *too* down or just slightly *too* away.

Before they moved on to the next hitter, Moyer added an afterthought. "At some point, Carl may try to bunt," he said.

"Why?"

"Because he's got great speed and he thinks he can beat me down the first base line," Moyer explained. "And he's left-handed. He can drag a bunt down the line and get it past me into that no-man's-land. Let's be sure to watch for that."

"I'll tell Ryan," Ruiz said, referring to first baseman Ryan Howard.

Finally, after numerous rain delays, it was time to get in full uniform and make his way onto the rain-soaked field. Fans were starting to enter the ballpark and the night was already alive and buzzing. Walking to the outfield, Moyer kept his head down, watching puddles of water splash over his cleats with every step. As he had all season, he placed his glove on the warning track and ran sprints in the outfield. In the bullpen, he threw well. The Imodium had quelled his stomach, but the more he threw, the more he broke into a cold sweat, and the more he told himself to ignore it. *This is just another game, just another game, just another game*, he repeated to himself over and over.

By now the fans were in full force, bellowing, waving white rally towels. They'd reached a crescendo when country music star Tim McGraw approached the mound. McGraw, son of the late Phillie legend Tug, who was on the mound when the Phils last won a World Series twenty-eight years earlier, secretly took out a small box and sprinkled his father's ashes precisely where Moyer would be pitching. Though baseball is full of gruff, chaw-chewing men, sentiment abounds. To Moyer, McGraw's moving act was another in a series of emotional connections — his own presence at the 1980 parade, his lifelong fixation on Carlton — that made tonight feel like a night of destiny, diarrhea be damned.

In an uncharacteristic nod to the emotion of the evening, Moyer made a conscious decision to look up on his walk in from the bullpen. It would be the one singular break in his routine. He wanted to take it all in. The stadium he'd pitched in for more than the last two years seemed brighter than it ever had. The noise was deafening. But now, approaching the dugout, as the fans behind first base stood and cheered the old warrior, Moyer looked down, not wanting to risk being taken out of his zone. This game was too important.

As Moyer predicted, Crawford was proving to be Moyer's biggest challenge. In the second inning, the outfielder doubled and stole third, scoring on a groundout. The Phils led 2–1 until sluggers Ryan Howard and Chase Utley gave Moyer a cushion with back-to-back home runs in the sixth.

Actually, pitching in the World Series turned out to be easy; sitting in the dugout, with a burbling stomach and the chills, was the real challenge. On the mound, Moyer was so focused that he forgot his stomach woes, and that he hadn't eaten all day. He didn't hear the fans, so intent was he on the mesmerizing sounds of the game—the hiss of the ball off the bat, the *thwack* of it into a glove—and on his own thoughts, an amalgam of self-pep-talk and strategic thinking. In a career that stood as a testament to the proposition that mind really can overcome matter, Moyer's valiant performance may have qualified as exhibit A.

Leading off the seventh with the Phils up 4–1, Crawford came to bat and made even more of a prophet out of Moyer. Just as the pitcher had predicted in his pregame meeting with Ruiz, Crawford dragged a bunt down the first base line, thinking he could beat the old man to the bag. But Moyer got a good jump off the mound and dove through the air for the ball as it nearly dribbled past him, fielding it and tossing it from his glove in one motion, ending up prone on the wet grass. First baseman Ryan Howard fielded it cleanly, and to all eyes both watching live *and* seeing the replays, Crawford was indisputably out by a fraction of a step. The crowd erupted with a roar, but first base umpire Tom Hallion was shielded by Howard's big body and didn't see the first baseman barehand the toss. He called Crawford safe. Even after the blown call, the fans wouldn't quiet, standing and applauding Moyer's all-out effort.

After giving up a double, Moyer got Gabe Gross to ground out, scoring Crawford. That was it for Moyer, who received a standing ovation on his way to the dugout. Relievers Chad Durbin and Ryan Madson, however, couldn't protect the lead, and by inning's end the game was tied at 4.

It would have been nice to have been the winning pitcher of record, and had it not been for Hallion's blown call, chances are that would have been the case. (To his credit, Hallion said after the game, "We're human beings and sometimes we get them wrong.") But Moyer was uttering his favorite phrase throughout the clubhouse after the game — "It's all good" — because Ruiz delivered the game winner in the ninth and Moyer had done what had seemed vastly improbable earlier in the day: he'd produced a quality start, especially after having been smoked in the National League Championship Series by the Dodgers. As had happened so many other times throughout his career, Moyer had proven something to his doubters. From all those talking heads who'd been clamoring for a change in the pitching rotation after the Dodgers had clobbered him, to even his own wife, who'd earlier thought he should be in a hospital room instead of on a pitching mound, he'd again embodied the sheer power of belief.

Two nights later, Jamie Moyer was a world champion. After reliever Brad Lidge struck out Eric Hinske to end the 2008 baseball season, after the champagne corks popped, after Moyer's dad and his two eldest boys — Dillon and Hutton, both in the clubhouse and in uniform for the game — came charging into the postgame celebration, Moyer embraced the man who had given him the dual gift of baseball and work ethic.

Seventy-seven-year-old Jim Moyer ambled into the clubhouse and his son's embrace. "This makes all those pepper games in our yard worthwhile," Jamie told his dad. Under his arm, Jim clutched the game program — like every other one he'd ever attended, he'd scored the game in real time.

While his teammates donned goggles and giddily doused each other with champagne, Moyer stood in the corner, surveying the scene. He joined in the celebration — shooting some champagne, taking some incoming — but as he watched his teammates, he saw a bunch of young kids celebrating without stopping to wonder just how fleeting this exhilaration would be.

That was as it should be. They were young and invincible, and to them this moment of triumph would now become the norm—for a time, at least. Moyer knew, however, that as moments go, it would need to be documented. Baseball is a game that has alternately broken his heart and sustained his spirits—sometimes at almost the exact same time—and he's learned that he needs tangible proof in front of him to accurately revisit its old emotions.

So, wading through a pack of jumping, screaming, soaked teammates, Moyer gathered his whole family and led them out to the Citizens Bank Park field, where they posed for photos near first base. The ballpark was still packed, the crowd still frenzied, when Moyer, eyeing the mound, got an idea. He grabbed a member of the grounds crew.

"Can I get a shovel or a pick to get the rubber?" he asked, motioning toward the pitching rubber.

"Let me ask my boss." Moments later, the worker returned, shaking his head.

"Major League Baseball wants it," he said.

"Awww, c'mon. Forget that," Moyer said. "*I* want it. I've got your back with the league. Please?"

The worker smiled. "Ah, what the hell," he said, before jogging off. He came back with a pick and shovel and started digging. "That's okay, let me do it," Moyer said, taking over. Now the crowd noticed—and the cheers started to pick up, gradually sweeping the stadium, as more and more fans noticed the spectacle in front of them. Moyer, grunting, head down, just went about his excavation. He started to run out of gas, and the grounds crew stepped in to help. When they'd dug enough and Moyer could wrangle the pitching rubber free, he flung it over his shoulder—it was nearly thirty pounds, owing to the cement-filled interior—and the crowd erupted as he jogged back into the clubhouse to chants of *Jamie! Jamie!* ringing through the air. He'd gotten the ultimate keepsake—something he'd place on the mantel in his bedroom in Bradenton, and in San Diego, after the Moyers would move there in 2011. Upon rising every morning, the first thing he'd look at would be his World Series pitching rubber.

The next day, Philadelphia came to a standstill as some two million fans came out to honor the world champions. The whole Moyer clan was on the float that slowly made its way down Broad Street, the city streets a sea of red Phillies jerseys and caps. On the floor of the flatbed truck, Yeni, just two years old, laid on her back, covered in confetti. Among the throng, one youngster held aloft a sign: "Jamie Moyer, I Skipped School To See YOUR Parade!"

Of the players who spoke to the crowd at Citizens Bank Park, second baseman Chase Utley would make headlines by exclaiming, *"World F'ing Champions!"* But it was Moyer's thoughtful comments that struck the most moving chord. He spoke at the end of the parade, referencing his own local childhood and the day twenty-eight years prior when *he'd* skipped school to attend the last Phillies World Series parade. "Twenty-eight years ago, I sat where you're sitting," he said to thunderous applause. "I was you. And I feel so fortunate to share this with you, my hometown."

As he spoke, and as the crowd cheered—here was one of their own, a fan, with a fan's work ethic—he looked at the man who had given him the game. He couldn't be sure, but it looked like Jim Moyer was tearing up, as were his own sons, Dillon and Hutton. Like so many men in America, sports had long been an emotional proxy for the Moyer men, who rarely told each other

"I love you." They never had to: baseball, which they shared so lovingly through the years, had said it all for them.

If the Seattle teams of the late '90s and early 2000s represented the last gasp of the game's era of camaraderie, then the Phillies of the late 2000s reflected something entirely new in Moyer's experience. While the team wasn't particularly close-knit in the way Seattle, or even Baltimore in the early '90s, had been—there were no group dinners out, for example—it nonetheless bonded over one common ethic: work.

Moyer had never been on a team that was more serious about its preparation. He'd get to the ballpark early to do his work and find twenty others there, doing the same. There was no Kangaroo Court, and there were hardly any clubhouse hijinks (save the comedy stylings of reliever Ryan Madson, who took it upon himself to try and keep things light). It was a deadly serious team of hard-edged competitors.

Despite what Billy Beane and some sabermetricians have held—that a player is what he is, early on—Moyer saw teammates push and prod and, yes, intimidate one another to get better. He saw players improve in all facets, and it all flowed from a group mind-set. "If you didn't work, you didn't fit in," he recalls today.

Home run hitter Ryan Howard was a subpar first baseman who made himself into a good one through countless extra hours of fielding practice. Chase Utley was a suspect second baseman who morphed into one of the game's best, and grew to become perhaps the greatest leader by example Moyer had ever seen. Utley was immensely quiet, but eventually his personality took over the team. He wasn't shy so much as silent in the placid, icy way of an assassin. He'd do whatever it took to win: lean his shoulder in front of 95-mile-per-hour fastballs to get on base, break up double plays either with cleats up or going for the body.

To Moyer, the ultimate gentleman away from the game, winning teams had to have an edge. As Harvey used to say, you have to be a bit of an asshole to succeed. The Phillies were just that—in the best sense of the word.

Unlike in Seattle, it was the players who dictated the team's personality, not necessarily the manager. Charlie Manuel was a good ol' country boy in his sixties, someone who upon his arrival in Philadelphia encountered ridicule for his malapropisms and his butchering of the King's English. But he was also a hitting savant—he'd once compared notes on the science of hitting with Ted Williams—and had a keen sense about people. Behind his amiable, duncelike demeanor, there lay a type of baseball psychologist in his own right. Cholly, as he was called, knew that a manager's first job is to create a culture where every player would, as the common sports parlance went, "run through brick walls" for his manager. He created a grandfatherly persona, someone players didn't want to disappoint. It was a stark contrast to the in-your-face intensity of Piniella, but it was the right demeanor for this group. Cold-blooded types like Chase Utley didn't need anyone in their face; they needed someone to have their back.

Moyer consistently took it upon himself to mentor the young pitchers on staff. Hamels was an early pupil; Moyer recommended Dorfman's *The Mental ABC's of Pitching* to him, which Hamels would page through before starts. When Hamels followed his breakout 2008 season with a lackluster one in 2009, it sent him seeking. He had learned the importance of the mental game by watching Moyer, and he set out on his own path, picking the brain of pitching coach Tom House and ultimately hooking up with a mental coach in his hometown of San Diego,

Jim Brogan, who tutored Hamels in concentration exercises and visualization.

Moyer introduced Kyle Kendrick, a young up-and-down sinkerballer, to Dorfman, recognizing in Kyle something quite familiar: the need to accept who he was. Once, he and Kendrick were seated next to one another in the dugout as the Phillies took on Atlanta. Braves pitcher Tim Hudson, who has won nearly 200 games over 14 seasons, was on the mound.

"You know, you can have the same results as Hudson," Moyer leaned over and said.

Kendrick, at the time not a particular favorite of the hometown Philly less-than-faithful, looked dubious. "You're a sinker/slider pitcher, like him, I don't care what ballpark you pitch in," Moyer explained. "Now look at your walk to strikeout ratio. It's about two to one. What happens if you cut out fifteen or twenty walks a year? That's something you can control."

Kendrick thought for a moment. "Yeah, I walked two guys Friday night and both of them scored," he said.

"A sinker/slider guy has to force contact by working the bottom of the zone, like Hudson does," Moyer said. "Yeah, you're going to get hit, but they're going to have to hit four singles to score a run. Unless you make a mistake and get the ball up in the zone."

Kendrick, who had given up 80 home runs in his first five seasons, nodded. Then, as if on cue, Hudson did just that—hanging a breaking pitch to their teammate John Mayberry Jr., who hit it out of the park. Kendrick smiled. "Nice to see Hudson make the same mistake I make," he said.

After the World Series win in 2008, the Phillies rewarded the forty-six-year-old Moyer with a two-year, $13.5 million deal.

On the call-in shows, there was some scratching of heads: why wouldn't Moyer now retire and go "out on top"? To Moyer, the media call for aging athletes to hang 'em up prematurely always seemed to have more to do with the media mavens making the argument than with anything having to do with baseball. It wasn't lost on him that many of those wondering if, at age forty-six, he ought to retire a World Series champ were themselves aging columnists and talking heads who wouldn't for a moment consider giving up their livelihoods—their passion—until they were damn good and ready. But Jamie wasn't ready yet. He'd just had a stellar season. If the batters weren't telling him to pack it in, why should anyone else?

Besides, everywhere he went in Philly, men and women his own age approached to thank him for getting them to join a gym, or start going for walks, or start watching what they eat. He'd inspired many of his generation-mates, it seemed, and in truth, he felt good about that.

Meantime, the Phils had some front-office change of their own. General manager Pat Gillick, who had brought Moyer to Philly from Seattle, retired, staying on in a consultant's role. The new general manager would either be Gillick's assistant, Ruben Amaro Jr., a former Phil who was young, good-looking, and charismatic, or Mike Arbuckle, the baseball lifer who was responsible for drafting many of the players who had ultimately led the Phillies to the World Series title, including Utley, Howard, and Rollins.

It was a tough call, but the Phillies went with Amaro Jr., with whom Moyer had a long history. Moyer had roomed with Ruben's older brother, David, on the Geneva Cubs in the New York Penn League in the mid-'80s. Ruben was the skinny Stanford freshman who would visit and sleep on their floor.

Just after signing his new deal, the Moyers celebrated like

only the Moyers can. Karen and Jamie gathered the brood, chartered a plane, and, instead of exchanging gifts themselves, spent a week in Guatemala. The plane was packed with presents for the kids at the orphanage where Karen had found Yeni. As a group, they went back to Yeni's old orphanage in a van stuffed with gifts for youngsters who had never experienced a real Christmas, who were living in total squalor, some of whom were stricken with AIDS. Ever aware of his own psychology now, Moyer found it the perfect cap to the year. "I was totally humbled," he recalls. "And just felt so fortunate and proud of my kids. It was out best Christmas ever."

Moyer, now forty-seven, got off to a terrible start in 2009. His command was shaky as was his control: balls that once were down were suddenly up in the zone. In April and May, he was 4–5 with a 6.75 ERA. But as was so often the case, he gradually started to figure it out. After six and two-thirds innings of shutout ball against the Diamondbacks in late July, he'd gone 6–2 with a 4.05 ERA in his next ten starts.

That didn't stop Amaro from signing free agent Pedro Martinez over the All-Star break. Manuel told Moyer he'd be moving to long relief. Martinez had once been a dominant starting pitcher, having won three Cy Young Awards for the Red Sox. But he was now a shadow of his former self, having been injured time and again. Moyer felt it was déjà vu all over again; that he was being judged and held to standards that don't apply to pitchers who throw faster. It was as if he were still always one or two bad starts from demotion—something that didn't exactly match his track record. He said as much in the press, even seeking out a *second* face-to-face with Manuel the day after being told of the decision. In that meeting, Moyer made his case: he was just starting to get back to the form he'd shown the previous year, when he'd led the staff in wins. Manuel didn't say it, but Moyer had the impression the decision wasn't his, that it came from Ruben.

Control what you can control. That's what Harvey would have said. So Moyer—one interview notwithstanding, in which he claimed that upon inking his new deal, Phils management had told him he wouldn't be put in the pen—decided to go to the bullpen and do his job. And do it he did: over nearly the last two months of the season, he recorded a 3.26 ERA and opponents hit just .206 against him, which included six shutout innings and the win in relief of Martinez against the Diamondbacks on August 18 and four innings to beat Atlanta ten days later, also in relief of Martinez.

He still preferred starting, for the security of knowing when he'd be pitching. But Jamie had fun in the bullpen, shooting the breeze with the other guys and the fans. He found that he laughed much more than in the ever-serious dugout.

On September 29, in relief of starter J. A. Happ, Moyer faced four batters and retired them all. The last one flew out to centerfield as Moyer fell off the mound. He had to be helped off the field. He'd torn muscles in his groin and lower abdomen. He was done for the season, and—count 'em—three off-season surgeries awaited.

Moyer watched the Phillies lose to the Yankees in the World Series. Before game four, he caught the ceremonial first pitch from his idol Steve Carlton, who showed Moyer the grip on his slider. Moyer knew that if you're not moving forward, you're standing still, and had already been asking himself, *What can I do this off-season to reinvent myself? What can I do that will set me apart?*

Like Karen, Moyer believes things happen for a reason. He

doesn't do Godspeak, like so many athletes who would have you believe that God was pulling for them when they hit that home run or struck out that batter. But Moyer, thanks to Karen's influence, believed in the mysticism of faith, and there had to be some reason why he and Steve Carlton, moments before that ceremonial first pitch, were limbering up by playing catch and Carlton's ball was breaking all over the place. "Could you show me that?" Moyer asked. What a kick it would be if he were to come back next year reinvented as Lefty.

But first came the three surgeries over the next three months. They treated, respectively: the groin, a postoperative infection, and a torn meniscus in his left knee. Come January, Karen watched as he started throwing his new cutter and began training to get prepared for 2010. "Oh my," she said to herself. "I'm living with freakin' Superman." She made a commitment to herself, even though she was raising eight kids and running a foundation and spin studio: *If he makes it back next season, I'm flying in for all his starts.*

It's the worst feeling in the world. It's like knowing you're dreaming when you're having a bad dream—you're powerless to stop it, which makes it even worse. You want to snap out of it, but you can't get out of your own way. You're embarrassed, ashamed to look your teammates in the eyes. You've let them down.

By 2010, Moyer had built a career on rescuing triumph from seeming failure. But sometimes failure would still happen, and it never got easier. To be shelled as a major league pitcher, to be unable to record a single out, to throw pitch after pitch and see them tagged to all corners of a ballpark, is to feel like you're racing downhill with no stop in sight.

June 11, 2010, at Fenway Park didn't start out ominously.

In fact, Moyer's 2010 was off to a good start. The experiment with Martinez ended the previous season, and Cliff Lee had been (inexplicably) traded to Texas when Amaro signed ace free agent Roy Halladay. That meant the fifth starter job was there for Moyer's taking, and his spring training performance cemented its capture.

Moyer entered the game against the Red Sox with a 6–5 record and a 3.98 ERA. He was coming off a complete-game victory at San Diego and opponents were hitting just .234 against him. The pitcher whose changeup had defined him for so many years was now throwing far less of them; instead, he was using his newfangled cutter to keep hitters off balance.

Before the game, Red Sox manager Terry Francona, who had played for the Cubs in Moyer's 1986 debut, couldn't believe his former teammate was still at it. "The thing that sets him apart is he just never gives in," Francona said.

While Moyer had been impressive in the season's early going, his team hadn't. Ever since Jimmy Rollins went down with a strained calf muscle, the Phillies had played listlessly, winning only five of 17 games and hitting an anemic .216. For the first time since his 2006 arrival in Philly, Moyer sensed a lack of passion in the clubhouse.

On this night, he felt strong in the bullpen. The Red Sox leadoff hitter, Marco Scutaro, had owned Moyer in the past. Rereading his old notes on Scutaro, he decided to ignore them—because nothing had ever worked. Scutaro set the tone for what was to come, never taking the bat from his shoulder. After six pitches—at least two of which appeared to be strikes but were called balls—Scutaro worked a walk.

Dustin Pedroia looked at an 82-mile-per-hour two-seamer on the outside corner for a strike. *They're not swinging.* Next came a 76-mile-per-hour cutter, a jammer. Pedroia pulled it sharply on the ground to Polanco at third, who threw to second for the force but not quickly enough to turn a double play.

Now it had been two batters and two breaks that hadn't gone Moyer's way: the strike calls against Scutaro and the seeming double play ball against Pedroia. Moyer took a deep breath, recognizing his negative thoughts, and tried to collect himself. Pitching from the stretch, he looked down at his hands holding the ball at his belt. Something was not right. He was not comfortable. Victor Martinez looked at three straight pitches; on the last of them, Moyer felt himself fading off to the left of the mound on his follow-through, instead of toward home plate. On a 2–1 pitch, Martinez clubbed an 82-mile-per-hour two-seamer off the Green Monster in left, just above the Granite City Supply advertisement.

As slugger David "Big Papi" Ortiz settled into the batter's box, with his .361 lifetime average against Moyer, Moyer noticed a powwow in the Sox dugout. Francona and four or five others were having an animated discussion on the dugout steps. Were they picking up signs? Where they plotting what was beginning to look like a purposeful strategy of not swinging the bat unless they were ahead in the count?

Indeed, Papi looked at the first three pitches. On 2–2, Moyer threw an 82-mile-per-hour two-seamer inside that froze the power hitter; umpire Paul Emmel clenched his fist as if to call a strike, but held back. Papi then ripped the next pitch, a cutter up in the zone, waist high, off the wall in left. The score was 2–0, Sox.

Adrian Beltre, true to form, took the first two pitches, before turning on a good cutter in tight, fighting it off down the leftfield line for yet another double: 3–0. When good pitches get turned into RBI base hits, it's often a sign that you're about to be in for a long night.

The Beltre hit confirmed that it was happening, that rabbit hole feeling, when nothing works and you start replaying all the "what ifs" in your head: *What if those pitches against Scutaro and that one against Big Papi had been called strikes? What if we'd turned that double play?*

The next hitter, Mike Lowell, looked at the first three pitches—no shocker there—and got ahead in the count 2–1. The defensive move would be for Moyer to give in and serve up a fastball in order to avoid going 3–1. He'd refuse—just like Francona predicted, and was likely telling his players. Moyer threw a cutter low and in for a strike, followed by a 74-mile-per-hour changeup high in the strike zone. Lowell wasted no time, crushing a two-run homer to left.

Moyer walked off the mound to curse himself: *I'm getting what I deserve. Look where that pitch was. Freakin' batting practice.* At times like this, he'd search the stands for something—anything—outside of himself to focus on. He saw a hot dog vendor. His eyes followed the vendor for about fifteen seconds. Out came pitching coach Rich Dubee.

"Awright, let's refocus here," Dubee said. "Concentrate on making quality pitches. Let's get an out."

Billy Hall looked at a called third strike—*They're looking at everything!*—and then a backdoor cutter induced a flyout from the number nine hitter, Darnell McDonald. Nine batters, five runs.

After the Phillies failed to score in their half of the second, the descent continued. The Red Sox stayed patient, the umpire remained stingy, and Moyer's response was to pitch angry, rejecting his own advice. *Don't try and get it all back with one pitch*, he'd tell himself, only to rear back and throw harder—precisely what the Sox hitters were looking for. Back-to-back doubles by Martinez and Big Papi made it 8–0. Moyer hadn't registered a single out in the second inning when Manuel took the ball and mercifully ended the carnage.

Sixty-one pitches. Ultimately nine runs. One inning. In the dugout, Moyer put his red Phillies jacket on and took a long swig of water before staring off into the middle distance. Dubee walked by with an encouraging slap on the knee, Charlie came by with a fatherly tap to the shoulder. Hamels and Blanton sat nearby. Not a word was spoken. They'd all been there and they knew there was nothing to be said.

Early in his career, the days between a performance like the shelling in Boston and Moyer's next start would be interminable. The shame and embarrassment, the feeling of having let down his teammates, the sense that all eyes in the clubhouse were on him because he had *failed* would last until he got the chance to make it right again five days later.

Ever since Seattle, though, Moyer had been able to lick his wounds overnight. As Harvey was fond of pointing out, other people aren't thinking about us quite as much as we think they are. What made Moyer think his teammates weren't as obsessed with their own challenges and failings, instead of fixating on *his*?

That realization helped ease the morning-after transition. The secret to handling such a public flogging is to begin to devise a positive plan forward. So Moyer asked Dubee if he'd noticed anything in his follow-through; he'd felt like he was "landing heavy" toward the first base side, which could explain the heightened elevation of his pitches. Dubee hadn't noticed it, but said they could look at it on tape. But Moyer didn't need to see it—he felt it. Besides, in the past, when he'd gone wrong, that trail-off had been a familiar rut. He'd work on it in his bullpen session.

Meantime, he'd start reviewing his notes on the Yankees. Yes, he was jumping from the frying pan into an all-out grease fire. But instead of shrinking from being on baseball's biggest stage, Moyer welcomed the challenge of pitching in Yankee Stadium. He'd always hated the Yankees. Like Dorfman, he felt Steinbrenner's team was too powerful, too arrogant, and too corporate. Years ago, they were the first team (of course) to have security cameras outside the clubhouse door. Moyer promptly dropped trou and mooned a hallway camera. When he shared the hijinx with Harvey, Dorfman's laughter filled the phone line and morphed into a part laugh, part coughing fit.

Gene Michael, the former Yankees general manager, had once told Moyer that though he was a good pitcher, he didn't have the mental toughness to succeed in New York. The media, the fans, the city itself—they demanded a certain type of personality in their athletes. Like so many other high achievers, Moyer has long fueled off a sense of umbrage, collecting old slights in order to push himself to higher heights. How sweet it always was to win against the Yankees.

In New York, Moyer often took the subway to games. He liked to be a fan, on his way to the ballpark, who just happened to pitch. On June 16, however, he took a cab to the Bronx from Midtown. Karen was flying in, but hadn't landed yet; in Boston, while her husband was getting beat up on the mound, her father had been undergoing prostate surgery. Now Digger was officially cancer-free and Jamie had a chance to erase the memory of the Boston massacre.

Moyer, meantime, wanted to be alone with his thoughts. For the first time since coming to Philly, his team was playing without fire. Was it that Jimmy was out? He didn't know, but he knew the night's big challenge was to somehow recapture the passion that had driven his team to the last two Fall Classics. Last night, they'd lost behind Halladay. In Seattle, and two years ago in Philly, Moyer had been the guy who took it upon himself to put an end to his team's slide. Could he be that guy tonight?

In their pregame meeting, Dubee conceded what Moyer had been feeling. "Look, I don't know why, but we're playing like crap," the pitching coach said. "But you can't let that get to you—"

"Don't you worry," Moyer snapped. "It won't. We're turning this damn thing around tonight." On his walk to the bullpen, he felt the anger coursing through his body: he was tired of the sluggish feeling, both in the dugout and on the field. *if you can control this feeling, this might be good. Let's be fed up. It might give us a little edge.*

When the game began, Moyer could sense the eagerness of the Yankees hitters. Many of them had long feasted on him: his old friend A-Rod averaged .389 with six homers against him; Jeter, .324; Jorge Posada, .333; Mark Teixeira, .306.

It's all good. Use their aggression. Jeter helped matters in the bottom of the first, grounding out to Utley on the first pitch, a fastball. Next up came Nick Swisher, who got ahead in the count 3–1. Rather than give in, Moyer placed an 81-mile-per-hour two-seamer on the outside corner that Swisher hit to centerfield for an out. Teixeira was next and Moyer could see his handwritten notes in his mind's eye: *Get in on him, make him speed up bat speed.* He opened with a fastball for a strike on the inside corner. Then came a cutter, down and in, the same pitch Beltre had golfed for a double in Boston. This time, Teixeira grounded it foul. After a high fastball came three straight inside pitches: two cutters and one two-seamer. Teixeira kept fouling them off, wondering, no doubt, when the deviation would come. That would be the next pitch: a backdoor cutter on the outside corner that froze Teixeira for strike three. Thirteen pitches, three outs.

In the dugout, Moyer uncharacteristically paced up and down, exhorting his teammates. "Let's go, no letup," he yelled. "Let's go, let's go!"

Ryan Howard and Jayson Werth homered for the Phils. Yankees starter A. J. Burnett labored just as hard as Moyer had in his last start, and the Phils built a 6–1 lead after three. And Moyer just continued to coast on the mound, while not letting up on his teammates in the dugout.

His tempo was quicker, his delivery quick and easy. He finished up square to home plate, ready to field a comebacker after each pitch, instead of falling off to the side after each release. The Yankees tried to do what the Sox had done—keep from swinging, wait him out—but Jamie kept the ball on the black and, critically, got those calls from the umpire. And he did the unexpected. The Yankees were sitting on his changeup, but that was the old Jamie Moyer. In this game, of 107 pitches, he would throw only two changeups and two curveballs. The rest were all two-seamers, straight fastballs, and—especially—cutters.

In the sixth, he got Jeter to again weakly offer at a first-pitch two-seamer away, lining out, before setting up Nick Swisher with a succession of cutters in on his hands, inducing foul ball after foul ball. Just when Swisher was looking for another pitch in tight, Moyer dropped yet another cutter on the outside corner for a called third strike. Before a packed crowd that included aging rock duo Paul Simon and Art Garfunkel, Moyer lasted eight innings, giving up just two runs and earning an improbable win.

Afterward, the New York media crowded around him—the same crew Gene Michael years ago said he wouldn't be able to handle. "I don't think that I'm old," he said simply, when asked for the secret to his unlikely success.

He'd continue his winning ways. Five days later, he'd go another eight innings against Cleveland, giving up one earned run. Five days after that, Toronto fell under his spell: seven innings, two runs. His only mistake was a two-run home run by Vernon Wells in the third inning, which made for some dubious history: it was the 506th home run allowed by Moyer, eclipsing the major league record held since 1957 by Phillies ace Robin Roberts.

Moyer didn't look at the new record as anything to be ashamed of; it was simply a testament to his longevity and resiliency. Had there ever been a pitcher better at taking punches? Karen promptly commissioned the printing of T-shirts that listed, on the front, the twenty-five players who had hit 500 or more home runs. On the back, it read, "But There's Only Two Who Have Given Up 500 Home Runs Or More: Robin Roberts (505) And Jamie Moyer (506 And Counting…)."

After the game, Moyer wouldn't be dragged into a discussion about the home run record. "I have a desire to be here, and I won't allow myself to get caught up in all the things that come with it," he said. He'd learned to avoid anything that took his focus away "from playing with these guys in this room." But there was a hint of the internal drive fueling his season thus far: "I really have to stay focused because whether it's the media, the coaching staff, the front office, if I have a bad game, they say, 'Well, you're too old, you're not going to do it.'"

It was the end of June and Moyer was now 9–6—among the National League leaders in wins—with a 4.30 ERA.

Some pundits called him the Phillies' ace—preposterous on a team with Halladay and Hamels—and the *Philadelphia Daily News* asked, is "Cooperstown now on his itinerary?" The story, by Ed Barkowitz, pointed out that he'd passed Hall of Famers Bob Gibson and Bob Feller in career wins. "Moyer is on pace to register the most wins he's had in a season since winning 21 as a spry 40-year-old with the Mariners in 2003," Barkowitz wrote.

But what Barkowitz didn't know was that Moyer was starting to feel a weird sensation in his elbow. He figured it was nothing, just some midseason dead-arm to work through. It felt like there was a rubber band in his arm, pulling and stretching. He took anti-inflammatories, but it continued to bother him through his next three starts, all losses. If anything, his elbow was getting worse.

Then came that fateful July night in St. Louis when it felt like something had snapped. And the taut words to Cholly in the dugout: "I can't throw." And the trip to California to see Dr. Jobe, while Ruben was prematurely telling the media the Moyer career was over. And the trip to the Dominican, to pitch for Moises Alou, only to have the flexor pronator and ulnar collateral ligament come clean off the bone.

Certainly, this was it. The end of a singular, improbable, thrilling career.

Wasn't it?

APRIL 2012

CHAPTER ELEVEN

Control is lost when a player's feelings and
thoughts focus on consequences.
— Harvey Dorfman

Well, that's not how I would've scripted this, Jamie Moyer thinks to himself as his 78-mile-per-hour fastball rockets off the bat of Jordan Schafer, the Houston Astros' centerfielder and leadoff hitter. Moyer doesn't even need to turn and follow the flight of the ball into deep rightfield. He knows. Welcome back to the majors.

First batter, 512th home run allowed, adding to the Moyer long ball record. Somehow appropriate. He gets the ball back from his catcher and walks behind the mound, bending down to squeeze the resin bag. He is wearing the stirrup socks that were all the rage when he was a fresh-faced rookie; now, with ash-colored stubble dotting his chin and wisps of gray peeking out from under his cap, the vision of Moyer on the mound in 2012 has a distinct Movietone feel to it.

The next batter, Brian Bixler, walks on a full count. Uh-oh. Much had been made of Moyer's pursuit of history tonight: he is trying to become the oldest pitcher in history to win a game, and he is doing it against the youngest team in the league. Karen, the kids, Mom, Dad, Jill, and Digger and his fiancée, Linda, are all in the stands. Getting roughed up in the first inning would make for a pretty anticlimactic first start.

But three pitches later, Moyer is walking off the mound relatively unscathed, having once again avoided deep damage. He gets J. D. Martinez to hit into a double play, and then slugger Carlos Lee grounds back to him for an easy out. He then retires the next six Astros he faces, two of them strikeouts.

In the fourth, in what would become a pattern, the Rockies' defense falters. Bixler hits a ground ball to third baseman Chris Nelson, who had been given the starting job at third base because of his superior glove; he promptly throws the ball well wide of first, and second baseman Marco Scutaro, trying to overcompensate for his teammate's gaffe, recovers the ball and mimics the play, throwing wildly to second. "They look like a damned Little League team!" Digger fumes in the stands.

Martinez follows by clubbing a home run to leftfield on a 1–1 changeup that Moyer leaves up in the zone. The inning ends with the Astros ahead 3–0, but not before another Scutaro error.

In the fifth, Houston manufactures a run after Marwin Gonzalez tags Moyer with a double in the left-center gap. Pitcher Lucas Harrell, trying to sacrifice, bunts his way on, and then Bixler legs out an infield grounder to Tulowitzki at short. Meantime, the Rockies can't touch Harrell, who would stymie them over seven innings. Moyer, lifted for a pinch hitter with a line of five innings, five hits, and three earned runs, takes the loss.

But he felt strong and had pitched competitively. After the game, manager Jim Tracy offers a ringing endorsement. "We're going ahead with Jamie," he says. "He gave us a competitive effort. Hopefully next time we'll get him some run support."

After he talks to the media and showers, Moyer emerges from the visiting team's clubhouse and his kids—the little ones—come running to him. They all pile into the Moyer-mobile, a van Karen rented to transport the crew from the hotel to the ballpark all weekend.

It's never quiet in the van—Hutton wants to talk about the game, Grady and Mac are bickering like an old married couple, and Duffy is making sure that Yeni and Kati don't squirm out of their car seats. Nonetheless, Moyer has a moment of reflection. "It felt right to be out there," he says. "Comfortable. Like it's where I'm supposed to be." History, though, would have to wait.

He hasn't even broken the record yet, but already Jamie Moyer is tired of answering questions about his age. It seems like every possible cliché has been exhausted. *How many ways can you find to write that someone is old?*

Behind the superficial story of Moyer's quest, though, *is* a fascinating one—but it's not solely about Moyer. It's more about the ghost that he's chasing.

On September 13, 1932, at forty-nine years and seventy days old, Jack Quinn pitched five innings and beat the St. Louis Cardinals, making him 3–6 with a 3.16 ERA and the oldest pitcher in history to win a game. Quinn was the last of the spitballers; when the trick pitch was banned in 1920, he and a handful of other pitchers were grandfathered in and allowed to keep throwing it.

To the Moyers, who would often comment on the role the mystical hand of fate has played in their unlikely journey, that Moyer was chasing Quinn had to be more than mere coincidence. Though salient facts about Quinn are still shrouded in mystery, like his real age and ethnicity, what is known is that he was the Jamie Moyer of his time.

Like Moyer, Quinn had played for eight teams. Like Moyer, he flummoxed batters with deft touch, movement, and trickery. Like Moyer, Quinn hailed from working-class Pennsylvania, having been born in Hazelton, just seventy miles from Moyer's Souderton.

Most of all, like Moyer, Quinn succeeded early because of physical gifts, and later thanks to mental ones. His career was launched, in storybook fashion, while he was watching a semipro game. A foul ball came his way in the stands and he threw it back to the catcher, the ball hitting squarely in the catcher's glove with a thud. The manager signed him to a contract on the spot, or so the story goes.

But, like Moyer, Quinn learned that early success offered no guarantee for the future, and that how he approached the game could be the tool that would set him apart from other pitchers.

"Nothing bothers me," Quinn once said. "Why should it? The undertaker will get us all soon enough. There's no need to meet him more than halfway. A lot of pitchers worry themselves out of the game. They cut their span of successful work by whole seasons. What a foolish thing to do! Pitching, with me, is a serious profession. I realize its importance and I like to pitch. Above all, I want to feel I can do good work."

Sound familiar? When he hears Quinn's long-ago quote, Moyer's eyes widen. "That's pretty cool," he says. Only the San Francisco Giants stand in the way of Moyer's rendezvous with Mr. Quinn and the record book.

As he takes his warm-up pitches in the top of the sixth inning, Moyer is reminded of something he felt just a few hours earlier: winded. It was his first experience with the thin Colorado air. Prior to game time, he had placed his glove on the warning track and proceeded to do his customary ten wind sprints. Only this time, afterward, he couldn't catch his breath. Even in the bullpen, minutes later, he was emitting small gasps, trying to get his equilibrium back.

Now it is 93 pitches later and he is starting to tire. He has kept the Giants off balance all night. The Rockies trail 2–0, but neither run came by way of hard-hit balls. One came with two outs in the fourth, a soft, seeing-eye grounder up the middle by Melky Cabrera. The other was a third inning pop fly to short center that dropped in for a single.

Otherwise, Moyer had battled Giants starter Madison Bumgarner in a pitching duel that—here's that age thing again—had the press box buzzing, given that the difference between the starters was the third largest since 1900: twenty-six years, 256 days.

On a 1–1 fastball to open the sixth, Ryan Theriot hits a routine fly ball to centerfielder Dexter Fowler, so routine that Moyer doesn't even follow its path. He's on to the next task at hand. Moyer has his back turned to the play when he hears the collective groan rise up from the crowd. He looks up to see Fowler chasing the ball, which had bounded clean out of his glove—the type of error you rarely see a major league outfielder commit.

Fowler, like so many of the game's new breed, had sought to make a one-handed catch of the ball. Through the years, still unable to shed Jim Moyer's teachings, Moyer had taken to calling out, "Two hands!" on routine pop-ups and fly balls. His teammates would rib him; didn't he know they were professionals? If only he'd thought to yell out his dad's catchphrase tonight.

Now, with Theriot on second, Moyer rests his hands on his knees. He knows he's starting to tire and he knows that getting out of the inning was just made more difficult by Fowler's miscue. This is his eleventh inning so far this season and his team has scored zero runs and just committed its fifth error behind him, but he doesn't think of that. He thinks of Brandon Crawford, whom he fools with a 67-mile-per-hour curveball for a weak ground ball back to the mound. He follows that with a strikeout of Bumgarner.

With a 2–2 count on Angel Pagan, Moyer is one pitch away from getting out of the sixth and erasing Fowler's mistake. But this is why baseball can be so tantalizingly heartbreaking. He's now thrown 110 pitches. A two-seamer gets too much of the plate. Pagan lines it to leftfield for an RBI. Cabrera follows with a double to right, the RBI Moyer would later be reminded of when it comes to light that Cabrera has tested positive for testosterone. Moyer's night is over. Five and two-thirds innings, four runs, only two earned.

After the game, Tracy fixates on the errors. "Jamie did a tremendous job," he says. "Unfortunately, we had a bad miss in the sixth inning that would have been a clean inning. Cost us two runs and ends up being the difference in the game....Asking Jamie Moyer to get four outs in an inning, or any of our starting pitching, it's going to cost you. It always does."

In the clubhouse, Fowler, an always smiling, easygoing presence, tentatively walks up to Moyer. Moyer knows stuff happens. After all, how many times had he given up walk-off homers, after all? The question is what you do with it. Does failure make you tougher, meaner, and more determined?

"I'm really sorry," Fowler says. "You pitched a great game—"

Moyer cuts him off. "Forget it," he says. "You'll catch the next one."

There are many reasons why Jamie Moyer has carried on a lifetime love affair with baseball, but the game's essential mystery may be chief among them. For over forty years, this most cerebral man has tried to master the game—sometimes succeeding—only to find more unanswerable questions following every answer. "It's unbelievable how much you don't know about the game you've been playing all your life," Mickey Mantle wrote in *The Quality of Courage*. For Moyer, baseball was like a lifelong puzzle that you could come close to finishing, but never quite.

In baseball, Moyer knows, there are answers he'll never know—no matter how hard sabermetricians and coaches and talking heads look for clues. Why does the Rockies' defense, in the words of *Denver Post* beat writer Troy Renck, seem "spooked" playing behind Moyer, committing five errors in his 11 innings? Why has normally sure-handed shortstop Troy Tulowitzki suddenly turned into an error machine?

Then there are the game's maddening matchups. Why did Moyer for so many years own the Yankees' Scott Brosius? When Brosius was at bat, Moyer had the feeling he could do anything he wanted. He could jam him inside at will, and when he needed to get him out, he'd throw soft away and watch Brosius slog his way back to the dugout. And why, in turn, did Brosius's teammate, Bernie Williams, drive every pitch Moyer threw at him off the fat part of the bat, no matter its speed or location?

Sometimes the answers are plain to see. Barry Bonds hit all five of his career homers off Moyer by 1991. Once Moyer started pitching Bonds inside, he let each at-bat play off against Bonds's jam point. He'd establish the jam point and attack it, pitch after pitch, making Bonds a tad bit slower in getting his arms fully extended once Moyer came back with something across the plate.

But often the reasons behind what happened on the field were more elusive. No matter what he tried against Manny

Ramirez or Carlos Delgado—the players who had hit the most home runs off him with ten and eight respectively—it didn't seem to work: they had his number. He'd prepare as usual—going over the notes from their past battles, searching for a pattern that held the key to success. He'd pay attention to each at-bat, to what their body language was saying to him. But they'd still get their cuts. They just saw the ball out of his hand better than most. Sometimes you just had to throw the ball and hope your defense could make a play behind you.

Moyer was reminded of just how often the laws of mystery applied to baseball when he was preparing for his April 17 start against San Diego, in what would be his third attempt to overtake Jack Quinn. He noticed that Mark Kotsay would be in leftfield and batting second.

In their pregame meeting, Moyer told catcher Wilin Rosario to not even bother discussing Kotsay. "Let's throw out how I've always approached him," he said, "'cause nothing's ever worked."

Kotsay was 19 for 33 lifetime against Moyer, a .576 average. The two hadn't faced each other since 2006, when Kotsay was in Oakland and Moyer Seattle. But they'd seen each other through the years—Karen is friendly with Mark's wife, also named Jamie—and when they'd all get together, Moyer would never hesitate to joke about Kotsay's success against him; maybe if he got him *thinking* about it, the magic would wear off.

But on this night, it didn't appear to be happening anytime soon. In the first inning against the 3–9 Padres, Kotsay singled to right on a 2–1 two-seamer that stayed low in the zone. Credit to Kotsay: he just went down and got it. He was shortly thereafter erased on the base paths, as Moyer cruised through the first two innings.

Now, in the third, Moyer decides he's got to do something— anything—to disrupt Kotsay's mental rhythm against him. His nemesis comes up with a man on first and one out. Moyer looks in for the sign from Rosario, but steps off the rubber.

"Hey!" he calls out to Kotsay. "Today's tax day. You declaring me on your taxes?"

Kotsay throws his head back in laughter, and even umpire Joe West chuckles. Moyer has again broken down the fourth wall, much like he did years ago with Justice and—as depicted in *Moneyball*—with Hatteberg, asking both batters to name their pitch. As Harvey used to say, "Self-consciousness will screw you up." By speaking directly to the batter, Moyer hopes to jolt awake Kotsay's sense of self-consciousness, by imposing his voice and presence into the comfortable zone Kotsay has established against him.

After two foul balls on cutters down and away, Moyer throws a two-seamer below the strike zone. Kotsay takes the bait and chops down on it, a routine grounder to Scutaro at second, who promptly turns the double play. Walking off the mound, Moyer throws his hands into the air in mock celebration—he's gotten him out!—and Kotsay laughs his way back to the Padres dugout.

In the bottom of the third, as if to make up for his miscue in Moyer's last start, Fowler crushes a two-run home run to right off Padres starter Anthony Bass, the first runs the Rockies have scored for Moyer all season. They add one more in the fourth on an RBI double by Rosario.

Meantime, Moyer has found his groove. After getting Kotsay to ground into the double play in the third, he retires seven of the next eight hitters—until Kotsay (of course) beats out an infield single in the sixth. But a low changeup at 73 miles per hour results in an inning-ending groundout by Chase Headley.

In the seventh, trouble. Moyer walks Jesus Guzman on four pitches. "That's my responsibility there," he'll say later. "There's no excuse for that."

After Nick Hundley flies out, Chris Denorfia hits a bloop single. *They're still off balance and not getting good wood on the ball*, Moyer tells himself. But then back-to-back Gold Glove winner Tulowitzki boots yet another easy ball, scoring Guzman. It's Tulowitzki's sixth error of the season, which is all of eleven games old. After the game, he'll have tears in his eyes and manager Tracy will give him the following night off to collect himself. Somewhere, Harvey is smiling at this latest example of just how much mind matters, for good or ill.

In the stands, Karen Moyer's phone lights up. It's an apoplectic Digger, watching via satellite in Indiana. "This Little League team is blowing it for him *again*!" he shouts.

After a sacrifice fly by Jason Bartlett to make the score 3–2, Moyer avoids further damage when pinch hitter Jeremy Hermida grounds out to Scutaro. Rockies fans stand en masse when Moyer walks off the field after seven, leaving with the lead, his fastest pitch having topped out at all of 79 miles per hour.

Now it's up to the bullpen. Karen is still fielding calls from Digger while watching nervously. Flamethrower Rex Brothers hurls a scoreless eighth for Colorado and then the Rockies' bats come alive in the bottom of the inning, with Michael Cuddyer scoring Tulowitzki and Rosario adding a sacrifice fly. The Rockies have a 5–2 cushion.

As the ninth unfolds, Karen is on her feet, cheering, and the TV cameras follow her every move between pitches. "No one knows how hard he's worked for this," she says, still nervous. Reliever Rafael Betancourt gives up a run, but with two down, Yonder Alonso swings and misses for strike three and Karen and Jill and the kids catapult out of their seats. The scoreboard screen blares the fact that Moyer—at forty-nine years, 150 days—is now the oldest pitcher ever to win a major league game and the fans are on their feet, cheering and chanting for the old man.

In the clubhouse, Rockies' PR man Jay Alves tells Moyer the Hall of Fame has called—would he donate his cap and glove? Moyer smiles. "The cap is no problem," he says. But asking a ballplayer to part with his glove—that could be heresy. Moyer doesn't use just any glove; his is oversized, the better to disguise his pitches. But he relents: "I'll give them the glove, but not tonight," he says. "It'll take me a couple of weeks to break in a new one."

When the glove does make it to Cooperstown, it will join a ball from 1929 signed by Jack Quinn, then a forty-six-year-old pitcher for the world champion Philadelphia Athletics. But before that can happen, the press is waiting. After Tracy declares the evening "a historic night for one tremendous human being," Moyer is asked for the secret to his longevity. "I don't have any secrets," he says. "I try to work hard. I try to dedicate myself to what I'm doing. Be responsible for what I'm doing. Be accountable for who I am and what I do and what I bring to the ballpark. And I try to have some fun with it."

He's asked about Quinn, whom he admits he'd never heard of until this chase began. "I kind of wish I was a baseball historian, and I am a little embarrassed that I don't know more about it," he says. "To have my name mentioned with the greats of the past is special." Upon hearing this, the Hall of Fame announces that it is inviting Moyer to be part of its ten-week internship program, in which students from across the country trek to Cooperstown to study the game. "Maybe in the off-season," Moyer jokes.

While he's holding court in the postgame interview room, Moyer can feel his phone vibrating in his pocket. There are hundreds of congratulatory texts coming in. "Congrats old man," writes Roy Halladay. "Pretty special accomplishment and I'm sure a special night! Keep it going, look forward to seeing you soon."

Raul Ibanez, his teammate in both Seattle and Philly: "Congratulations! You continue to be an inspiration to everyone, especially me. I am proud and honored to know you and be able to call you my friend. You are and always will be the man."

Unnoticed in all the hype surrounding Moyer's record-breaking win are a couple of equally stunning facts. The victory, his 268th, moves him into a tie for thirty-fourth on the all-time list with Jim Palmer. And though his record is 1–2, his 2.55 ERA leads his team.

But once the writers have gone upstairs to file their stories, Moyer doesn't have time to think about all that. It's time to party. It is, after all, Kati's sixth birthday, so the whole crew heads back to the airy house the Moyers are renting in Denver's Cherry Creek neighborhood for ice cream and cake. Kati blows out her candles and then the Moyer kids watch *SportsCenter*, the lead story of which is their father's win for the ages.

"Thanks for giving me an ending to the book," I say, after the little ones have gone to bed.

"What do you mean, an ending?" Moyer asks.

"Well, I figure making history like this, it's pretty climactic," I explain.

Moyer shakes his head. "I don't know," he says with a wry smile. "I plan on winning a lot more games."

By the end of April, despite the defensive breakdowns and inconsistent hitting, the Rockies are flirting with .500 and Moyer has been the team's best pitcher. He follows his record-setting win over the Padres with a six-inning no-decision against the Pirates, in which he allows just one earned run. That is followed by a five inning no-decision against the Mets, in which he is hit harder than in his previous starts, but he works out of trouble time and again and keeps his team in the game.

Meantime, some in the Denver media start referring to Moyer as the team's ace—as much a commentary on the Rockies' sub-par starting pitching as on Moyer's surprising results. The saber-metricians weigh in, seeming to second the notion. Rob Neyer, who apprenticed under Bill James, writes, "I didn't think he could still pitch. Not well enough, anyway. But yes, he (arguably) *has* been the Rockies' best starting pitcher this season."

Over at FanGraphs.com, Bradley Woodrum writes, "Not only has the near-half-century man earned a spot on the Rockies rotation, he is pitching like their ace." Woodrum points out that Moyer's ERA is beating both his FIP and SIERA (skill-interactive earned run average) numbers—the two stats that take fielding and luck out of the pitcher performance equation by focusing on those things a pitcher controls: strikeout, walk, ground-ball, and fly-ball rates, for example. "The last time Moyer had an ERA above his FIP, people could still greet their family at the airport gate," writes Woodrum. "So whether it's good fielding on his part or just some other-worldly, quasi-voodoo trick, Moyer beats his FIP, his xFIP, and his SIERA. He beats them so consistently, in fact, that we can probably estimate his ERA this year by just subtracting his standard margin from the more stable predictors like SIERA. In other words, if we subtract 0.40 from his 4.56 SIERA, we get a 4.16 ERA, which absolutely boggles the soul and mind when we consider not only Moyer's age, but his role as a starter (no one his age has ever been an MLB starter), and his home park."

With all this talk of his astounding month—Moyer ends April with a record of 1–2 with a 3.14 ERA—there is one person un-convinced of the hype: Jamie Moyer himself. He appreciates statistics like FIP and SIERA because they account for some of the variables that are not in his control, but in general he subscribes to what Harvey used to say about baseball's overreliance on complicated formulas: statistics can be used "in the same manner a drunken man uses lampposts: for support, rather than illumination."

Even as the sabermetricians marvel at the numbers he is putting up, Moyer senses that something is not quite right. There is the small matter of his groin, which has never fully recovered since spring training. It doesn't affect him on the mound, but it is an ongoing, nagging irritant. There is the bigger matter of his velocity, or lack thereof. His fastball is averaging just shy of 77 miles per hour, four miles slower than in 2010 and six miles slower than in 2002. The combination of pinpoint location at alternating speeds is Moyer's whole game. If the speed differential between his fastball and changeup is now going to be five—instead of ten—miles per hour, it means there is less margin for error in terms of his location.

And that, so far, is the biggest trouble spot. Even when struggling early in his career, Moyer had always been able to hit his spots with stunning repeatability, as Dom Johnson would say. He still has better control and command than most, but now when he misses with a pitch, he misses bigger than usual. There are times when a pitch called for low and inside ends up high and out.

Moyer knows that one of the last things to return after Tommy John surgery is full command. But he feels this isn't a physical issue so much as a mechanical one. It doesn't feel like he has yet consistently found his arm slot, that same release point for every pitch, over and over again. While he works on finding it in his bullpen sessions, he wonders how long he will have to find it. Clearly, this Rockies team, with its horrid defense, irregular hitting, and batting-practice pitching, is not going to compete for anything this season. The question is—how long will they stick with a forty-nine-year-old starter?

In early May, the Atlanta Braves come to Coors Field, and Moyer is seeming to continue his early-season mastery. Moyer cruises through five with an 8–3 lead.

But trouble awaits in the sixth. Atlanta's Matt Diaz and Jason Heyward crush back-to-back home runs off Moyer, and when Tyler Pastornicky follows with a single to right, Tracy slowly walks to the mound and pulls his starter. Moyer leaves with an 8–5 lead, but reliever Esmil Rogers can't hold it. Moyer gets another no-decision and the Rockies lose, 13–9.

Five nights later, Moyer is in Los Angeles, where the lineup contains stark reminders of his longevity. After all, he faced Dodgers manager Don Mattingly two decades ago, not to mention the fathers of current Dodgers Tony Gwynn Jr. and Scott Van Slyke.

Through three innings, Moyer has given up two hits and one run on a Mark Ellis homer. He seems to have better stuff tonight—which may be a function of venue. At Coors Field, he's finding, his two-seamer doesn't sink and his cutter doesn't move quite as much as on the road. Tonight he gets ahead of five of the first seven hitters he faces.

Sitting behind home plate is super-agent Scott Boras, Harvey's old friend and boss. "Remarkable, just remarkable," Boras comments, watching Moyer. "I used to tell Harvey, when Jamie was representing himself, to tell him I could make him a lot more money. He should have done a lot better than he did through the years." (Of course, Harvey never said anything to Jamie. "He wouldn't," Moyer says. "Harvey would have never put business into our relationship.")

Moyer retires both Ellis and Matt Kemp to open the fourth inning. Andre Ethier hits a two-out double to right center, bringing up Bobby Abreu. Moyer starts the veteran lefty with two perfect cutters on the outside corner: 0–2. A fastball follows, high and tight. That sets up another cutter, again on the outside corner. But home plate umpire Ed Rapuano doesn't ring up the batter. Moyer comes back with the same pitch—again, he doesn't get the call. Now, with the count full, he has a decision: in tight or stay away? He opts to stay away—if Abreu takes again, in a battle between veterans, he's bound to get the *third* border-line call—but Abreu is sitting on the location. He sticks his bat out for an RBI single the opposite way, over Tulowitzki's out-stretched glove. After Juan Uribe flies out to end the inning, Moyer berates himself on the walk back to the dugout for letting Abreu outthink him. *A good hitting veteran like Abreu is going to make an adjustment if all you do is stay away*, he thinks. *Why not keep him honest?*

In the fifth, trailing 2–0, Moyer gives up three runs, all with two outs, the big blow a two-run double by Ellis. Moyer is done after five, having struck out seven Dodgers but giving up five runs. The loss drops his record to 1–3 and raises his ERA to 4.66.

Still, Moyer senses some progress has been made. His arm slot felt better, which might also explain the better movement on the ball, as evidenced by the high number of strikeouts. "But again it was the flippin' fifth inning," he says two mornings later in a San Francisco diner. (On the street, a passerby does a dou-ble take and mutters, "I love you, Jamie!" Moyer thanks him before observing, "You gotta love San Francisco.")

On the plane from Los Angeles, Moyer listened to the book-on-tape version of Dorfman's *The Mental ABC's of Pitching*. Given his troubles in the fifth inning of late, he listened to the chapter entitled "The Big Inning." Dorfman captures the sinking feeling of helplessness a pitcher gets when everything starts to slide downhill. "The first order of business for 'stopping the big inning' is for the pitcher to stop himself," Dorfman writes. "To gather himself—get off the mound, collect his thoughts, recognize the situation and have a plan before toeing the rubber again.... Pitchers do not 'stop the bleeding' if they do not stop themselves. The tendency of pitchers in trouble is to speed up. They want to get out of the inning quickly, to get off the mound, to get into the dugout—now! The greater a pitcher's sense of urgency, the more he rushes his mind and muscles. Self-control leaves him. The inning 'wins'; the pitcher loses.... We get outs by paying attention to the task in front of us, not the runners behind us."

Moyer asked twenty-four-year-old pitcher Alex White to join him in listening to the Dorfman chapter. White faced the Dodgers the night after Moyer and, like him, was knocked out of the game in the fifth inning. The two dissected White's thinking on the mound.

"I was kind of pitching around Tony Gwynn," White said.

"Why pitch around Gwynn? He's the leadoff hitter. He's not going to hurt you with a home run, but he might hurt you with his legs. If you walk him, there's no defense for a walk."

"I thought I could get Ellis out," White said. "I thought I could get a double-play ball."

"See, to me, you didn't give yourself enough credit and you gave the hitter too much credit," Moyer said. "Instead of letting the situation dictate to you—'Oh my gosh, I gotta do this, I gotta do that, I gotta get that double play ball'—what Harvey is saying is *you* dictate to the situation. Take a step back and analyze what's going on."

The two talked pitching into the night. White might just as well have been speaking for Moyer when he observed that there always seems to be one moment in every game that will determine how your outing is going to go. It's the tipping point: get past it, and you're likely to cruise on your way to a good night. If, for example, Moyer had gotten that called third strike against Abreu in the fourth against the Dodgers, he might have had a vastly different result.

Five nights later, back in Colorado, Moyer notches his second win of the young season. He goes six and a third innings, giving up just one run in a 6–1 win. But it's not his pitching that makes headlines. In the fourth, leading 3–0, Moyer bats with two outs and runners on second and third against twenty-two-year-old lefty Patrick Corbin. He squibs a 2–2 fastball off the end of his bat on the ground between Corbin and first baseman Paul Goldschmidt. Goldschmidt fields the ball and lunges for the hustling Moyer—who would later call his sojourn down the first base line a "slow crawl"—to no avail. Fowler, on second, never hesitates; the infield hit drives in two runs and Moyer has set a new record: the oldest player ever to drive in a run.

Moyer's influence on his teammates was borne out by Fowler's hustle on the play. "I was shocked that Moyer beat it out," Fowler would say after the game. "The guy was hustling.... He's a bulldog. The guy never quits."

The Rockies are 15–21, and Moyer is now 2–3 and his ERA 4.20, still tops among his team's starters.

They say that no matter how experienced the fighter, the knockout in a boxing match comes as a sudden, shocking surprise. Even if you see it and you're bracing for that ultimate punch, you never fully expect the end to come when it does.

Jamie Moyer is more pugilistic than most major league pitchers, having taken more than his share of punches through the years, always to rise again. After the Arizona win, right when he's thinking he may have turned some kind of corner, he feels the sting of a powerful one-two combination.

First comes an outing in Miami, where Giancarlo Stanton hits a mammoth grand slam against him in the fourth inning, after Moyer had carried a 4–0 lead through three. He ends up giving up six runs and taking the loss. Five days later, in Cincinnati, as at Miami, every pitch seems to be up in the zone. The Reds tee off, crushing four home runs in his five innings. The two losses are part of an epic Colorado slide. After beating Arizona, the Rockies win only two of their next ten games.

Moyer has a feeling about what's coming. It's only ten days since the encouraging signs in Los Angeles and at home against Arizona, but in the high-stakes realm of professional baseball, whole fates can be determined in such a short time span. Particularly if you're a forty-nine-year-old pitcher on a bad team that shows no signs of getting better.

When Moyer is called into general manager Dan O'Dowd's office, Jim Tracy is there, choked up. They say the most complimentary things about his work ethic, his class, his effort. But they're a bad team that won't contend and they have young arms to develop. Moyer thanks them from the bottom of his heart for the opportunity.

He cleans out his locker while Tracy makes the announcement. "He was up against the odds of late," the manager says. "There is no difference in the man, there's no difference in his will to compete. There is a difference in that the 82- or 83-mile-per-hour that he had as a fastball had started to come back and get closer to where some of his off-speed pitches were. There's very little variance between his pitches."

When Moyer takes the podium, he's smiling. He thanks O'Dowd, says that Tracy "stuck his neck out for me," and—as

Harvey would have had him do—he takes responsibility. "Unfortunately, I didn't hold up my end of the bargain," he says. "That's what happens in this business."

Ever the glass-half-full type, Moyer drinks a beer on his way to the airport and focuses on the positive. "I get to sleep in my own bed tonight," he says. "And I get to go to Hutton's high school graduation. That'll be pretty cool." After that, Hutton's high school—Cathedral Catholic in suburban San Diego—will play in a playoff game that, were he still employed, Jamie would have kept tabs on via text messages from Karen. Instead, he'll be able to see his second-born play playoff baseball.

Within minutes, many of the stories that start to move on the wire include the words "Career Likely Over" in their headlines. Of course, that's what they wrote when the Rangers released him in 1990. That's what the smart money thought when Joe Torre sent him packing in 1991. That's what even his closest friends and relatives thought when the Cubs cut him out of spring training in 1992. That's what the Seattle media assumed when he was traded to Philly in 2006 for two no-name minor leaguers. That's what Ruben Amaro Jr. said when he blew out the elbow in 2010. But surely, now that he had made history, and now that his comeback *was* history, surely this would be it. Jamie Moyer would finally be a former professional baseball player. Right?

As he approaches the airport, one other positive of this latest roundhouse suddenly dawns on him. "This could give me some time to get with Dom, have a few bullpens, and work on some things," he says.

JUNE 2012

CHAPTER TWELVE

> The player who can retain his joy for baseball
> is the one who has not let others' needs in-
> trude upon his own.
>
> —Harvey Dorfman

On Tuesday, June 8, at 12:13 p.m., Jamie Moyer texts a friend: "In Atlanta, should I continue to Buffalo or go on to Grand Cayman?" He answers himself thirty-three minutes later: "Decided on boarding to Buffalo. I'm in my seat."

He's joking, but the ambivalence is real. It's been nearly two weeks since the baseball know-it-alls yet again pronounced his career DOA, two weeks in which he'd carried on an internal wrestling match: *Should I pull this plug?* Yet here he is, boarding that connecting flight for Buffalo, where he'll pitch for the Norfolk Tides, the Baltimore Orioles' Triple A team.

Back in Rancho Sante Fe after his release by the Rockies, Moyer had once again comfortably slid into his Mr. Mom role: golfing with Mac, picking up Grady at gymnastics and Duffy at soccer, helping Kati and Yeni with their Kumon. Meantime, the Orioles called, who were surprisingly in first place in the AL East and looking to add a pitcher to eat some innings in anticipation of the Yankees making one of their inevitable runs. The Blue Jays also expressed interest after a handful of starters went down to injury. Both were intrigued enough by Moyer's early results for Colorado to want to see which was the outlier: April or May.

Part of Moyer wondered just what the hell he was doing. Being there for Hutton's graduation reminded him of all that he'd missed through the years, plays and games and birthdays he'd have to listen to over the phone or through the filter of Karen's texts and jpegs. As his agent, Jim Bronner, called with the details behind what would be a brief minor league showcase—two or three starts, $5,000—he wondered, *Why would you get on a plane and leave these kids, when you just got back to them? Why?*

He wished Harvey were still around. But he knew what his mentor would say. Harvey's response would no doubt be identical to the advice Dorfman once gave to Jim Abbott, when Abbott was contemplating stepping away from the game after a disastrous 2–18 1996 season. "Using your family as a way out," Dorfman told the pitcher, as recounted in Abbott's memoir, *Imperfect*, is "a cop-out...we invent motives for our behavior. You use the separation from family in one context but not the other? Does that make sense? If you were pitching well, you'd still live for your family. To what extent will you regret this? What about in five years? Can you live with it appropriately? Use all the info, then you'll have no regret."

Ah, yes, the absence of regret. Two months ago, Moyer was baseball's feel-good story. Now, the media narrative had ever so slightly turned. "Jamie Moyer embodies the sort of player who has competed for too many years," one blogger opined. Another concurred: "It's getting hard to watch as the 49-year-old desperately tries to prolong an amazing and historic career."

But for Moyer, desperation didn't enter into it. He knew that had he listened to the press, he would have retired long ago and that those who chronicle the game seem somehow threatened by the example of aging in it. Moyer had heard the pundits' clichéd calls to "go out on top" at least since 2006. It had always sparked a defiant streak in him. Besides, for him, this wasn't about "going out on top"; it was about going out on his terms.

Harvey used to say, "If you want to know who a person is, watch how he responds to adversity." Moyer had gotten clocked at the end of May; did that mean he was done showing who he is, someone who gets up time and again after being knocked down?

Harvey would also say, "Good learners risk doing things badly in order to learn how to do things well." Moyer asked himself, *Do I still have room to learn?* As for his family, Karen and Dillon and Hutton were pushing him to give it one last shot. So he made his way across the Ted Williams Highway to the tiny hamlet of Poway, where he found Dom Johnson in his backyard, as if the pitching whisperer had been visited by a vision of an aging seeker's impending arrival. There was no gopher this time, just Moyer on the mound and Johnson eyeing the mechanics. Johnson noticed some of the same things Moyer had been working on: the hand coming too slow, too passively out of the glove on the windup, leading to a lessening in arm speed through the motion. Similarly, when his left hand reared all the way back, Moyer would stop for a nanosecond, instead of continuing in one uninterrupted flow; again, deceleration. Finally, when stopping at the back of the delivery, the left arm was swinging too far toward third base, giving batters a clean "back window" look at the grip on the pitch about to come.

"I had a feeling Joey Votto picked up the grip on that homer in Cincinnati," Moyer said.

"That's how, no doubt," Johnson said.

So they went to work. Keeping the arm in, shielded by the

body, while refraining from any stop-motion. After two bullpens together, it felt crisper, cleaner—and maybe even faster.

Those bullpen workouts led Moyer to determine that there was indeed a project to be finished. Ever since coming under Dorfman's spell, Moyer had been a testament to the notion that process matters—even more than results. Forget about what the media said: did *he* really think his process was over? Standing on Dom's mound, it didn't feel that way. He might not get back to the majors, but he *could* get better.

Karen was ecstatic, seeing her husband's quest not as some abandonment of their kids, but as a teachable moment for them. Their father would be modeling a whole range of character traits, from persistence to preparation to self-confidence to, perhaps most important of all, seeing something through to the end, even in the face of potential ridicule.

So now he's about to meet his new team, the Norfolk Tides, in Buffalo. He gets picked up at the airport and is taken to the team's hotel. The wire services are reporting that he ain't done yet. Jamie is now forty-nine years old—and he's back in the minors. *There's something appropriate about that*, he thinks, smiling to himself as he walks over to a local steakhouse, where he'll sit at the bar, have a beer, and watch *SportsCenter*.

It's *Star Wars* night at Coca-Cola Field in downtown Buffalo, which means it's a stadium packed full of relics. Not only Darth Vader and Jamie Moyer; the Tides also have on the roster veteran Miguel Tejada and Moyer's former teammate in Philly, J. C. Romero, not to mention Bill Hall, who was one of the few Red Sox not to hit Moyer in that 2010 shellacking administered by Boston in Moyer's last season in Philly.

It's the biggest crowd of Buffalo's season. Families are drawn to see the *Star Wars* promotion, but baseball aficionados are here to see this forty-nine-year-old pitching curiosity. Most of Moyer's teammates weren't even born when *Star Wars* debuted. Moyer was in high school.

On this June night, Moyer is masterful. The bullpen sessions with Dom appear to have paid off: his fastball in the first inning is clocked at 82 miles per hour—the hardest he's thrown since 2010. He pairs the fastball with 72-mile-per-hour changeups and 76-mile-per-hour cutters. As Harvey would have it, Moyer is basking in the moment on the mound. At one point, he doesn't hear the home plate umpire's call.

"Ball or strike?" Moyer asks.

The ump comes out from behind home plate, removes his mask. "Ball," he says.

Moyer smiles. "You lose your hearing when you get to be my age," he says.

The Bisons, who are managed by fifty-three-year-old Wally Backman, seem helpless, hitting only one ball hard, a single back through the middle, the only hit Moyer surrenders. Fifty-two of Moyer's 84 pitches are strikes over five shutout innings, with five strikeouts and no walks. He gets the win.

After the fifth, Moyer sits on the bench in the dugout as his teammates—all of whom seem to have Dillon's fresh, ruddy cheeks—parade by to offer high fives. He runs a towel through his soaked hair. Pitching coach Mike Griffin sits next to him.

"How'd it feel?"

Moyer takes a deep breath, looking off into the expanse of outfield green. "I've got to tell you, this feeling is just…" He trails off, searching. "Priceless. It's just priceless. I'm in a minor league ballpark, with a bunch of kids not much older than my son, and it's just you and the game, you know what I mean? There's nothing here between you and the game."

Griffin is fifty-five, a lifer who pitched six years in the majors. The two are silent for a moment, looking out at the outfield lawn. Finally, Griffin speaks. "Helluva job tonight," he says, getting up to go.

Afterwards, in the clubhouse, four local reporters crowd around Moyer. They ask what keeps him going. "This," he says. "Playing for a team, taking on another challenge."

But he doesn't want to talk about tonight's game. Instead, he turns the tables on his interlocutors and Bison PR man Brad Bisbing. The return to the minors has kick-started his memory. "Hey, the Earl of Bud isn't here anymore?" Moyer asks the group, referring to the legendary Bisons beer vendor back in the old War Memorial Stadium. Moyer, who visited Buffalo as a minor leaguer in the 1980s, remembers how the Earl's dancing antics would bring the crowd to its feet.

"We're having an Earl of Bud bobblehead night in August," Bisbing says. "He's coming back for it."

"I remember once our manager Mark DeJohn got up and danced with him," Moyer says. "And what about the Butcher?"

The Butcher was another icon, a 425-pound bat boy who would eat ten or twelve peanut butter and jelly sandwiches in the clubhouse before each game—egged on by the players— but would nonetheless delight the crowd with his athleticism. He'd sprint behind home plate to catch foul balls rolling down the backstop net, but he'd do so behind his back, or in his cap. When he'd miss, the PA announcer would intone, "The Butcher—no range!"

"He's fallen on hard times," one of the writers says. "They had a fund-raiser for him not that long ago."

Meantime, in his office, fifty-five-year-old manager Ron Johnson has googled Moyer's career stats. "Wow," he says, eyeing them. Johnson had a three-year stint in the majors in the early

'80s, and was once the first base coach for the Red Sox. "This guy makes me want to start working out again," he tells the local reporters.

Outside the stadium, a handful of fans wait for autographs. Moyer signs each one before hailing a cab over to Gabriel's Gate—he has a hankering for what he hears are the best wings in wingtown. When they come, they don't disappoint. Neither does the beer, which is cold and thirst-quenching. After a couple, for the first time since he blew out his arm nearly two years ago, this most present-tense of thinkers—a man who has trained himself to focus only on the task at hand—pivots to the future. He starts talking about what could be next. About maybe teaching pitching to kids from Little League to the pros. About rounding up guys like his buddy Trevor Hoffman and starting an academy that teaches mechanics, the mental game, and arm maintenance. Videos. Classroom instruction. Bullpen sessions.

Moyer takes a long pull on his beer. A host of practical concerns invade. "Of course, I'd have to find a facility somewhere," he says. "And I bet a lot of major league pitching coaches wouldn't want someone like me in their pitchers' ears. Teams can be territorial about that." He takes another swig. Those challenges are far off. Tonight was a good night. Because he was back on a baseball field.

"It's crazy to say, and I know I can't do it," he says. "I doubt Karen would want me to. And I have responsibilities. So I can't do it. But if I could, you know what? I'd play the rest of the season in Triple A. It's just so…pure. It's just…baseball. *It's what baseball always was to me.*"

In two days, the Tides will board a bus for the eleven-hour ride back to Norfolk. "I can't wait," Moyer says, and there is not a hint of sarcasm in his voice; he knows his baseball days are waning, and he's going to embrace every detail of this twilight, even if it leaves him tired and his legs stiff and sore.

There are two outs in the seventh inning of Moyer's second start. This time, he has befuddled one of his many former teams, the Toledo Mud Hens. He has given up two earned runs and seven hits, and has struck out seven while walking none.

He takes a deep breath on the mound. Behind home plate, just to the right of Karen and the kids, are a group of college-age kids chanting, "JA-MIE! JA-MIE! JA-MIE!" He makes eye contact with Toledo coach Leon "Bull" Durham, his teammate on the Cubs in the '80s. Earlier, when Durham was tossing batting practice, Moyer had teased him: "Throw strikes, Bull!"

Now, with the Mud Hens flustered and the kids in the stands making a ruckus, Moyer looks at his old friend and slightly shrugs, as if to say, *You believe this?* He throws a two-seamer and the ball is smoked right back to him on a line, but the old reflexes aren't shot yet; he snares it and theatrically flips the ball back toward home plate while sprinting off the mound to the dugout, the chant of "JA-MIE! JA-MIE!" now catching on among the eight thousand fans in attendance.

Five days later, Moyer pitches four innings, giving up one run on three hits and striking out four without issuing a walk. In 16 innings, he now has a 1.69 ERA with 16 strikeouts and not a single walk. Most important, his velocity is back to 82, and he feels he's found his arm slot again.

In the press box, the speculation is that Moyer has been removed from the game after four innings because a call-up to the Orioles is imminent. That's what Moyer's agent, Jim Bronner, has been led to believe too. Over the next few days, however, the call doesn't come. Orioles general manager Dan Duquette is unavailable to speak to Bronner and doesn't return his messages. Finally, Duquette tells Bronner they'd like Moyer to make one more start.

"That wasn't the agreement," Moyer tells his agent. The Tides have already left for Toledo; Moyer has been holed up in his Norfolk hotel room, waiting for a call-up that isn't on its way. He's feeling disrespected, used: he's an insurance policy, while Duquette—who wasn't exactly straight with him some seventeen years ago in Boston—tries to map his next move, thinking he can buy time by asking for another start.

Moyer loves the minor league experience because of the purity of the game on the field, but he's getting too old for the cynical machinations that too often define the game in its front offices. "I'm forty-nine years old and I'm waiting by a phone in a hotel room like a rookie," he tells Karen, who is in Philly for a Moyer Foundation charity event. He could stay and putter around his hotel room, or he could tell Bronner to tell the Orioles to stuff it, rent a car, and be in Philly in six hours—in time to make a different kind of pitch, an exhortation to donate to the cause of helping kids in distress. In other words, he can either be played with or do something good for his soul.

"I'm free!" he texts a friend as he makes his escape from Norfolk. The next day, the story moves across the wire: Jamie Moyer Requests Release from Baltimore Orioles.

By that night, the Blue Jays have called. Two starts for the Triple A Las Vegas 51s await.

Maybe knowing that the curtain is coming down on him is making Moyer feel overly nostalgic, but shortly after walking into the 51s' clubhouse he feels transported back in time once again to a simpler baseball era. He'd grown weary of the big league post-camaraderie atmosphere; those Mariner teams more than a decade ago were the last to feature teammates who worked *and* socialized together. In his last years in Philly, he'd have dinner on the road with the announcers or the team's video coordinator, because the players tended to go their own separate ways. (And when they did get together, they went out to clubs—not exactly Moyer's speed.) By then, the game had become a business, and teammates whom you used to live, argue, drink, and form lifelong bonds with had become merely colleagues and passing acquaintances.

But when Moyer meets up with the 51s in Tacoma, Washington, where he'd be making his first start in the Seattle area since he'd left the Mariners six years prior, he finds a group of young guys who pull for each other even though they know they are competing against one another for a shot at that big career break. They eat together, they come to the ballpark together, they work out together, they play cards together, and they wile away the hours before a game by watching movies together in the clubhouse.

It takes Moyer back to his earlier minor league days, in small towns like Geneva, New York; Pittsfield, Massachusetts; and Winston-Salem, North Carolina, where he and his teammates would live, two or three to an apartment, where they'd pile into his light blue Pinto station wagon to get to the ballpark, where they'd eat at IHOP, often running into other teammates— because they all shared the same moment in time. They'd corral a booth and drink coffee, refill after refill, while reliving at-bats and cursing out managers and commenting on girls in the stands, until it was time to go to bed so they could do the same damn thing tomorrow.

As at Norfolk, these kids ask questions of this oldster in their midst, looking at his concentration cards like maybe they hold the all too elusive secret, mining his memory for tales about the game's greats. (When Moyer regales a couple of young pitchers about how Bonds had owned him until he got over his fear of coming inside to the slugger, he could see a few faint light switches turn on.) One night, he goes to a nearby sports bar for a burger, where he runs into two teammates, a couple of pitchers from Texas. They invite him to join them, and they all watch a game on the big screen while Moyer tries his best not to remind them of their fathers.

Moyer's first start for Vegas contains a dramatic Mariners past-versus-future story line. He is facing off against pitcher Danny Hultzen, who is twenty-seven years his junior and Seattle's much-heralded top draft choice in 2011. Hultzen had posted a 1.19 Double A ERA and had just been promoted to Triple A, where he had five days earlier been shelled in his first start.

He is no stranger to Moyer. In 2010, Dillon's Cal-Irvine team faced Hultzen, the University of Virginia ace, in the NCAA baseball tournament. Moyer was impressed by Hultzen's arm— the kid could touch 96 miles per hour—but felt his secondary pitches needed some work, which Moyer had volunteered on an ESPN broadcast of the game.

Before the game, as Moyer begins to make his way down the leftfield line from the bullpen to the dugout before the singing of the national anthem, he becomes aware of a stirring in the stands. It starts with some applause in leftfield and it begins to build in intensity; by the time Jamie reaches third base and looks up, over 7,000 fans are standing and cheering for him, one bearing a sign that reads, simply, "Thank You." He wants to stop and take it all in, but he refrains from breaking stride. Instead, he tips his cap to the crowd and the cheers grow louder. *I wasn't expecting this*, he thinks, feeling the emotions well up.

Moyer starts shakily—could it be due to the unexpected ovation? He gives up a mammoth home run in the first and another in the second. He surrenders three early runs but once again rescues victory from seeming failure, holding Tacoma scoreless thereafter through five, at one point setting down eight in a row, good enough for the win.

"That was awesome to watch and really cool," Hultzen, who had trouble with his command, says after taking the loss. "Not only to get to play against him, but against a guy you looked up to growing up."

If the end was near, at least he'd gotten to feel the love of the Seattle fans, and to play for them one last time.

Five nights later, Moyer is cruising, holding Reno scoreless through four innings and leading 3–0. But then Moyer's old nemesis—the fifth inning—decides to make one final appearance. A fly ball to shallow center that should be caught drops among a trio of timid fielders. A potential double-play ball becomes a fielder's choice. Meantime, pitches that worked the low part of the strike zone in earlier innings are suddenly belt high. A double is followed by a homer and Reno leads, 4–3.

It's more of the same in the sixth. Reno starts to pick up Moyer's rhythm. Pitches that hitters were out in front of earlier are now struck on the meat of the bat. Moyer, trying harder, is up in the zone. A double, a suicide squeeze, a pair of RBI singles. Moyer gets out of the inning, but he leaves the game trailing after having pitched six innings, surrendering seven runs in his last two.

On the bench in the dugout, he drinks his water, looks out at the field in front of him, and thinks, *If this is it, I'm cool with that.* Bronner will hear from the Blue Jays tomorrow; they'll tell him that since the All-Star weekend is upon us, they won't need a starter for another week or ten days. So Jamie would be more than welcome to stay on with Vegas until then—but no guarantees.

But in his heart, Moyer doesn't need to hear from Bronner to know that this is it. *He feels it*. He'll call Karen after the game. "I think I'm done," he'll say. But for now, sitting in the dugout, he wonders if this mystical minor league tour these last weeks hasn't been some type of subconscious goodbye on his part, a way to say thank you to the game, while simultaneously reconnecting to it.

He knows that when he gets older, he'll have to go back to the discs of all his old games to truly remember the on-field exploits; he'll have to watch that ninth-inning punch-out of Bonds that followed a towering Bonds shot just three innings earlier in order to fully relive what he did.

But he won't have to search around the house for the memories that have been swirling around his head these last weeks. The time Harvey Dorfman's brusque voice inserted itself into his consciousness—*"What are you going to do about it?"*—and he was suddenly not so alone anymore. The time Lou Piniella said, "We brought you here to pitch," not even understanding the momentousness of such a simple statement: Moyer had waited ten years for someone to show him that kind of faith. The bullpen sessions where—aha!—a centimeter difference in the placement of a pinkie finger could be the difference between Bonds going yard or Bonds heading back to the dugout. The female beat reporter who always wore sunglasses, and whom the guys referred to as the "Pecker Checker." The cramped, late-night bus rides in the minors, with silly, farting teammates.

These are the memories that come now, sitting in what very well could be his last dugout. It's taken Moyer four decades in the game to understand that these are the memories that truly matter, because he and his teammates were young men together, very publicly trying to excel at something that invites error day after day, and their only response to that could be to have fun together, to be bonded by this weird life they'd chosen, and by the work they could never quite master.

At the end of the classic *Ball Four*, Jim Bouton writes that "you spend a good piece of your life gripping a baseball and in the end it turns out it was the other way around all the time." Moyer begs to differ. It's not about the ball, just like it's not about your physique or your speed or your gun of an arm. It's about what you think and what you believe. He faced 8.9 percent of the game's batters, gave up more home runs than anyone in history, won more games than all but thirty-three pitchers before him, and it was all accomplished despite a cavalcade of doubters, right up until the very end. No, it wasn't the ball that held him; it was his own oceanic curiosity that clutched him, his own insatiable need to get better. It was the challenge of doing the hardest of things the absolutely best way you could while people screamed at you that you were destined to fail.

Now, taking off a baseball uniform likely for the final time— who would have thought that it would have been a Las Vegas 51s jersey?—Jamie Moyer knows that when he thinks back on this long and singular career, it won't be a specific memory that comes to him. It will instead be a feeling. It will be the feeling he had on that fall night in Philly while he dug up the World Series pitching rubber; it will be the feeling he had in Seattle when he won his twentieth game during that magical 2001 season; it will be the feeling he had in his driveway so many years ago, with his father crouched down against the garage door, that shrunken glove awaiting each pitch.

And it will be the feeling he had just four weeks ago in

Buffalo, after he threw five shutout innings for the Tides and, looking out at the breathtaking sight of a baseball field, he tried to find the right word to capture his lifelong love affair with the child's game that has dominated his thoughts for close to fifty years. "Priceless," he said, as he looked at that field. "Priceless."

NOVEMBER 2012

EPILOGUE

Everybody needs closure," Karen Moyer says. As the driving force behind the nation's largest collection of child bereavement camps, she should know. She has seen the positive effects of closure firsthand every summer.

Walking away from the game in July was a loss of sorts for her husband, though it was hardly as traumatic as the loss Karen is used to counseling. Still, it was the likely end of something big—likely because Jamie hadn't decided that he was absolutely, positively retired yet. But Karen knows that if it is the end, it needs to be marked appropriately, and so she does what Karen does: she goes all-out and throws a "Moyer Foundation Roast & Toast" to honor "Number 50 Turning 50."

Nearly two hundred guests flock to Las Vegas's MGM Grand for a dinner, fund-raiser, and good-natured roast of Moyer, who sits on the stage—often with Mac or Grady perched on his lap—and takes abuse from a who's who of the baseball world.

Chase Utley regales the crowd with tales of the lengths Moyer would go in order to pitch. "A trainer would tape his whole body, making sure that the legs were taped to the hips, so nothing fell apart," Utley says. "And then the trainer would take handfuls of Icy Hot and rub down both arms and shoulders. All to just pitch *one* game."

In the live auction, Cliff Lee outbids all bidders for a framed collection of Moyer-signed milestone baseballs, to the tune of $20,000. A video from former Yankee slugger Bernie Williams delights the crowd. "When I heard about this evening, I really thought I should be there with you," says Williams, who hit .389 with eight home runs—the third most—in his career against Moyer. "Not really to pay tribute to all you've done, but to thank you for all you did for my career....I really owned you. There's no way around it. You were the guy who did more for my career than anyone else in baseball." He closes by conceding that Moyer "will go down in history as one of the better magicians this game has ever known."

Rick Sutcliffe talks about the first time he saw Moyer throw in spring training with the Cubs in the '80s. The kid struck out a batter with a beautiful 3–2 changeup. "I went up to him and said, 'That was a great changeup,'" Sutcliffe recalls. "And he said, 'That was my fastball.' I thought, 'I don't need to get to know this guy. He won't be around long.'"

Gregory Chaya and his older brother Chris fly in for the event. Gregory, in his twenties now and still cancer-free, is thin and shy. When Moyer and he embrace, Gregory nuzzles his face into Moyer's neck. Also in attendance are Michele and Jerry Metcalf, Erin's parents. They've brought a collage of all the photos taken through the years of them and Erin with Jamie.

Lou Piniella and Charlie Manuel make video presentations. The Phillie Phanatic holds up a sign that reads, "I Miss You." Afterward, a clearly moved Moyer is stunned. "Wow," he says. "This was clearly a Karen Moyer production. My wife didn't miss a thing. To have so many ex-teammates show up, it's just really special."

He pauses. "She even thought to pay respect to people who were important in my life but who are no longer here," he says.

"Like [former Baltimore manager] Johnny Oates. And Harvey? Did you see the photo of Harvey?"

Back home in Rancho Santa Fe, it's a typical Wednesday. The smart board on the kitchen counter details the day's activities:

12:00: Dillon Doctor Appt
2:00 Pick Up Duffy
2:45 Pick Up Mac, Yeni, and Kati
3:30 Mac Golf
3:30–4 Kati Swim
5–8:30 Grady Gymnastics
6:30–8:15 Duffy Soccer
Make It A Wonderful Wednesday!

The clan will gather tonight—with Hutton, now a freshman at Pepperdine University, on Skype—for dinner to mark Yeni's "Gotcha Day," the anniversary of her adoption. She'll lead the family in grace while everyone holds hands, closing with, "And special attention to me for my Gotcha Day."

But first Moyer goes on a succession of errands, picking up a kid here, taking a kid there. Then he goes for a walk on the beach, even though, ever since he stopped playing some five months ago, his feet have ached to no end. He has played catch with Dillon and Hutton a couple of times, only to wake up the next morning more sore than he's ever been in his life.

Dillon and Hutton keep asking hopefully whether he'll make yet another comeback. It's a question he wrestles with. Unlike so many who call it quits, he's still mentally able. But the body is breaking down before the spirit. He doesn't think his health would carry him through an entire season.

"If this is the end, I'm pretty good with that," Moyer says while strolling the beach. "I like flipping the TV on, looking at highlights at night, and then flipping it off and walking away."

Then again, while watching TV one night, it is not at all clear that his playing days are done. Just before spring training 2013, he watches his one-time teammate Tim Wakefield teaching the knuckleball to a lineup of former NFL quarterbacks on MLB Network's *The Knuckler. I can do that*, Moyer thinks. *How cool would it be to reinvent myself at fifty years old as a knuckleballer?* He goes so far as to throw the pitch out back with Mac. And he checks his address book and there's a number for Charlie Hough, who he played with in Texas—one of the great knuckleballers. Maybe a road trip is in order: visits to Hough and Wakefield. Just to see. He's intrigued by the prospect of another quest and the challenge of learning something new.

But Moyer's time is not spent exclusively fantasizing about becoming the next Phil Niekro. After a lifetime of obsessing about one thing, he's finally a different kind of free agent. Since coming home in July 2012, he has mostly been a dad. Finally, he has lunch with Dom and then with Yousef. He lays out his very nascent vision for the Jamie Moyer Pitching Academy and talks to them about putting the old band back together again. Yousef takes it upon himself to put together a business plan.

If it happens, it will mark the evolution of Jamie Moyer into something approximating the professional reincarnation of Harvey Dorfman. Who else is more qualified to teach pitching than the craft's ultimate student?

Dorfman has generations of disciples, and there were likely players he was closer to and spoke to more often than Moyer. But there has never been one who so fully embodied the Dorfman ethic. Moyer went to Dorfman a frightened journeyman who was paralyzed by the fear of failure, and he became...

well, he became the living apotheosis of Dorfman's definition of mental toughness on page 179 in *The Mental Game of Baseball*:

"We reject, rather than accept, pressure," Dorfman wrote. "We control pain, rather than be controlled by it. We grow, rather than shrink, through adversity. We become further motivated, rather than defeated, by failure."

For both Moyer and his mentor, it has always been about the work. Moyer shuns the spotlight just as Dorfman did. After all, it is customary at roasts for the subject to get the last word, to commandeer the microphone and exact some revenge. But at the Vegas event that would have been out of character for Moyer, just as it would have been for Dorfman. Instead, he took the mike and did as Harvey would have had him do. He refocused everyone on the task at hand. "I hope everyone has learned something about the foundation and about our passion, which is helping kids in distress," he said. And then his family joined him onstage and the crowd sang "Happy Birthday" to the fifty-year-old pitcher, who very purposefully has refused to announce his retirement. Because, really, who knows?

APPENDIX

Moyer's Easiest Outs

- **Scott Brosius**: .146 (7 for 48), 16 K's. "For some reason, when Scott came to the plate, I was very comfortable. I felt like I could throw my changeup to him anytime I wanted and get a lot of weak pop-ups or rollover ground balls to third. I'd catch him in between a lot: he'd be covering away, and I'd throw in. He had a tough time staying back and waiting on the change."

- **Lance Berkman**: .083 (1 for 12), 5 K's. "Lance was a switch hitter who had more power as a lefty than on the right side of the plate, where he'd bat against me. I'd rock him back and forth: in and away, in and away. Like Scott, he had a tough time not jumping out at the changeup. When guys complained that I threw too slow, that's what I liked to hear."

- **Cecil Fielder**: .189 (7 for 37), 1 HR, 3 RBI, 10 K's. "He had a long swing with his arms extended. He'd chase the ball when it was off the plate. I'd throw him a lot of changeups away, and when my catcher and I thought we could get inside, I'd get in under his hands and tie him up for a swing and a miss. The key was to throw him pitches that looked like strikes but that weren't when they got to the plate."

- **Glenn Wilson**: .120 (3 for 25), 6 K's. "Glenn was a good mistake hitter. You'd have to be careful coming inside to him. He'd hurt you if you got too much of the plate. I'd get him to roll over on the changeup a lot."
- **Kirby Puckett**: .176 (3 for 17). "His strike zone was from his shoelaces to his chin. He was a free swinger—which I liked to see—with real power, and short arms. Throw him a short curveball at his shoe tops and he'll chase it. If I went inside against him, I'd have to get in deep. Anything middle-in, he'd make you pay."

Moyer's Toughest Outs

- **Wade Boggs**: Hit .382 (21 for 55) versus Moyer with two home runs and eight RBI. "Wade had one of the best eyes at the plate I've ever seen," Moyer says. "He knew the strike zone and was disciplined about it. He didn't care if the count was 0–2 or 2–2. He had a plan and he was going to execute."
- **Mark Kotsay**: .583 (21 for 36) with an OPS of 1.451. "He covered both sides of the plate very well off me and didn't try to do too much, other than hit the ball where it was pitched. He had an uncanny knack to square the ball up. And on occasion, he'd lay down a bunt just to keep me honest."
- **Mike Schmidt**: .444 (12 for 27), 2 HR, 9 RBI, .704 SLG. "He was in his prime and I was young and inexperienced when I faced him. He took advantage of that. I had to prove I was going to beat him on the inner half of the plate, and at that time I didn't have the confidence to do that. He wouldn't panic. He knew he was going to get a pitch to hit."

- **Bernie Williams**: .389 (35 for 90), 8 HR, 21 RBI, 1.245 OPS. "As a young player in the minors, Bernie didn't really know how to hit. But he grew into a very good hitter with power. I faced him in a lot of really tight situations, often with runners on, and he always had a good at-bat. He'd sit on a pitch until you threw it to him."

- **Manny Ramirez**: .352 (19 for 54), 10 HR, 21 RBI, .963 SLG, 1.389 OPS. "Another one of those guys who would just sit on a pitch—sometimes for a whole day. If he got it, he'd hit it hard. He was a great mistake hitter. Back in his Cleveland days, every borderline pitch seemed to be called in his favor. Frustrating."

Regular-Season Career Statistics

Year	Team	GP	GS	IP	W–L	HR	BB	SO	WHIP	ERA
1986	Cubs	16	16	87.1	7–4	10	42	45	1.71	5.05
1987	Cubs	35	35	201	12–15	28	97	147	1.53	5.10
1988	Cubs	34	30	202	9–15	20	55	121	1.32	3.48
1989	Tex	15	15	76	4–9	10	33	44	1.54	4.86
1990	Tex	33	10	102.1	2–6	6	39	58	1.50	4.66
1991	St L	8	7	31.1	0–5	5	16	20	1.72	5.74
1993	Bal	25	25	152	12–9	11	38	90	1.26	3.43
1994	Bal	23	23	149	5–7	23	38	87	1.32	4.77
1995	Bal	27	18	115.2	8–6	18	30	65	1.27	5.21
1996	Bos	23	10	90	7–1	14	27	50	1.53	4.50
1996	Sea	11	11	70.2	6–2	9	19	29	1.20	3.31
1996	TOT	34	21	160.2	13–3	23	46	79	1.39	3.98
1997	Sea	30	30	188.2	17–5	24	43	113	1.22	3.86
1998	Sea	34	34	234.1	15–9	23	42	158	1.18	3.53
1999	Sea	32	32	228	14–8	23	48	137	1.24	3.87
2000	Sea	26	26	154	13–10	22	53	98	1.47	5.49
2001	Sea	33	33	209.2	20–6	24	44	119	1.10	3.43
2002	Sea	34	34	230.2	13–8	28	50	147	1.08	3.32
2003	Sea	33	33	215	21–7	19	66	129	1.23	3.27
2004	Sea	34	33	202	7–13	44	63	125	1.39	5.21
2005	Sea	32	32	200	13–7	23	52	102	1.39	4.28
2006	Sea	25	25	160	6–12	25	44	82	1.39	4.39
2006	Phi	8	8	51.1	5–2	8	7	26	1.09	4.03
2006	TOT	33	33	211.1	11–14	33	51	108	1.32	4.30
2007	Phi	33	33	199.1	14–12	30	66	133	1.44	5.01
2008	Phi	33	33	196.1	16–7	20	62	123	1.33	3.71
2009	Phi	30	25	162	12–10	27	43	94	1.36	4.94
2010	Phi	19	19	111.2	9–9	20	20	63	1.10	4.84
2012	Col	10	10	53.2	2–5	11	18	36	1.73	5.70
TOT		696	638	4074	269–209	522	1155	2441	1.32	4.25

Playoff Career Statistics

Year	Team	GP	GS	IP	W–L	HR	BB	SO	WHIP	ERA
1997	Sea	1	1	4.2	0–1	1	1	2	1.29	5.79
2001	Sea	3	3	19	3–0	1	3	15	0.79	1.89
2007	Phi	1	1	6	0–0	0	2	2	1.17	1.50
2008	Phi	3	3	11.2	0–2	1	4	10	1.63	8.49
TOT		8	8	41.1	3–3	3	10	29	1.14	4.14

Minor League Statistics

Year	Team	GP	GS	IP	W–L	HR	BB	SO	WHIP	ERA
1984	Geneva (A–)	14	14	104.2	9–3	5	31	120	0.860	1.89
1985	Wnstn/Slm (A)	12	12	94	8–2	1	22	94	1.106	2.30
1985	Pttsfield (AA)	15	15	96.2	7–6	4	32	51	1.355	3.72
1985	TOT	27	27	190.2	15–8	5	54	145	1.233	3.02
1986	Pttsfield (AA)	6	6	41	3–1	2	16	42	1.049	0.88
1986	Iowa (AAA)	6	6	42.1	3–2	2	11	25	0.850	2.55
1986	TOT	12	12	83.1	6–3	4	27	67	0.948	1.73
1989	Rangers (RK)	3	3	11	1–0	0	1	18	0.818	1.64
1989	Tulsa (AA)	2	2	12.1	1–1	1	3	9	1.541	5.11
1989	TOT	5	5	23.1	2–1	1	4	27	1.200	3.47
1991	Lville (AAA)	20	20	125.2	5–10	16	43	69	1.337	3.80
1992	Toledo (AAA)	21	20	138.2	10–8	8	37	80	1.190	2.86
1993	Roch (AAA)	8	8	54	6–0	2	13	41	1.019	1.67
1997	Tacoma (AAA)	1	1	5	1–0	0	0	6	0.200	0.00
2012	Norfolk (AAA)	3	3	16	1–1	1	0	16	0.688	1.69
2012	Vegas (AAA)	2	2	11	1–1	3	3	9	1.818	8.18
2012	TOT	5	5	27	2–2	4	3	25	1.148	4.33
TOT		113	112	752.1	56–35	45	212	580	1.132	2.76

ACKNOWLEDGMENTS

Jamie Moyer

As the previous pages show, it's been a long, long journey. There are many people to thank and acknowledge, but I want to start first with a nonperson—the game of baseball itself. It is my oldest companion, and it has both driven me mad and made me deliriously happy. The game has such an imposing history that I'm constantly humbled to have had a minor role in it.

Of course, baseball is made up of people, and there are so many responsible for my education in it. First and foremost is my father, Jim Moyer, who not only gave me the game, but also the work ethic needed to succeed in it. And my mother, Joan, who when she committed to keeping scrapbooks of all my clippings, never dreamed it would be a lifelong endeavor.

I've had countless teachers and mentors through the years; space prohibits me from naming everyone. But a few bear repeating: Lou Piniella, Dick Pole, Pat Gillick, Johnny Oates, Roland Hemond, Gordon Goldsberry, Billy Blitzer, George Bennett, Mike Cooper, Bryan Price. Clearly, I learned the game from some of its all-time greats. Outside the game, a young man named Gregory Chaya taught me more than he'll ever know about courage and positive thinking. Jim Bronner has been much more than an agent. He's also a trusted friend who I know always has my back. And of course, Harvey Dorfman taught me lessons about life I'll forever carry throughout mine.

I can't put into words what Harvey meant to me; hopefully, this book will show it. He was my savior, my friend, and my teacher. Baseball is littered with Harvey's intellectual offspring. We're a tight-knit band, a group of players who will always share a special bond.

I especially want to thank Harvey's widow, Anita, for her blessing of this project. Over two decades ago, a scared, losing thirty-year-old pitcher showed up on her doorstep and she kindly took him in for a weekend of introspection. Two decades later, I continue to be moved and inspired by her hospitality and kindness.

I also want to thank my teammates through the years. When a team is going right, teammates make one another better, and I was lucky enough to play with countless athletes who pushed me to higher heights. I can't name them all, but people like Jay Buhner, Chase Utley, Cal Ripken, and Rick Sutcliffe all know the effect they had on me.

Fans see the finished product of our games on the field, but they don't see the work that goes into it or the behind-the-scenes people who prepare athletes for peak performance. I've had an all-star cast around me for decades, including Peter Shmock, Yousef Ghandour, and Liba Placek, as well as great doctors like Lewis Yocum, David Altchek, and Mike Ciccotti.

My wife, Karen, and our eight wonderful children have not only put up with my baseball journey (I've lost count of how many moves we've made), they've encouraged it. They'll never fully know just how much strength they've given me through the years. I'm incredibly grateful and lucky to have them.

Rick Wolff at Grand Central Publishing, who understood this project from the beginning, shares my affinity for and allegiance to Harvey Dorfman. Agent David Black made our concerns his, like all great agents do. And writer Larry Platt challenged me to think outside the box for this project and created the type of book-writing experience I had hoped for. Through it all, we created a mutual respect and friendship.

Finally, this book is for any young kid who first picks up a baseball and wonders if it might be fun to toss this thing around a little. The pure joy of that sense of discovery and experimentation is something to hang on to. You're in for a heckuva ride.

Larry Platt

"The guy who has a book in him is Jamie Moyer. How the hell does he do it?" Those words from agent David Black in the summer of 2010 gave birth to this project. As always, I'm indebted to David for his vision and judgment, not to mention his friendship and—when necessary—his Harvey Dorfman–like fits of tough love.

Rick Wolff at Grand Central Publishing instantly saw how Moyer's story was really the story of the mysterious mental game of baseball, and—a disciple himself of Dorfman—he was instrumental in constructing a narrative that captured Harvey's singular influence. Throughout, Rick's enthusiasm and encouragement never wavered. I'm deeply thankful for his passion and support.

Speaking of Harvey, I regret that I never met the man. But I'm indebted to him for his wisdom and I hope his portrayal in these pages does him justice.

Mike Tollin is a talented filmmaker, terrific friend, and tortured Philadelphia sports fan. It was Mike who first introduced me to the Moyers and whose advice throughout the writing of this book has always been dead-on. No matter how busy Mike's

Hollywood mogul life becomes, he always has time to bemoan the state of Philly sports teams—a constant reminder of what really matters in life.

Then there's my literary posse: Ben Wallace read early versions of this manuscript and offered insightful feedback. And in addition to contributing some typically astute reactions to early drafts, Andy Putz, one of the best young editors in America, expertly pushed me to focus on the human drama of the Moyer story above all else. My designer friends Tim Baldwin and John Goryl of B & G Design Group weighed in with some typically brilliant suggestions on the styling of the cover. And my very dear friend Zach Bissinger always kept my spirits high with his unique brand of comic relief.

Hannah Keyser is a dedicated, hardworking assistant who researched, fact-checked, and transcribed more audiotape than any one person should be subjected to. She also has a bright future as a writer in her own right. And Mike and John Vagnoni's Ambrosia Key West was the perfect place to pen many of these pages. I don't hold their affiliation with *my* Harvey Dorfman— wild man Pat Croce—against them.

At Grand Central, a tip of the cap goes to Meredith Haggerty, Bob Castillo, Jimmy Franco, and the rest of their remarkable publishing team.

I owe a special amount of gratitude to my parents and to my wife, Bet Mizgala, who never tired of hearing my tales of life among the Moyers. (And who is rooting for Duffy Moyer to one day beat me in Ping-Pong. Not gonna happen.)

Finally, when this venture started, I told Karen and Jamie Moyer that I didn't just want to conduct a few interviews, transcribe notes, and write a book. I wanted to embed myself in their lives, to walk in Moyer's cleats, if you will, and come up with the most intimate account possible of what pitching is and what it takes to do it so well for so long. They let me into their life to the point that I often felt like the ninth Moyer offspring. Their level of trust extended to the page, where their only edits consisted of factual corrections.

I can't thank them enough for their kindness, their trust, and their friendship.

INDEX

ABOUT THE AUTHORS

JAMIE MOYER is thirty-fourth on Major League Baseball's all-time win list with a record of 269–209 compiled over four decades for eight teams, including the 2008 World Series champion Philadelphia Phillies. He is the oldest pitcher in history to have won a game, which came in April 2012 for the Colorado Rockies. Off the field, Moyer is the president of the Moyer Foundation, where, along with his wife, Karen, he has raised over $22 million to serve the needs of children in distress. Among his many honors, Moyer has been the recipient of baseball's Roberto Clemente Award, for exemplifying sportsmanship, community involvement, and dedication, and the Branch Rickey Award, for exemplary community service. He lives with Karen and their eight children in Rancho Santa Fe, California.

LARRY PLATT is the former editor of the *Philadelphia Daily News* and *Philadelphia Magazine* and the author of *Only the Strong Survive: The Odyssey of Allen Iverson* and *New Jack Jocks: Rebels, Race, and the American Athlete*. He is a columnist for the *Philadelphia Inquirer* and his writing has appeared in *GQ*, *New York*, the *New York Times Magazine*, and *Men's Journal*, among other publications. He lives outside Philadelphia with his wife, Bet.